"In a series of engrossing open letters to his estranged middle son, a father recounts the painful events that led to his self-acceptance later in life. This memoir is, in turns, heartbreaking, hilarious and poignant and fills a void in the Christian literary canon at the intersection of LGBTQ+ fatherhood and Christianity, illustrating that the two need not and indeed are not mutually exclusive. A gifted story-teller, Gregory Elsasser-Chavez dispenses advice with wit, grace and humility, allowing the reader to join him in his journey to enlightenment. This is a must read for Christians, non-Christians, and for anyone who hopes to understand the fierce love a father has for his children."
– William Dameron, author of the New York Times Editors' Choice, The Lie: A Memoir of Two Marriages, Catfishing & Coming Out

"Terms of Estrangement describes in terrifying detail the precise cost of conservative Christian rejection of LGBTQ+ people and of the reality of their lives. Brilliantly written, these letters from a gay father to his estranged son offer a new genre to tell an old story – traditionalist Christian teaching kills people and relationships. A crucial contribution to literature. A cry of anguish from a father's broken heart. A must-read."
– David Gushee, author of Changing Our Mind and Kingdom Ethics

"The harm done by religious teachings of terror regarding sexual and gender minorities tears through families. Here a dad—a gay man and a skilled writer--expresses that grief (and so much more) in the form of letters to a son who may never read them. Many have gone through this in secret. Now we have a window into what it must be like, at least for one dad, in this affecting book. If you know this fraught heartache, Terms of Estrangement bears witness that you are not alone."
– Ken Wilson, author of A Letter to My Congregation

"To think this book is only relevant for gay and lesbian people from strongly Bible believing backgrounds would be a mistake. The experiences of loss, grief, relationship/family breakups, mental health issues and finding authenticity are human experiences and, therefore, relevant to all…there are no chapters, so the reader must decide when it's time to have a break, close the book, and go to sleep. Believe me, you'll need those breaks."

– Anthony Venn-Brown OAM, author of the bestseller A Life of Unlearning
– a preacher's struggle with his homosexuality, church and faith and founder and CEO of Ambassadors & Bridge Builders International (ABBI)

"Despite the heavy subject matter, Terms of Estrangement is a powerful and ultimately uplifting read that sheds light on the struggles faced by those who identify as LGBTQ. Gregory's letters are raw and honest, and readers will be moved by his vulnerability and his unwavering love for his son. The book also offers valuable insights into the complexities of family relationships, the power of determination, and the importance of choosing our own paths in life. Overall, Terms of Estrangement is a beautifully written and deeply affecting book that will resonate with anyone who has experienced the pain of a broken relationship with a loved one."

– Pastor Danny Cortez, Director, Estuary Space

Gregory Elsasser-Chavez is an award-winning playwright of eight plays and the novel, *The Field Trip.* He has three sons and one husband and lives in Southern California.

Gregory has been a high school and junior high teacher in Los Angeles County for thirty years and is currently teaching English.

He still writes to his son.

For *Beverage*

Gregory Elsasser-Chavez

TERMS OF ESTRANGEMENT

AUSTIN MACAULEY PUBLISHERS™

LONDON * CAMBRIDGE * NEW YORK * SHARJAH

Ordering Information
Quantity sales: Special discounts are available on quantity purchases by corporations, associations, and others. For details, contact the publisher at the address below.

Publisher's Cataloging-in-Publication data
Elsasser-Chavez, Gregory
Terms of Estrangement

ISBN 9781685625795 (Paperback)
ISBN 9781685626235 (ePub e-book)
ISBN 9781685625801 (Audiobook)

Library of Congress Control Number: 2023906375

www.austinmacauley.com/us

First Published 2023
Austin Macauley Publishers LLC
40 Wall Street, 33rd Floor, Suite 3302
New York, NY 10005
USA

mail-usa@austinmacauley.com
+1 (646) 5125767

Special thanks to Tiffany Dorin who stepped up, thoroughly editing the first draft of these letters without asking for any financial compensation in return. She claims to have done it because she "weirdly loves this stuff," but I think she did it simply because she is kind.

Gina Madison also combed through the first draft, checking for inconsistencies in the narrative portion and keeping me honest. We've known each other for a couple of decades, so her insight as an outside observer was extremely valuable.

Lily, Jessica, Monica, and Cyndi: thank you for reading the book early and for all the encouragement that followed. I've saved all your notes.

Erin and Summer: I have no words. You both are a huge reason why this book is on the shelves. I promise you this book will change some lives, and your investment will be immeasurable.

While I'm grateful to all the readers of this book spending a couple hours with me as I detailed some of the most painful and embarrassing moments of my life, the majority of my gratitude is left for my husband, Abraham Chavez. Man or woman, gay or straight, husband or wife…it doesn't matter: Abraham is one of the best *humans* I know. From the beginning, he advocated for both me and my children and stood quietly by while I took two years out of our lives to spend the time it required to candidly unpack my life to my son night after night—and occasionally through weekends and holidays. He was *always* present, graciously enduring my various regrets, my lows, and the grief that would inevitably accompany each letter, ensuring me that I was never alone through this process.
I owe him pretty much everything, so everything left of me is his.
Except the TV remote control. That he can't have.

Disclaimer

Many names and other identifiable information have been changed to protect the identity of the author's children, family, friends, and various institutions.

If you can't annoy somebody, there is little point in writing.

– Kingsley Amis

Day After Halloween, 2009
Travis was 5:

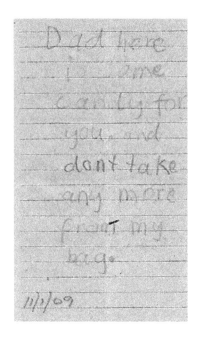

My Response:

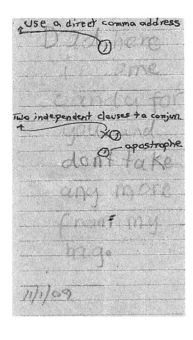

Dear Travis,

For several blocks of hours, over a period of almost two weeks, I've sat in front of a blank Microsoft Word screen, staring at either the blinking cursor or the small crack on the upper left-hand side of the screen, wondering if, like a windshield, the crack is getting bigger. If the crack reaches down into the "Auto Save" feature in Word, no doubt the whole thing will have to be replaced.

By the way, do you remember how many times I had to replace the windshield(s) in my Jeep(s) as the result of some pissed off freeway pebble? When I finally sold this last Wrangler, I knocked a couple hundred dollars off the price because of what was probably my fourth or fifth crack. Actually, it hadn't turned into a crack yet, still a hole, but the guy I sold it to—a fire captain who works out of a station right by your house—didn't seem to care; in fact, he agreed to buy the Jeep over the phone without even having seen it in person. He just had two kids who wanted to take the roof off, and a slightly used Jeep with a hole in the center of the windshield was the only way he could talk them into going to the dentist.

If you drive by the station, you can see the Wrangler behind an iron-wrought fence. I mean, if the captain is working that day, I guess. I'm assuming it's there. When I drive by, I never look.

Travis, you know I'm never at a loss for words. Never. Last week I found a reason to tell the mail lady that they spell it "G-R-E-Y" in Britain. Once I told a homeless person I could give them $5 but I'd need change back. But when it comes to you, the son whose linguistical (dictionary.com) talents were most like mine, I have now discovered that I simply don't have the words. I mean, I have words, but I'm not sure if they're the right ones. And I want to be very careful.

After my suicide attempt in our home, I was placed in a second mental hospital where patients were encouraged to attend various daily group sessions; the more sessions I went to, the better the chances of getting out sooner. During these sessions, one of the more prevalent, common themes woven into all the curriculum was that of apology and forgiveness. At some point, all of us in that room had at least a handful of people who needed to hear our apologies. Many of us needed to be recipients of apologies ourselves.

The plan here is to write you a series of letters that, for now, will have to act as a one-way dialogue, providing me a platform to seek your forgiveness for numerous hurts and injuries directed at you, your brothers, and your mom. Certain offenses that I'll confess to will come with some explanations. Others will reveal a variety of reasons behind my actions. None of them will offer excuses.

As I start "monologuing" with you, a framed picture of you on my desk to the right and the ugliest succulent on my left—which makes sense because the word "succulent" itself if the ugliest word in the English language—there's no doubt I will unearth many more offensives that I haven't yet considered. Writing can do that.

To a certain degree, I can accept your estrangement and silence as way for you to exact punishment, a retribution for breach of contract between a father and his son, a son who expected his dad to live up to certain unwritten standards of behavior. But, Travis, if all my letters are mere apologies, all of them saturated with words of repentance and regret, I'll be missing an opportunity to share with you certain valuable insights and wisdom that might help you make sense out of the messiness that is life.

Regardless as to how you might feel at the moment, I am still your dad, and estrangement or not, I have a job to do. I have things to teach you, and if I have to do it through letters like this one, or through blocked text messages, or even through *skywriting*, I'll do it. Your distance will not stop me from resuming my duty to you. It will not stop me from pursuing you. It will not stop me from loving you, even if it's from afar.

Travis: one season of bad behavior shouldn't quash a lifetime of love, and my prayer right now is that you'll be able to put aside your anger and your pain and read with an unbiased heart as I unfold for you my history and yours in a way I think can give you, first, some peace, and second, some context to a complicated, somewhat counterfeit life that was rapidly unravelling in front of you before it buckled and collapsed, imploding right in front of you, seemingly without any warning.

Regrettably, you and your brothers were unwilling prisoners of war in your father's battles, captives to a secret, internal fight that your dad was wrestling and crying and drinking and yelling his way through.

For that, and for many other things, I am deeply, *deeply* sorry. You didn't choose to have a dad who would drag you through his struggles. You didn't choose to be a witness to your parents' failing marriage.

And just like I didn't choose to be a gay man, you didn't choose to have a gay father.

But here's the good news in all of this: there are situations in this world we *can* choose.

Please give me a chance to show you *exactly* what they are.

Love you,

Love, Dad

Dear Travis,

Everyone has a COVID story. Literally, everyone. I can almost guarantee you that the monk born and raised in the deepest cave in the deepest part of Montenegro knows someone who knows *someone* that had the worst case of COVID on record…but didn't realize it until they took the antibodies test.

I, too, have a COVID story too. But let me back up first.

It was going on about two months of zero communication between you and me before I officially started…stalking…you. Sounds weird, but I can't think of another word. Thesaurus.com likes "ambush," but "stalk," while still a little disturbing, is a lot less OJ Simpson.

Shortly after my texts were blocked…way after your answers were whittled down to one sentence responses…I decided I would purposefully walk the halls between class periods—in close proximity to your classrooms.

I used that word on purpose. Don't be lazy. Look up "proximity."

I'd walk behind you close enough to grab that small duck tail on the back of your neck if I had wanted—which is somewhat problematic since you hunch your head and shoulders so far forward all the time. Son, you gotta learn how to straighten up your posture; keep this up and you'll be swinging from a bell tower by the time you're 50.

Anyway, I maintained a safe distance; last thing I wanted was an uncomfortable scene in case you spun around and crashed into me.

I also had a favorite blocked pillar on the second floor of the L building that provided a decent vantage point to the stairway you had to go up before 3rd period. I usually stood behind it a couple of times a week on my way back from the faculty bathroom.

By the way, this is something I'll bet you didn't know about your dad: surreptitiously following and tracking you is actually a learned skill I developed in college when I worked as a private investigator.

I did tell you that part of my history, right?

Well, in case I didn't…

For $8 an hour, when I was about 20 or so, I was an employee of a private investigator—he was a church friend of Grammy and Papa. Exciting stuff? Not really. Forget what you *think* you know what a private detective's day is like because Hollywood glamorizes the job like they do with those sappy warm-hearted movies about sassy, naively idealistic teachers taking their first teaching job in an inner-city school. Truth? It was just a lot of sitting around.

For the most part, the job entailed hours of spying on clients who were on disability leave. Many of them had claimed to be practically bed-ridden, so my job was to park outside their house and wait around for the suspect to go outside and mow their lawn or, best case scenario, bungee jump off a bridge. I had a video camera and would record it all.

One time I caught a guy moving a tire. Saw a guy walk his dog once. That's about it. Whatever the job was, it wasn't *Moonlighting*, that's for sure.

But like I mentioned, in my training period, I was schooled in the "art" of following people, mostly in cars, and after some time I was actually pretty good at it. Once I followed a guy from Long Beach to Big Bear, and he never saw me, although I did have to get out of my car and climb up a small mountain to watch and subsequently film him sitting all day at a fricken' meeting in a fricken' chair.

Ugggh, a *chair*. He was in the mountains in the winter. You'd think he'd at least take an hour to go skiing.

However, the whole private investigator thing ended when I turned 21 and someone put a gun to my head. I'll tell that story later, but that's the background as it applies to how I learned to spy on you without you being aware.

But back to following you at school. On the occasional day I found myself emboldened by an extra Bang or Mountain Dew Zero, I'd find a way to walk *toward* you from the other direction to see if your eyes would meet mine. Did they? I mean, was it obvious I was seeking you out? Did it piss you off further or was there a small part of you that was hoping I'd come find you?

Regardless, after a while, that got boring.

No, "boring" isn't right. "Unfulfilling" is better.

That's when I came up with the whole parking lot "shadowing" idea, and I *know* you knew what I was doing then.

It's not as creepy as it sounds. I'll finish my story tomorrow, and I will relate it to COVID.

PS: I don't expect you to understand the *Moonlighting* reference, but please tell me you know who OJ Simpson is.

Love, Dad

Dear Travis,

The teenage years are hard enough even without being dragged through your parents' divorce.

And while your dad comes out of the closet.

And while he's teaching English at the same high school you and your brother attend, your brother sitting every day at the front of your dad's third period American literature class.

And, of course, having all your friends find out the truth of it all before you've even had a chance to process it. Wow. The sheer embarrassment you and Andrew must have felt as the story slowly crawled its way through 3,800 students in unfathomable. In my defense, I did my best to keep things quiet until you both had graduated, but scandal like that has an energy of its own.

I think this was a part of the reason why you chose to cut-off all ties with your dad. Self-preservation is a requirement and asset in the teenage years, and the public intrusion into your life, exposing family troubles that should have remained private was no doubt humiliating for you. And I am very, very sorry for that.

If you let me, I can make it up to you. Ask me how.

Your silence didn't stop me from pursuing you in whatever way I could, however, and that's when I resorted to the stalking.

The first time it happened was by accident. It was a Wednesday, and I always get to school early on Wednesdays because that's the only day I give out make-up exams, and on that day, I was giving *Pride and Prejudice* tests. Honestly, I'm not quite sure how I am easily able to recall which tests I was giving that particular morning, especially since this is coming from a man who has been known to order tacos at fast food drive-throughs...only to pay at the first window before driving home, sans food.

That morning I parked as usual, and as I glanced through my rearview mirror, I saw you carrying bricks outside your construction classroom. Although maybe it wasn't bricks but wood. I don't know—as you well remember, I was never much of a "handy construction-y" dad.

By the way, our construction tech classes at Marshall High School highlight what is probably the most impressive career program at any high school in California. I've been at Marshall twenty years, and never have I seen anything more practical and well-suited for our student population. When I was a kid and took "woodshop"—a rudimentary precursor to the intensive program you have now—the only thing I remember constructing was a drink coaster, the wood I was given to work with a leftover piece already cut out by a circular saw. Basically all I had to do was sand it, and voila: I had a coaster.

Still got a "C" on it though.

I watched you working outside that morning for a good twenty minutes; I was late to that make-up test Wednesday. From then on, I'd get to work ten minutes early every couple of days, camouflage my car behind another vehicle at least the size of my Jeep, and sit and watch you work outside.

I know you saw me because within a week or so, you had stopped sweeping or constructing or something and you would go back into the classroom. So, I was forced to switch it up; I'd come at different times. Most days I'd get to see you for at least a couple of minutes before you'd disappear inside. Sometimes I took pictures.

You often wore safety glasses but a good portion of the time you opted for sunglasses instead. I would have preferred the safety glasses. But was that on purpose? Did you wear sunglasses so you could look over at me without me *knowing* you were looking?

In March of 2020, COVID took all that away as the world began to quarantine. The last thing you were working on, I think, was some brick structure. Not quite sure what that was. At first, I thought it was a chimney, but even with my limited knowledge I understood that you don't build chimneys on the ground.

…You don't, do you?

The last day I saw you was March 13th, 2020, the final day of school before the world decided to play a pretty serious game of hide-and-go-seek. I haven't set eyes on you since that day.

It has been a tremendous loss. For both of us, I think.

Love, Dad

Dear Travis,

Your oldest brother and I talk a couple of times a week, and when Andrew isn't working thirty/forty hours a week catching people shoving garden mulch under their shirts at Walmart, I get to spend a quality five…ten…minutes with him, just catching up.

One night a girl "friend" came to the house with your brother, and as we were all sitting in the living room after dinner, I started thinking about *you* instead of *him*.

It dawned on me that I have no idea if you've found love yet.

Son, for me, not knowing if you have yet to experience God's greatest creation and gift to mankind, not walking alongside you as you join the rest of the world's philosophers and mailmen and poets and car salespeople and gym trainers and grandmothers and ranchers and presidents as we all wrestle to define, then redefine, then give up on, then give into…well, not knowing if you have found *love* is somehow more painful than if I had discovered you were struggling with…depression, for example. More difficult than knowing you might be having doubts about the future or are overly ambivalent about the present.

So I'm asking now: do you have someone?

I mean, I know it's hard for people to connect during a massive pandemic, but that aside, do you somehow find yourself talking to one girl a little more than others? If so, is it just through text? Phone calls? Zoom? Do teenagers even date anymore? My students say kids don't really date. They just call it "talking." That's weird.

Well, even if you don't have a special girl in your life, you will at some point, and I want to, for five seconds, pretend like you are living here with me in my house and you have just announced that you're going on your first official…"talk."

Because I have some advice.

Now I know your personality and hear your protestations, so hold up. Let me just get the terms and conditions out of the way before I write anything else because, after all, you may cut me out of your life as you deem necessary, but I'm your *dad*, and our estrangement doesn't release me from acting out my responsibilities to guide and walk you through certain experiences. Although you are quickly becoming a man, I still have much counsel to offer, counsel you need to get from the one person you need to hear it from the most.

So, I want to imagine you coming to me and saying, "Dad, tonight I'm going out to talk with Clara, and I was wondering if it's a good idea to buy her some roses."

"No. You'll look desperate."

"Oh. But you told me you brought a girl flowers when you were in high school."

"You really want me to be your credible source when it comes to dating women?"

"Yeah, but isn't it all kind of just the same? I mean, dating either men or women?"

Lord have mercy, no.

"Yes."

"So are flowers a good idea or bad?"

"I went out with a girl named Allegra one time."

"Did you bring her flowers?"

"No."

"Then what does that have to do with anything?"

"It doesn't, but can you imagine the jokes I could have thrown around if the allergy medication had been invented by then? There are at least fifteen puns that can come out of the word 'pollen' alone."

"Dad, I love you and you're my hero until the day I hold your hand on your deathbed, but if I'm gonna get flowers, I need to go now."

"How much money do you have for flowers?"

"$3."

"Then say 'flower' not 'flowers'."

"Dad—"

"Allegra had a goat; she introduced me to it before we went on our first date which was, I believe, the mall. We had just walked past Miller's Outpost, and I reached down and tried to hold her hand. She jerked that hand back as violently as the way my head jerked back when I was ten and licked the end of a 9-volt battery."

"Were you embarrassed?"

"No. I was…confused. I mean, when a girl named Allegra who owns a goat and introduces said goat to a guy on the first date but refuses to hold his hand…well, it messes with the self-esteem a little."

"I'm going now, Dad."

"OK, wait. On a first date, you technically can take *one* rose. One. But you need to be very careful on the color of the rose."

"So no red then?"

"Exactly."

"How about yellow?"

"Yellow? Son, do you like Claritin more than other girls?"

"It's 'Clara'."

"Girls tend to overthink. Get her yellow, and she'll spend all night thinking you just want to stay friends."

"How about something, like, fun. Like, green?"

"Does she have a red beard and stare down at you from a cereal box?"

"Dad…"

"No weird colors. No orange. No stripes."

"Obviously no black."

"The mob sends a single black rose to certain people only…another piece of advice: you don't want to be one of those people."

"Pink?"

"Pink is fine. Tells her you're definitely interested in her more than others, and yet it doesn't carry the heavy-handed message that a red rose does. White is good. One white rose expresses volumes: of your respect for her, of her brilliance. It's a symbolical way to say how you how you value her *goodness* and her *perfection*."

"I'll go with that."

"But the best is purple. Find the deepest purple rose you can. In the 1600s, do you know who wore purple?"

"Royalty?"

"Yeah. The dye used to make purple cloth was so expensive it was universally acknowledged as the finest color, the color of the wealthy."

"So which one do I get?"

"Here's twelve bucks. Buy her a white, pink, and purple rose. Put the purple rose in front."

"Thanks."

"Have a good talk, Son. Love you."

"You too."

Travis: that's my favorite memory of something that hasn't happened yet.

Love, Dad

Dear Travis,

If you ever have to tell someone you're "free" from them, then you're not free from them.

Love, Dad

Dear Travis:

After you blocked my phone number some time ago, I started sending you messages through various "texting" internet sites, mostly for free. A few of them cost a buck or two. I'm hoping you got at least *some* of these messages—a couple of those sites were a bit...*shady*, and I ended up on some pretty interesting email lists as a result.

That's a letter for another time.

When that didn't seem to be working, I started mailing you physical letters. The one you set on fire then took a picture was memorable not just because of the stark shock of seeing my words in flames but because of the caption you wrote underneath: "Keep 'em coming!" you said.

By the way, were you at least impressed that I Fed-Ex'ed you another letter after that incident? The one written with a Sharpie on a metal door kick plate?

Yeah...you remember that one. Know this, son: you *are* clever, but you learned from the best.

To sum up, the following is a list of the various ways I have tried to keep lines of communication open between me and you. I tell you this not to make you feel guilty but to prove to you that I have never given up trying to reach out to you; after all, I don't want you to come back to me in 20 years and ask

"Where were you? I was 17 years old and pissed off! Why couldn't you have been the adult in this situation?"

So please take note of the methods in which I've undertaken to keep in close contact with my favorite middle son over the last couple of years:

1. Sent you texts several times a week, even though I was blocked.
2. Left you voice mails.
3. Texted you through various internet web-based texting sites (see above).
4. Texted you from other people's phones.
5. Mailed you actual notes and letters. Since I wanted you to actually open and *read* these letters, I opted to use envelopes with the return addresses printed from our school, my dentist, and Hawthorne Unified School District.

I hope the one from the police department didn't freak you out.

6. The metal door kick plate (again, see above).
7. Since you were such a huge fan of *The Office*, I even reached out to Steve Carell's manager and asked if Mr. Carell would consider helping bridge a conversation between the two of us.

OK, that one was a little weird, but I was getting desperate. Not surprisingly, I didn't hear back on that one.

However, creative yet practical father that I am, I needed something to give you that I wouldn't worry would end up in the trash or in flames like your 9th grade copy of *Romeo and Juliet*. That's when I got the idea for the Bible.

I took an old study Bible that I've had for years, and, starting much like God did, I started in the beginning. Genesis—*that* beginning. Now this particular Bible, *The Quest Study Bible*, has liner expository notes, the notes contributions from scholars and theologians, in order to give the reader a better understanding of difficult texts and the Bible as a whole.

There are these huge spaces in between the notes on every page, and since I wouldn't dare let one of my letters even come close to touching any of the words in God's Word, I've used the leftover space on the sides in order to write you daily letters, Bible verses, copies of memes, affirmations, advice, grammar tips, dating tips, grooming tips, more grammar tips, and snippets from the stories of my life and experiences, hoping these anecdotes will help you understand how we got to the place where we currently find ourselves as a family.

At this point, I've written up through 2 Samuel, and it is my great hope that I will someday get to hand you this Bible in person. Your mother and I taught you well—I know of your great respect for God's Word, and I know you won't burn it or throw it into the recycle bin.

I hope I can get this Bible to you soon. Please don't let me get to Revelation before I can see your face and hug you.

I seemed to miss you more than usual today. Don't know why.

Love, Dad

Dear Travis,

Most days, like today, I postpone writing to you for up to two or three hours at a time. I sit down at my computer, put on my writing music (always instrumental movie soundtracks), open this file, move the cursor, and I write "Dear Travis."

Then I check Instagram.

Then I check Facebook.

And Twitter. Which is a quick distraction because I only follow about 100 people.

After all this, I then look at my phone to see what's on my weekly calendar, which leads me to logging on to three different websites to see who Trump has recently pissed off. And those fricken' websites! More than once, those news pages have suckered me into clicking onto their sponsored advertisements to read about the "22 Reasons Why the 'Desperate Housewives' Cast Didn't Get Along" or "Where is Honey Boo-Boo…Paula Abdul…Michael Clarke Duncan (dead) Today?"

Speaking of Trump, do you remember in December 2016 when I took you to New York and Trump Tower, and we sat with the press in that plaza Starbucks waiting for him to come out of the elevators? You kept saying "We are not leaving here until we see Uncle Trump." Secretly, I myself couldn't care less about seeing Trump—I was holding out for my own reasons, waiting to see if another famous resident, Kathleen Turner, might come out of the elevators instead. Turner is an actress I had always liked and who had the honor of being one of my "confused adolescent crushes" when I was 12.

More of that to come. Definitely.

About a month later I discovered that waiting for the *Romancing the Stone* actress was about as useless as waiting for Trump since she had moved out of the Tower years earlier. Guess I should have clicked on one of those sponsored "Where Is?" ads before we sat there for two hours.

Anyway, back to wasting time.

Sometimes I pick up the kitchen. On my *third* letter to you, I cleaned all the baseboards for a half-hour before I wrote one word, and right now I just ordered two boxes of dishwasher pods and a 450-count case of Christmas ornament hooks from Amazon.

The point is, over the years, I've written a novel, eight plays, and four pilot episodes of a TV show, and, for the most part, while I often struggle with characterization, I've never had much trouble with the *words*. Writing scenes with pissed off Muppets attacking a penthouse suite in New York, creating character scenarios for people with OCD or caffeine addictions…all of that is so much easier than writing simple letters to the son I used to know almost as much as I know myself.

Which, as you will see, isn't saying much.

But Travis, the words don't come to me like they used to not because of a sloppy "writer's block" excuse or something like it. I *know* what to say. I just don't *want* to say them. Not to you. Not to the son who's still a kid in my eyes instead of the man the government has claimed you now are. The following words are difficult, and they may be as difficult for you to read them as it is for me to write them. Maybe more. And to be completely honest, I'd rather brush my teeth with the toilet brush I just bought on Amazon than to have to finally tell you the very…uncomfortable…truths regarding all of my past untruths. But if I'm going to help you make sense of *your* present, I have to take you back to my past.

So for now I'll put those long-reaching, fireplace matchsticks, the jug of casein, and the Kindle edition of *American Heiress: The Wild Saga of the Kidnapping, Crimes and Trial of Patty Hearst* into my wish list, and I will stop throwing away this time I now have with you.

I think back to that day in New York, sitting there at that Starbucks overlooking the lobby, and while at the time it seemed like we wasted way too much of an already rushed four-day visit, I'd give up almost anything just to sit there with you again, waiting for Donald Trump to not come out of those elevators.

Even now. Even after his tax plan screwed me royally.

Love, Dad

Dear Travis,

I don't think it's possible for me to tell you exactly when I understood I was gay. After all, I don't think *you* could pinpoint a time when you knew you were straight. Yeah, that's a pat response, one that is quickly starting to stale, but asking at what age I knew I liked guys instead of girls is generally the first thing people want to know. So I think it's only fair to answer the question.

By the way, when did you find out you liked *girls*? Was it in 7th grade when you kept getting out of your seat in your history class to get tissues to talk to some girl or did you really have bad allergies?

8. For me, I think I was 8.

Full disclosure though: I have a really weird thing with the number 8. To this day. I truly do remember being in kindergarten when I decided that since I was working with numbers for the better part of the day, I had to have a favorite number, so I picked the number 4. Naturally my hatred of the number 8 followed since it was twice the 4s, feeling that two 4s would, yes be greedy, but more than that, the number 8 was unsettling: it had no sharp lines and would take up far more space on that cheap brown paper with the broken lines that looked exactly like the 5 freeway at 2 in the morning. The 8 was too round; the 4 was streamlined.

Huh. Looking back, I may not know how old I was when I found out I was gay, but I guess I *can* tell you when I realized I was a minimalist.

So I always tell people I knew I was gay when I was 8. I just don't know if that is actually true.

Age aside, I *do*, however, remember the first time I could… *recognize*… that something was…*off*. Again, I don't exactly remember how old I was, but the man for whom I had my first "non-sexualized" crush was really my first foray into what would become a lifetime of deep, warring confliction: see not only was he a male, but he was also a fellow Christian…and a youth pastor. Thirty plus years later, I think it would have been an easier transition if my first crush had been on a teenage puppy-mill-owning-atheist, but that, like most everything else at that time, was not under my control.

Again, this was way before puberty, so while there weren't any sexual feelings that I could connect with the…*pull*…toward this man, this youth pastor *that had just been hired by our church, came to our* house to meet my parents, and almost immediately I understood something to be "wrong." Because although he wasn't the first man I had ever looked at—nor was he the first youth pastor I had met—he was the first male I had glanced at and then "studied…"and then the weird little bubbles of some unrecognizable stomach malady suddenly came from nowhere.

Some of us gay folks now call those bubbles *shame*.

Here's an easy way to put it: remember the "circle of life" in *The Lion King*? You know, "first the grass grows, then the animal eats the grass, then the man eats the animal, etc., etc., etc.?" Gay Christian boys and girls have their own similar circle, but it goes like this:

From out of the mulch of Youthful Confusion, a stem from a tiny grain called "embarrassment" pokes its green head up through the brown muck. After the stem has been strengthened by the tears that flow into the bag of Reese's Pieces at the precise moment E.T. tells Gertie to "Be Good," it is eventually classified as a weed called "shame." This shame grows strong as it is lovingly nurtured by the combination of the way you secretly looked at River Phoenix in *Stand by Me* and the desperate, around-the-clock prayers directed to the God you have wanted to follow since you could talk. The God you are sure no longer loves you like He did before. Because you have thoughts and desires that you still can't define but somehow knows He disapproves of even though you asked for nor desired any of it.

So you try and manipulate that weed into a flower as the deal making begins: you promise to read your Bible every day. *All* of the Bible. Even the slow parts that start halfway through Exodus. You give more than 10% of your allowance. You go to church three times a week and summer camp most years where you fill out the card and repeatedly ask Jesus into your heart at the end of every camp. Once home, you keep your eyes on the ground when certain scenes pop up in movies. Ignore book covers at Waldenbooks that might make you stumble. Focus your eyes on the magazines *only* on the 1st and 2nd shelf in the liquor store, for you know if you look up further you are in danger of watering these odd inclinations you silently carry that don't have a name yet but definitely fall under the category of "Things We Don't Speak Of."

Things that will send you straight to Hell.

Through God's silence, the deals fall through and the shame, not even having mercy enough to at least blossom into a dandelion, takes a header back into the dirt where it stays put, year after year after year before someone eventually comes along and plants turf on it—because after all, it's California and never rains, and it's too expensive to water real grass year round.

We call that turf "depression," and since the shame is now smothered under a thin layer of tar and whatever goop that makes the turf stick, the shame stays put, depression making sure it is always kept in its place.

That's the gay circle of life.

And that, my son, is called an extended metaphor.

I don't know about you, but I think reading about your father's first crush on a man is enough for one day. More later.

Love, Dad

Dear Travis,

When you have more than one child, the inevitable conversation as to which child is the favorite will at some point take place—and hopefully not in front of your children. And this conversation will happen more than once, trust me. When I get asked, I always tell the truth, and nine times out of ten, no one believes my answer. And it irritates the snot out of me.

Of course, I guess my track record for telling the truth is a little suspect at this point.

It's like that episode in *I Love Lucy*—which happens to be in my top five favorite *Lucy* episodes in case you were wondering—where Lucy tells Ricky, "You can't tell people the truth, they'll think you're lying; you have to lie to make them think you're telling the truth."

Let me tell you something: I have recently discovered that people get so worked up about the truth because sometimes the truth is so unbelievable that a lie is much easier to accept. And when you lie—and people know it—you're just giving others an unspoken permission to lie to *you* about things they find unbelievable about themselves. At that point, everyone wins. Right?

My honest answer is that out of the three of you boys, I never had a favorite child. I *related* differently to each one of you, but if you put a gun to my head, I honestly wouldn't be able to pick. And no one ever accepts that answer.

However.

You, Travis, did stand out amongst your brothers. Not in that flashy, middle child cliché kind of way; instead you, on your own, separated yourself from Andrew and Christopher in subtle ways, and only in the private, quiet moments among family was I even able to tell. It was sort of like those activity papers I did in kindergarten where there was a picture of a train, a plane…and an alpaca. And I had to circle which item just didn't…group…with the others. And unless someone has figured out how to ride an alpaca forty years later, the answer will *always* be the alpaca.

You're the alpaca, dude. Yes, we need the train. We need the plane. We love and are awed by both. But the alpaca is the one we want to know more about on Wikipedia. Since it looks like nothing else we usually see on a farm, we find ourselves drawn to the alpaca over the cows and the horses and the pigs.

Because it's odd looking but beautiful.

Distinct and very social yet slightly guarded and careful. A gentle animal that will violently spit the moment it feels threatened.

Travis, if our family is going to move past this, we need a person who stands out from the rest of us. If there is ever going to be acceptance, forgiveness, and understanding from all sides and perspectives, you will be the one to spearhead it because you aren't *like* the rest of our family. And while most people are arguing as to whether it's the mom or dad who truly holds a family together, I am here to tell you that it is *you*.

It has always been *you.*

As you read these letters with your name on each one, I hope you see what I'm talking about. Even if my letters don't serve their intended purpose, I at least pray that you will understand that I've been watching you from the moment you came screaming into this world, Lionel Ritchie's "Dancing on the Ceiling" playing on the operating room's overhead speakers. Yes, I've been watching and studying you from the beginning, and I hope you realize that I *know* you.

You're the son who refuses to tiptoe through life—instead you go out of your way to make sure every person hears each one of your steps.

I love you, and I hope you never look at another alpaca the same way ever again.

Love, Dad

Dear Travis,

The last time I seriously had considered ending my life was in September 2019; now that I sit here today, fully alive and appropriately medicated, I can confidently say that it was the last time I would contemplate suicide. Besides, I think my desire was less about wanting to die and more about not wanting to *live*, and that is two very different things. So sometime soon after the last time I seriously mulled over death by my own hands, I made a verbal vow to God and a silent vow to you boys that taking my own life was no longer on the table.

April 2019 was a close call, however, for that was when I knew for certain that the family dynamic I had created with you and your brothers and your mom was no longer a temporary solution to a problem that couldn't be fixed with more therapy…more Bible reading…more prayer. It was now permanent. And the finality of letting go of pretty much the only life I had ever known was overwhelming.

It was too much. I had lost my family. I had lost my God. I was alone.

However, I must give credit to three things that kept me alive through April 2019. The first was God. In his omnipotence, He kept me alive.

The second reason I held on was for you kids. I just couldn't put you boys through any more trauma. You had been through enough, and I wouldn't inflict any more pain on you and your brothers.

Now I don't want to make light of the situation, but the third reason I decided to reject suicide was because I absolutely needed to be alive for the finale of the best TV show in the 21st century…which was still several months away.

Yeah, I know how it sounds, but it's true.

I remember sitting on my bed, getting out my journal to write a few instructions down, when I began to understand that if I did overdose once again—without making the mistakes of last time—my life would truly be over. Heaven or hell would be next.

And I wouldn't know how *my show* ended.

So this odd and twisted little fleshly desire preempted any further harmful, selfish actions on my part. Months later when the finale finally aired, I was in a much better place than I had been in April. A friend of mine joked later that the ending was so bad that I must have regretted not going through with the April plan, but, actually, I thought it was a great ending. Well worth the life that I am still lucky to have.

Again, there was one more deep moment that next September. I wrote you a letter that same night; I still have it. As painful as it might be for you, I'd like you to read it someday.

I'm bringing this up because a good portion of my story includes several incidents of attempted suicide and weeks…and months…and years…of thinking about death on a daily basis. And, as my son, I am very, *very* concerned you may struggle with the same feelings of hopelessness. The idea that you could get to the point where I have been scares me to death.

A little pun intended.

I'm not physically with you anymore to check on you, so I will offer my help through this medium with the hopes you will read the letters, for if my story can shine a little light through your own dark times, and, quite possibly, keep you on this earth, then all my history will have been worth it.

I haven't said it in a while, but I love you. I miss you.

I'm not sure if these letters are helping or hurting. You or me.

Love, Dad

Dear Travis,

With some confidence, I can make an estimate as to the number of therapists I have frequented in my fifty years, and that number equates to approximately twenty-eight counselors, therapists, psychiatrists, marriage/family therapists, pastors, psychologists, and licensed clinical social workers. There have been so many "counselors" that if my life were a screenplay, the writer would have to make a couple composite characters out of the many. They all pretty much said the same thing anyway.

If Abraham Lincoln and Einstein were to have a baby, he'd look like my very first counselor, a bearded man who I worked with for less than two months. I was in 9th grade. All I can remember is his office had all these dark spots, no windows, no sunlight, and he was very, very emotionless.

I also remember that he was the first of many counselors I would lie to. By then, I knew a little bit as to why I was "different," but I never discussed "that" with any therapists until my early twenties. I instead opted to blame my depression solely on the relationship I had with my dad, which had been rocky, to say the least, for as long as I could remember.

Side note: I'm not going to spend much of the time I have here with you rehashing my relationship with my dad, your Papa. It's a common crutch, cliché or otherwise, to analyze one's current hang-ups and neurosis as consequences of the parent/child relationship, but I don't want to put blame on my father for the way my life turned out mostly because I don't want you, or your brothers, to do that to me. My father was human. He was imperfect, like the rest of us. He also had lousy role models, but that didn't stop him from taking the only parental model he had ever known and making some improvements. He did the best he could. And much like we all do, he's mellowed out with age and my relationship with him today is the best it's ever been. That's what I choose to focus on. End of story.

Ok, so our time together, the therapist and I, was not successful because I chose to avoid the truth, and I made a conscious decision to reveal very little. To be fair, I hadn't told *anyone* the truth, and there was still that part of me that wanted to please this stranger; he was yet another man in my life that I wanted to impress, and I wanted him to see me as someone other than an angsty teenager taking up space and wasting his time especially in light of all the lies I was telling, lies that I'm now convinced he knew I was telling all along.

I especially did not want to risk the chance that if he knew what I was discovering about myself, he would cancel our sessions, or, worse yet, tell my parents. Needless to say, my time with him was quick and fruitless, so I moved on. I can't recall when I found out that he had committed suicide some years later, but I do think about it whenever I drive by his old office. And I know that his death still bothers me.

I hope you are well. Earlier today I thought about that time we went camping and horseback riding in Santa Barbara. Remember how we passed that field of trees way off the main highway? The trees that had been cut down to their trunks and were stark white from decay?

That was probably the creepiest thing I had ever seen. I always think about those trees at weddings for some reason. Weird, I know.

Love, Dad

Dear Travis,

One of the many things I want to teach you through this limited but, hopefully, effective way of keeping us close is the idea of *perspective*. Once these letters are finished (and I pray all the time that these letters will no longer be a necessity and will see an end date), but I'm hoping a motif (not a *theme*— they are different; look them up), will form, and you won't just have a *head* knowledge of the concept of perspective but an *experiential* knowledge of what it means to look at something from a vantage point you never even knew existed.

Think of a little kid looking through a knothole in a fence leading into a park. He bends down, smacks his eye flush against the wood, and from his limited view he can see a man standing over another man, this one sleeping, and after muttering a few short words that sound like complete gibberish to you, the standing man takes a knife from off his belt and begins violently stabbing the sleeping man to death.

Now unless you're a stock 1990's John Grisham character, running away from this sudden violence doesn't occur to you. Within ten seconds, you are over that fence and looking for your own weapon, ready to jump in and stop the murder unfolding in front of you.

The first thing you see when you land is that the "dead" man has no blood on him. Nor does the guy stabbing him. Then you look out and see the crowd of people sitting on the grass In front of the elevated platform, now understood to you as a stage, where the stabbing took place.

And you notice that no one is screaming or running to stop the assailant. No one is even calling the police.

Of course, now the actors and the perplexed crowd is staring at *you*, most of the audience figuring your entrance was a part of Macbeth since none of them have ever truly understood Shakespeare nor do they particularly *like* him even though they have to *pretend* to like him.

No one watches a Shakespeare play for anything but bragging rights, Travis.

As it all sinks in, you recognize your surroundings because you and I visited Central Park years ago. We saw the *Catcher in the Rye* carousel, had food at the restaurant they filmed *Ghostbusters*, and then I think we debated whether to ice skate at the frozen pond or go to the zoo.

We went to the zoo, remember? It was winter and we mostly saw seals and fish.

You understand what I'm getting at? Sometimes your understanding and perspective is limited, much like your eyesight becomes when choosing to observe life only through a knothole in a fence. No, life requires you to get out in the open and take in the broader view.

I think you get the point.

So, I have an assignment for you, and I think this will solidify your understanding of *perspective* and then I'll leave it at that. The following is a list that I've drawn up and then narrowed down under the heading of "The Ten Worst Fathers That Have Ever Existed: Real or Fiction." Google all of them, read up about each one, and then I want you to compare and contrast fatherhood performances—mine against theirs. That's it.

Here's the list:

1. Herod the Great
2. Jeffrey MacDonald
3. Tywin Lannister
4. Woody Allen
5. Neil's father from *Dead Poet's Society*
6. Lt. Col. Wilbur "Bull" Meecham
7. Jack Torrance
8. Ivan the Terrible
9. Joseph Fritzl
10. Joe Jackson

Love, Dad

Dear Travis,

At some time during my early, solo therapy sessions, around 14…15…I attempted suicide for the first time. And as is common with certain activities a person tries for the first time—a true rookie I was—the attempt failed, and instead of taking my life, it just cracked the door open to a new idea, the idea that killing myself on my own terms was an action that would give me, for the first time in my life, 100% control.

But that night, Divine intervention, the pre-internet era, and lack of experience was what saved my life. Thankfully, I had no idea what I was doing.

As I was getting ready for bed that night, I went into the kitchen cabinet and took Grammy's bottle of Anacin, a popular over the counter headache medication at the time, and after making a few cryptic "goodbye" phone calls, I took a handful of them. Probably twenty or so. I went to bed that night, and I don't even remember being scared.

I did not wake up dead the next morning. Instead I was greeted with a high-pitched ringing in both my ears. Tinnitus on steroids. And the ringing wasn't just a constant *tttttiiiiinnnnnggg*, but an all-out television Emergency Broadcast system test, sound turned all the way up, freaking me out not because it wouldn't *stop* but because I couldn't hear anything *else*.

In addition to the ringing, both ears were stuffed and throbbing, my stomach was cramping up, and my jaw was sore from clenching it in my sleep.

Shout out to the makers of Anacin, however, because I didn't have a headache, that's for sure.

Emotionally, I don't know if I was disappointed or relieved or both. I do remember being freaked out that I had done something permanent to my hearing, and I knew I had to tell your grandmother something. So I got up and went into her strawberry themed bathroom. Her portable black-and-white TV was turned on, placed on the counter next to her vanity mirror as usual, and while the newscasters' lips were moving, nothing was coming out.

Me (louder than normal): "Mom, I woke up this morning, and there's this loud ringing, and I can't hear much!"

Grammy: (Words)

Me: "It feels like someone left a buzzer in both ears and then stuffed them with cotton!"

Grammy: (Words. Some I believe were moderately anxious)

Me: "I don't think it's a cold because it's mainly just the ears!"

Note: this story would be much more humorous had she offered me a couple Anacin for my earache, but she didn't.

Me: "Mom, I feel lousy, but I don't want to miss school because I borrowed some girl's homework to copy, and if I don't get it to her, she'll get a '0' on it!"

Now I, of course, didn't really say this, but the cheating part was true, and it was on my mind. And the girl *did* get a zero on it and was pretty pissed off about it, and I *did* tell her the whole story when I ran into her at Walmart about six months ago.

Within a few hours, Grammy and I were in the doctor's office, and, assumedly using words, the doctor diagnosed me with something that had nothing to do with a suicide attempt or homosexual suppression, and by the next morning everything had returned to normal.

Anti-climactic, but that really was the end.

However, this "incident" is something I tend to think about whenever the subject of my first suicide attempt or "gay cures" comes up; I've always said if there really was a "gay pill" out there that could cure homosexuality, it sure isn't the ingredients in Anacin because if it *could*…well, considering the amount of pills I took that night, it would have been enough for me to find even Susan Wymark* attractive.

Love, Dad

*Name may have been changed, but Uncle Jim knows exactly who I'm talking about.

Dear Travis,

The only time I ever liked horseback riding was when you and I went on that trip to Santa Barbara and "glamped" in those oversized tents with the carpet, a heater, and the electrical outlet for my phone which sat right next to my queen-sized bed.

That was also the same trip we took with the dead, white, tree trunks.

In retrospect, that long three-day weekend marked the end of two things for me: traditional, "roughing it" camping and horseback riding. I have vowed I will never ride another horse again unless we ride together.

Ok, that's shmaltzy, but it's also symbolic.

Love, Dad

Dear Travis,

To be fair, as a closeted teenager who didn't really know he was closeted, my four years of high school, smack dab in the middle of the 80s, wasn't quite the traumatic event as experienced by many other gay folks.

Side note: from here on out, whenever I use the term "gay folks," I'm going to go ahead and lump all people who fall into the LGBTQ+ category because, seriously, every time I have to type "LGBTQ+" I have to stop and 1) remember the correct order of the anacronym, and 2) stop to search out the "+" symbol on my keyboard which takes about an extra five seconds. True story: when I took typing (now called "keyboarding") in 9th grade, I skipped the two-day lesson covering the top row where the numbers and symbols are located on a standard keyboard. To this day, I have to look at the top row before I use it.

Example One: &7

Example Two: 93@*

Like I predicted, that took some time.

Second side note: whether or not you go to college, take a keyboarding class. Besides "checkbook math," "keyboarding" was the most practical and useful class I have ever taken. In my adult life, I've never used algebra or looked under another microscope, but my keyboarding skills came in handy when writing eight plays and a novel. And now these letters to you.

So I mean no disrespect when I single out "gay folks." I'm not really ignoring the entirety of the LGBTQ+ community or downplaying their importance as less equal to "gay folk": I'm just lazy.

Back to high school: I knew several straight kids whose high school experience seemed far worse than mine. Yeah, I had a shaky relationship with my dad that would take years to sort out, but I wasn't beaten or ignored by either of my parents. I knew I was loved. You've seen my old house: mid-size, middle-income home in a nice suburb in Los Angeles. I was fortunate. The gay accusations had pretty much stopped by high school. I was still called "nerd" once in a while, but even I couldn't argue with that. After all, I *was* that one freshman who was using the urinal in the locker room and peed all over myself when someone was pushed into me.

I was liked by my teachers and my friends. My friends and I were a small but tight group and some of my best days were lunches in the drama room with the eight of us and my theatre teacher, Ms. Emerson, who I remain friends with to this day.

As a teacher at the same campus where I went to school—and now the same school in which you will soon be graduating from—I have often watched you and your friends whenever I had supervision duty. I did that before our family life blew up, and I did it after, always curious as to whether or not your teenage experience was anything like mine.

You and I are so different, but studying you at your lunch table over a four year period, I picked up some similarities in the way we both interact with people. I kept my social circle pretty small…as have you. Whenever I sat down to eat with my friends, I always found myself sitting in the middle of them. You do that too, except you guys always stay standing for some reason. When others would talk, I couldn't stop my thoughts and emotions from playing out on my face no matter how hard I tried. But while for me the depression was on full display from an early age, your face these last couple of years has been an expressive mix of teenaged practice aloofness and what I best describe as…indifference. There were moments that your feelings were as transparent as if you took a Sharpie and wrote "Why Bother?" across your forehead.

Travis: is that how you've felt about life in general, or are you just indifferent to *your* life? Is that where our DNA and shared experience closely ties us together? Perhaps after all these years, it wasn't depression and shame and suicidal ideation that was in my psyche's driver's seat during my teenage years—maybe I just couldn't find a reason to live. At least, not until I was 31 years old.

You know what? This was a lot today, and I'll end it here a little early.

Love, Dad

Dear Travis,

Listen, I know it was the 70s and 80s where information about homosexuality was buried in a few chapters in medical books, in journals, and on the occasional after 9:00pm TV show or movie, but COME ON, how did my family, even though we were *very* Christian, never suspect that I was gay until I was in college? I've recently asked them, and they *swear* they didn't know that "I struggled" (we still don't use the word "gay" much. It's still too new). No, my family never really questioned my sexual identity—they really just thought I was "creative." And "troubled."

Keep it in mind that your Papa was a police detective.

The following is a list, in no particular order, of gay stereotypes I fulfilled. Fulfilling them proudly or with embarrassment is not at issue, but instead "it is what it is"…as every news commentator and every teacher at the end of a semester likes to say.

Yeah, I know if anyone but you reads this list I'd take some flak for giving into the stereotype that there *are* gay stereotypes. But we also live in a world where a good portion of British people really *do* like to talk an awful lot about the weather. Where plenty of Americans talk too loud. And where white people aren't as close with their families as they could be.

Note: gay stereotypes I did *not* fulfill will be in a future letter.

Here's my list:

1. I was twelve or so, and I had to write a short essay about the story of my life thus far. One of the memories included a story of me, at four years old, pretending I was Snow White, where I'd fall asleep and wait for "the handsome prince to come kiss me awake." I got a B on that paper. Homophobia.

2. I saw the movie version of the musical *Annie* about three times. The obvious gay component clue was when I bought the soundtrack and played it over and over until I drove everybody nuts. In fact, I was such a fan, Grammy and Papa bought these fancy plates—the kind you display and not eat on—with scenes from the film plastered all over them. I imagine I'll see these plates someday when the Living Will is read. Don't start Googling: I already did and they are worth nothing.

3. I can't fix anything. Even something as simple as hammering a nail into a wall can go wrong. I have more handymen in my Contacts than I do take-out restaurants.

4. I have always loved many a musical, but *The Wizard of Oz* was my Super Bowl. I watched it religiously every year in March and, like that scene in ET, I always cried at the end.

5. I had crushes on girls with blonde hair. Now I'm not sold on this one, but I've heard from more than one source that if you can get a gay man to admit he had a crush on any one girl, he'd claim a blonde one.

6. I have cared about my appearance since I came out of the womb; I've over-obsessed about my body shape and weight, my nose size, and the

way I looked in clothes for as long as I can remember. I have no memory of ever *not* caring what I looked like.

7. I tried to get a subscription of *Tiger Beat*. Look it up.

8. I was, and still am, very sensitive and care too much about what other people think of me.

9. I like Jeeps and apparently Jeeps are to gay men what a Subaru is to lesbians.

10. I tend to be a bit self-absorbed. Not sure? Go back to this list and see how many times I started each sentence with "I."

11. I had a rough relationship with my dad, but I was close to my mom.

12. Playing any sport was as rough as you could imagine. Combine very little athletic skill with a bit of femininity, and I spent a lot of years crying in my room before baseball games. Those days were brutal.

13. In 5th grade, the whole class caught me making-out with my desk. Literally opening my lips and dry sucking the lacquered wood. Ok, maybe that wasn't a gay thing and just a weird thing. MAN that was odd.

Travis, I tell you these things to not only inject some humor into what was partially a painful part of my history, but to also get you to understand that I didn't *choose* to hope the prince from *Snow White* would come kiss me. I was 4. I didn't ask to be obsessed with *Annie* or the Tin Man (he was my favorite) any more than your brother chose to be obsessed with pirates and *Star Wars* when *he* was 4.

And certainly no one urged you to be drawn to skateboarding and wakeboarding and violent military video games at an early age. Your mom and I didn't need to stoke those desires in you—they came naturally.

And I didn't choose to be attracted to men any more than you chose to be attracted to women.

Listen: undoubtedly, life would have been so much easier if DJAA didn't have to make an exception for me, allowing me to play T-ball at 6 years old. I would have *loved* to find going to a Dodger game enjoyable instead of wishing I was at home listening to "It's a Hard Knock Life" every night before I went to bed. How much easier it would have been to be like every other boy and just basically skate through life. How fewer insults I would have had to endure.

But I'm 49 now, and I'm not going to regret or apologize or change my natural inclinations any more than you should at 17.

I love you, son. I hope to see you soon.

Even if you never accept who I am, I hope you always accept who you are. I truly mean that.

Love, Dad

Dear Travis,

In 2018, I wrote and produced a play called *The Games People Play*. The story centers around a desperate man who, with the help of his psychiatrist best friend, uses modern psychotherapy findings combined with medication in order to have all existence of his dead son erased from his grieving wife's memory.

I didn't understand at the time I was writing the play that it would be my most personal; never before had I attempted to write a *metaphor*, nor did I try here, but that's the way it turned out. It took a close friend, an actor in the play, to point out to me the parallels to my own life and the life I had with your mother and you boys. Subconsciously, the play, thematically, had a lot to say about my refusal to deal with my homosexuality and the subsequent consequences once I gave up the "struggle" in order to accept who I was, and while there is not one element of sexual identity in the play, do a close read and you'll see it.

One last thing: I wrote the play about four months before I had any idea I was going to move out of our home, so coincidentally or not, the portion of the storyline concerning the death of a child ended up a grim foreshadowing of what would happen between you and me just eight months later.

I mention the play only as an artistic illustration of what my life was like as a closeted gay man, and while a Tennessee Williams example would have been more appropriate and less self-promoting, I can also appreciate that I'll never get you to read *Cat on a Hot Tin Roof*; however, I *might* be able to get you to read *The Games People Play* since the play has *you*, Travis, written all throughout—you'll recognize yourself in the dead son even though the character never makes an appearance and has no lines whatsoever. And while I might be patting myself on the back here, it is my most mature work and one

I'm most proud of…but like every Travolta movie, it came and went and we all forgot about it.

Due to the psychiatric experimentation of the husband and his friend, the wife in the play, Allison, has not only forgotten her son's death but is unable to remember having a son in the first place. But while any trace of the boy, Jacob, was erased, the men were unable to take away the grief that was buried too deep into Allison's psyche. She walked around for most of the play knowing she was grieving and suffering the byproducts of grief but not really understanding why.

When it comes to how I handled my sexual confusion as a teenager, I was much like Allison. To this day, when people ask me when I discovered I was gay, I can't give them a real solid answer. Listen Travis, I didn't even acknowledge in my head that I liked *men* until I was halfway through college, so I couldn't spend a lot of my adolescent and teenage years mulling philosophically whether I was gay or straight. In *my* Christian world, a person couldn't be gay and follow Jesus any more than a practicing serial killer could follow Jesus.

Yes, that comparison has been made before, I promise.

And since I definitely *was* a follower of Christ, by my own free will (ssshhhh Calvinists, ssshhhh), the option to *practice* homosexuality didn't exist for me. So, if being a gay man was off the table for me from the get-go, I unconsciously understood that I could *not* entertain the idea that certain models on the *Men's Health* covers were…interesting…to look at. I would look at them super-fast, but I never let myself think "Jeesh, I find that dude attractive. Maybe I'm gay." Instead, I would think, "Maybe I should buy that issue: I really do need to increase my bench press by 25% and find the 32 foods that will burn fat while I sleep."

That worked at school too; I never allowed my thoughts to go farther than "Hmmm, I'm super drawn to the way that older guy looks. He is *cool*, and I *wish* I could be that cool. If only all the girls stared at me like that." And then I would make sure I walked down a certain hall after third period every day so I could see David or Brett* pass by and look right over my head, leaving me with the delusion that I just wanted to *be* these guys instead of wanting them to simply like me back.

No, that kind of thinking would send me straight to hell.

So I chose to live my hell now instead of going there later.

Like Allison, I knew there was something lying underneath my safe, boundary pushing thoughts that were breaking me down every single day, shoving me into therapists' offices where I blamed my struggles on the broken relationship with my dad, thinking about death more than, I figured, the average teenager did. I walked around like a person who had been numbed up at the dentist's office: I knew I had a lip even though I couldn't feel it, but I was also careful enough to know I shouldn't reach up to *try* and feel it, and I definitely shouldn't drink anything for a few hours lest I draw attention to it when I dribble all over my face.

Now I can blame evangelical Christianity, my parents, or Reagan or Bush at the helm of the very sexually conservative 80s, but when it all comes down to it, the fear of losing my God, my parents, my brother and extended family, and my friends lay on *me* because I never gave anyone a chance to let them know what I was suffering through. It's not fair to place reactionary expectations on people based on what you *think* they will say or do. Even with the burgeoning years of Oprah but before Dr. Phil, I was savvy enough to understand that I had people in my life that loved me for who they *thought* I was and would continue to love me when they found out *what* I was, and if it had come down to it, there were enough people who would have stuck around to cover for the people who didn't.

If you have two people in your life who love you, Travis, then you are a blessed man.

Consider yourself a thousand times blessed.

Miss you.

Love, Dad

*Names haven't been changed here. These guys didn't know I existed then…and they don't now. Facebook has assured me of that.

Dear Travis,

One of the teachers at your old middle school told me, not verbatim, that "it would have been better had I killed myself rather than be a homosexual." If I had committed suicide before I "gave in to my fleshly desires," if I had conformed to traditional ideological and theological thought before I took my life, then I would have "gone to heaven. I would have been with Jesus."

The implication, of course, is now I'm not. I'm *not* going to be with Jesus when that time comes.

This was just a few months after my last and final suicide attempt by the way.

He told me this at the gym too, not that it really matters, I guess. It's just another reminder that I spend way too much time talking at the gym and not enough time working out.

This teacher, Mr. Hoover, was teaching at your first public middle school during your 8th grade year. While you were never in his class, you are very familiar with him—you couldn't stand him actually—and since I knew him personally and considered him a friend, I would always defend him whenever you had some complaints.

Now do you remember who I'm talking about? Sure, you do.

He and I would run into each other at various work-related conferences and committees since we both work for the same district; we worked especially close since his school was a feeder school into our high school.

But I don't think I had seen him during the early months of 2019 right after I had moved out of our house, and by the time I ran into him, the rumor mill had done its job so well that we just called it "The Mill."

I'll save you the gist of the entire conversation, mostly because I just can't remember all of it.

I tell you this story for a very specific reason, and it's not to garner sympathy. In reality, it's sort of the opposite. I'll explain.

I have an almost 50-year-old world view that has been largely influenced and developed by many antithetical belief systems: there have been strong biblical and parental influences, liberal and conservative platforms, and across the spectrum friendships and job experiences. Raising kids will change the way you think about the world too. Naturally, there is also my own particular strand of DNA that forms the way I think and feel. The point is that when it comes down to me sharing my particular views on any controversial topic, I basically please no one.

My gay friends disagree with me on most things most of the time.

My liberal friends want to pull their hair out and gnash their teeth at me when politics come up in the conversation.

My remaining conservative Christian friends say one thing, my more liberal Christian friends say another…and sometimes I end up agreeing with all of them.

However, the majority of the people listed above have stuck by me and tolerated what they deem my "intolerance" of (pick a subject), and (pick a subject), and most definitely (pick a subject). Think of a current controversy, name it, I'll share my thoughts, and someone in a crowded room will look for rocks to throw.

Even those friends I have lost throughout the last couple of years—mainly conservative Christian friends—have never showed me hate. They never yelled at me for the decision I made to embrace the fact that I'm gay and that I openly have proclaimed "gay folks" can be Christians. They have never gotten into my face about what I have done to our family. Yeah, a few of them softly said their piece (wait, is it "peace?"), but it wasn't done viciously—love was most definitely the motivation behind their beliefs and words. And to this day, I didn't part with *one* person due to a heated argument over this monumental shift in the way I decided to change my life; most of us just drifted apart like people do when their lives take them on different paths.

And that's what's missing in our world, Travis: the art of loving someone regardless of what they might think.

Haven't the Trump years taught any of us that?

Yes, "love covers a multitude of sins," but I'll make it even simpler, lowering the bar even further: love covers humans when they say dumb things—even when they basically tell you they think being gay is worse than being dead. That it's a worse sin than taking your own life.

It's just a variation on that whole "sticks and stones" thing, but why shouldn't it apply to adults?

I'll put it this way: how did Mr. Hoover actually hurt me, mentally or physically, when he said what he said? Just consider being on the receiving end for a second. What he told me amounts to nothing more than a strong opinion—albeit a completely un-Christlike and ludicrous one. True, he was a complete buffoon when he said that, and it highlights some weaknesses in his overall character. However, perhaps minutely stung after that confrontation, I still stuck it to him by not offering to share the bench press.

But I did another day.

And I'll do it again if he starts remembering to bring a towel to wipe up his own sweat.

And you know what? Overall, he's still a good guy.

He tells jokes in the funniest deadpan way.

He loves kids, and his frustration with them comes from a good place, a place that wants to see kids learn while they're in his class.

He rolls his eyes at the exact same time I do during meetings and will back my opinions whenever I give him a certain look.

He has taught me some things from the Bible that have blown me away.

And he's a stupid human sometimes. So am I. So are you.

Listen, I know there are exceptions, and this isn't about letting people walk all over you, never pushing back when that needs to be done. But I don't want to talk about those rare incidents because based on knowing you like I do, you have placed the right people in your life and you've already weeded out the harmful ones. But I also trust that you will hear people out…and then apply grace as needed.

Now because of this line of thinking, I've been accused of not truly being "gracious" but of being more concerned with how I'll be perceived by people in my life: I've been told by more than one person that I don't pronounce judgments on people because I want to be liked.

But for the most part, it's just not true…in most cases…for at my age and my experiences, it is very hard for me to judge too harshly people's thoughts and actions; over and over I find myself searching and then applying the same amount of patience that I've demanded of others these last two years. I have done so much harm to people in fifty years: family, friends, co-workers, students…and I've been afforded an incredible amount of grace from God and from those who love me time after time after time.

You have been given much grace yourself, Travis. Throughout this ordeal, you and your brothers will have done some things that you will later step back and all say you weren't so proud of.

But as a fellow stupid human, I know there is still much grace you will be granted in the years between now and dead.

Find patience for people.

And pay it forward. Great piece of advice. Decent movie.

Love, Dad

Dear Travis,

As promised, here is the list of gay stereotypes I never really thought applied to me. Yes, I need to put the disclaimer out that stereotypes are generalizations that can bring pain and they aren't 100% true, which IS true, yada, yada, yada. But I'm sure your issues with me go far beyond any inappropriate usages of stereotypes.

Here you go:

1. I have no fashion sense, and I generally don't care where the furniture goes or what colors compliment which piece of art on a wall. I don't even really like art. Actually, I'm not even a fan of colors either. I still wear a lot of grey and black.

2. Clothes. I don't care what I wear as long as it's comfortable. I couldn't care less (remember it is ALWAYS "couldn't care less" and not "could care less") about labels or designers.
   a. However, when I first came out, I played with my style a little and tried a few things, but I never took to it. I look back at those pictures and I look ridiculous.

3. Like clothes, I don't care about shoes.

4. My love for all three of the *Indiana Jones* films. Let's pretend there's not a fourth or fifth film, ok?
   a. But I'd say liking *Indiana Jones* is pretty butch.

5. I have never, nor will I ever, have a diva. Or a "hag." Google those terms.

6. I still have many conservative views, and not just fiscally conservative—I often find the Log Cabin Republicans too liberal. Look them up too.

7. I firmly believe marriage is between two people, and should be, if possible, for life.

8. I have never once said, "Hey Gurl!"

9. I believe churches should have the right to determine whether or not they marry a gay couple. I also think they have a right to determine homosexuality is a sin, and as a private organization, churches should have the right to deny gay folks attendance or membership.
   a. CAVEAT: I think if churches are going to take the actions above, they must stop taking federal money through their tax exemption

status. If any organization is going to discriminate people based on sexual preference, they should not be getting a tax break when they are blatantly denying people their Constitutional freedoms.

10. I have acknowledged and now have written up a list of gay stereotypes that I believe have some truth to them. That's enough to get me permanently kicked out of the gay folks club.

Hey, I know you're struggling with your grades: please push through—you're almost finished. Travis, you are too stubborn to let our family problems stop you from taking a solid hold of your future, and I know you have big plans after high school; don't let ANYTHING get in your way of starting your own life.

Love, Dad

Dear Travis,

A friend recommended I sign-up for a co-parenting class through Zoom. The weekly volunteer or court ordered group therapy sessions are designed to help divorced parents knock off all the nasty behavior we ex-married couples enact on each other, thus harming our kids further. I enrolled in this course strictly because my getting help will only benefit you, your mom, and your brothers. I know I have some anger issues to work out, Travis (even before I moved out), and I want nothing more than to be a better father to you once you and I are reunited.

Well, I think on the second week of the course someone in the class said something pretty profound—it wasn't even the therapist. Even though I wrote down what this lady had just said, I don't think I got it word-for-word. And I think she stole it from a meme, but then, again, I do that all the time. It went something like this:

"People will only miss you if they fail to replace you."

For once, I'm not going to get too long-winded or philosophical here, but Son, I need to be very clear with you here: no matter what happens with us, even if we are never brought together again, I swear to you that you will *never* be replaced.

I lied. Let me go into some detail.

Modern Christian churches often twist a few scriptures by claiming we have a "God-shaped hole in our hearts" that we fill with sex, drugs, food, alcohol…whatever brings us physical pleasure. And while I'm not a huge fan of this particular "Christianeze" phraseology, I can understand the *concept* behind it because as a Christian, I have never felt I had a "God-shaped hole" but once I saw you on August 12, 2003, I discovered I had a hole of which up to that point I was unaware of—until you came screaming into this world. You immediately filled in that hole and it became forever yours. And I will never give that spot to anyone else.

It doesn't matter if I'm reunited with both your brothers.

It doesn't matter if I get close to another thousand high schoolers in my classes.

It doesn't matter if I have dogs and dress them up as humans.

And it doesn't matter if I ever get married again someday.

There is not one human being on earth who can take your spot.

That is reserved for you.

And if that spot stays empty forever, then it stays empty. But there is no expiration date: you can come claim it anytime.

No Matter How Long it Takes:

Love, Dad

Dear Travis,

On 2 February 2019, I finally admitted to myself that I wasn't a guy who "struggled" with same sex attractions (commonly referred to in the ex-gay movement as "SSA")—no, I instead decided I was a just a plain ole' ordinary gay man, and there wasn't anything I could or would do about it anymore.

And you know what brought the most relief? Although the admitting to myself that I was gay released a little pressure, like a bike tire if you push that little phalange thing when you put just a tad too much air, honestly, I didn't derive a lot of satisfaction from just making a personal announcement to myself.

It was knowing I was giving up the *fight*.

It was finally an acknowledgment that I didn't have to struggle with pretense anymore. I could finally quit that character I had been playing from a very young age.

Saying "a weight had been lifted" doesn't do it justice.

One of the most valuable lessons I've taught you boys—and tons of teenagers before and after you—is to acknowledge things about yourself before others have the chance to do it. As a fellow *Friends* watcher, you will recall the episode where Phoebe tells Monica she is "high maintenance" only to turn around and then label Rachel a "pushover." After some conferring, Rachel and Monica march in and admit to Phoebe's accusations, but then proceed to try and hurt her feelings back by calling her "flaky." And Phoebe's response resonated with me probably around the tenth time I saw that episode. She said, "I know."

Dude: make sure you are the first person to know who and what you are—the good *and* the bad stuff.

If you didn't already know you're a decisive and goal-oriented person, how are you going to stoke that gift to its full potential and use it to glorify God and help others?

What if you didn't intuitively know that you can be sullen and quick to anger, and you have to wait until another person in your life points it out? How much time would be wasted, time in which God could be working on you in these areas!

Years ago, I was teaching dead front and center and a booger flew out of my nose and landed on a kid's tie. Anyway, instead of a) pretending it didn't happen or b) leaving class out of embarrassment, I chose to instead address it right then and there. I said, "Dude, I just boogered all over your tie."

And you know what happened then? The kids laughed. But they laughed alongside me, not *at* me. At that point, it was *my* joke and I owned it.

Like Chandler said to Ross in another episode of *Friends*.

So that's what I wanted to do with my sexual identity—I didn't want to experience the real or imagined whisperings following me down the halls at schools or flat out truths in the form of insults hurled in my face. I wanted to *own* that I was gay instead of feeling that rush of pain knowing that everyone was blatantly aware of who I was—except me. That was the real shame. The real pain was that everyone was in on the "joke" but me.

52

Finally, Travis, I could put years of cruel behind me. People wouldn't be able to hurt me anymore with snide side remarks of "GAY!" and "geek!" and "nerd!" I could finally say, "Um, I know that I'm gay. I know that I'm a geek. I know that I'm a nerd." And if God is ok with those things and so am I then what does it matter if no one else is?

My shame was nailed on the cross 2,000 years ago, and I would no longer feel ashamed.

So, I could not fake anymore who I was, and I was at the point that literally taking my own life was no longer going to be a youthful cry for help. And after a few months of therapy, I opted out of suicide and made the decision to live for you and your brothers.

And, yes, I did choose to live for myself.

Up until that horrible day where I packed up my things and moved out, I had done everything in my power to change my sexuality and live and identify as a straight male—I really want to press this point with you. And while the proceeding letters are not about making a statement as to whether a person can change their orientation from gay to straight, I want you to be aware as to what extent I went through for almost thirty years to try and change my sexuality.

Travis, while these days I don't care too much about what other people think of me anymore, I *do* care what *you* think of me, and I'm speaking about all of these things because I want you to know how hard I tried, how much effort I put in to being a straight man—if for the only reason to be able to stay in a marriage where both people were infinitely unhappy, so I could keep you, Christopher, and Andrew in my life.

Since the moment I knew I was different, it was a concerted effort to try and change what was "wrong with me"—even before I knew anything about being gay or straight. Like I said earlier: I didn't even know what sex *was* before I knew there was something different with my sexual identity, but whatever it was, I knew I had to change it if I was going to be able to live and function in the world that was created for me, a path laid out for me from birth of which I had zero input. So I began the work required of me to change for God. And I did it for my parents. Later, I did it for your mom. And you boys. And while there are many gay folks out there whose experience has mirrored mine, I can only truly know what I went through, so, according to me, it feels like no one in the world worked as hard to change than I did.

Tomorrow, I will start with an explanation of classic "conversion therapy," but before I do, I'd like you to do your own research and start by Googling the phrase "praying the gay away."

Love, Dad

Dear Travis,

The following is a list of Christian based books I read from age 18 to 46 that guided me through the process of erasing my homosexual nature. From what my quick research has informed me, however, major online booksellers were no longer going to carry books as it pertains to changing one's sexual orientation, but I did manage to find several during my search on Amazon.

1. *Desires in Conflict: Answering the Struggle for Sexual Identity* by Joe Dallas. Coincidentally, he was one of my therapists and a truly kind, well-intentioned man.
2. *The Gay Gospel?* By Joe Dallas.
3. *A Strong Delusion* by Joe Dallas.
4. *Growth Into Manhood: Resuming the Journey* by Alan Medinger. This one did more damage than most.
5. *Reparative Therapy of Male Homosexuality: A New Clinical Approach* by Joseph Nicolosi. Couldn't get through this one; way too clinical.
6. *The Broken Image* by Leanne Payne. I believe this was the book that talked about anointing myself with oil as a means of healing, although I could be wrong. All it did was give me a zit on my forehead. True story.
7. *Pursuing Sexual Wholeness* by Andrew Comiskey.
8. *Leaving Homosexuality: A Practical Guide for Men and Women Looking for a Way Out* by Alan Chambers. Incidentally, Chambers was the founder of *Exodus International*, the largest "ex-gay" organization in the world. It closed in 2013 when Chambers publicly admitted that conversion therapy was not an effective way to change a person's sexuality.
9. *Love Won Out* by John and Anne Paulk. John and Anne, a gay man and lesbian woman, were married after they renounced their sexual

"disorders." The book, *Love Won Out*, was responsible for this very large *Focus on the Family* umbrella ministry and had conferences all over the world. Years later, John was caught at a gay bar, apologized, and he and his wife divorced. I believe his wife still renounces her lesbianism and is the founder of *Restored Hope Network,* an ex-gay ministry headed up by many of the leaders of *Exodus.*

10. *The Battle for Normality: A Guide for Self-Therapy for Homosexuality,* by Gerard J.M. Van Den Aardweg, Ph.D. Man, this book was just plain goofy. I can't wait to tell you what it wanted me to do to "cure" myself.

11. *Bringing Up Boys* by James Dobson. I read this book, especially to focus on the chapter "The Origins of Homosexuality" so I could make sure any boys I had would not "turn out gay."

12. *Coming Out of Homosexuality: New Freedom for Men and Women by Bob Davies and Lori Rentzel.*

13. *Naked Surrender: Coming Home to Our True Sexuality* by Andrew Comiskey.

14. *Healing Homosexuality by Leanne Payne.*

15. In addition to books, I took a self-study course over the internet—and was also provided a free online accountability mentor—from a web-based organization called *Setting Captives Free.* The site is still running today and has so many free gospel-centered courses which still provide the free mentor, but the SSA course is gone…it may have gone underground. Once I completed the course, I actually became a mentor for a while and taught their material in conjunction with all the information I had been studying from the resources that I mentioned above.

Besides the curriculum and the over thirty therapists and pastors I mentioned in an earlier letter, I also went to group therapy for men with my same struggles:

1. I took a very private men's SSA group at a local church where the pastor gave us biblical guidance and accountability; I'll go into more of that later.

2. Another private men's SSA group at a large megachurch in Anaheim had us watching *What About Bob?* during a session.

3. I went to one other men's sexual brokenness Bible study at some church, but I only remember going once, and I don't remember why I quit.
4. I later led a similar private men's SSA group at Fair Oaks First Christian for several years where I went through various steps men could take to convert their homosexual behavior and/or attractions. You two older boys went with me and went to the kids' ministry at the same time.

Although I do want you to take some time and research some of the ideas in the books above, providing you with an understanding as to what the reigning Christian thought on homosexuality was at the time, most of these books are repetitive and offer basically similar theories. Here is a non-biased overview of the theories:

1. Male and female homosexuality do not have roots in biology, meaning there is no scientific evidence that humans are "born gay."
2. Homosexuality is, according to the resources above, a psychological condition generally found in gay men and women who did not have healthy and satisfactory relationships with the parent of the same sex. When I went through these books, I believed this to be the case, and that is why I blamed Papa for years—I considered him the primary "cause" of my homosexuality. However, I'm saying this now, in print: I was wrong about that. I truly regret placing this burden on my father's shoulders.
3. For gay men, the combination of a domineering mother and a passive father could be the causation of one's distorted sexual orientation.
4. Since the gay person did not have a bonding relationship with the same sex parent, they often attach to the other parent in an unhealthy way— gay men embracing and adopting the feminine side projected from their mothers, the lesbian from her father.
5. Sometimes, molestation by an adult person of the same sex can also create homosexual desires once the child hits puberty.
6. Since homosexuality is a "malformation of the psyche," the idea that various "reparative" therapies (such as "aversion" therapy) could be performed in order to cure people with same sex attraction. You can

Google stories about people getting electroshock therapy and hydrotherapy; there are many accounts describing different type of beatings and other physical tortures.

7. Deemed cruel, most of the above mentioned "therapies" went out with the 80s and were replaced with different, less violent, forms of changing ones sexual preferences. Different packaging, same contents.

Looking back, the worst part of the theories from Christian pastors, psychologists, ex-gay authors, and lesbian celebrity mothers was that the gay man or woman was not just "struggling with sinful same sex affliction," but the one word used over and over and over again was the word *broken*. Homosexuals weren't just sinners: we were broken. Some of the book *titles* even contained a form of the word "broken."

In my many years of being a Christian and reading countless books on many aspects of Christianity, rarely did the authors use the word *broken* like it was ascribed to Christian gay men and women. Very few of the theological books I read on lack of faith, greed, abortion, sins of the past, or sexual purity among heterosexual male and females described those Christians as "broken": that is a term left exclusively for gay men or women.

In the Christian universe, being called a "sinner" lessens the sting of the pronouncement because it just makes you one person in a billion of other sinners. In a sense, you're in "good company."

But homosexuals are "broken."

Which implies damage that can never truly heal.

A "normal Christian" is a sinner…but they can be forgiven. They can be "lost" but "found." A *broken* person can be fixed, yes, but have you ever tried to fix a crack in a windshield? I have. No matter how good the patch job, I would always see that little glued hole, so if I would have been "healed" from homosexuality, people would still have been able to see the remnants of my brokenness forever.

The above theories presented in those books—now almost unanimously debunked by Christian theologians today—did not heal me in the slightest.

They did break me in a different way however, but the breakage did not stop with just me.

Not sure? Look at our family, Travis.

Love, Dad

Dear Travis,

What kids don't understand until much later in life is that parents have grandiose visions of miraculous achievements and romantic, supernatural accomplishments bestowed upon them by their children. Watch the graduation scene from the movie *Parenthood,* and you'll know exactly what every father secretly dreams for when it comes to their children, especially from boys.

However, sometimes misguided fathers want to raise their sons as personal "do overs;" for reasons only known to them, dads want to a see a repeat of their childhood performed by their kids, with some improvement, of course. I, nevertheless, wanted the exact opposite: I didn't want my interests and personality and temperament foisted on *anyone*, especially my children. I prayed instead that the three of you boys would have completely different childhood experiences because I had *hated* myself growing up, and, as you are well aware of now, I spent years in dark depression and teenage angst that I didn't grow out of until your oldest brother was born.

I was into acting and writing and directing. Nothing wrong with those things because I have some talent there, but since I equated those things with the mania and trauma I was experiencing, as a dad, I threw the baby out with the bathwater and wanted you guys to be completely different. I wanted you to steer clear of anything that resembled my life.

So I wanted you to be an *athlete*, and a great one, preferably a football player because that would be an experience that was far removed from anything I accomplished in high school. See as an adult, I would go to the occasional football game and ask when "Intermission" was instead of "Half-Time," so I wanted you to be either the best quarterback or the best running back our school had ever seen since I went to school there myself. I didn't want to live my childhood *over* by living vicariously through you—I wanted you to live the life I had always dreamed of having myself.

The vision I had for you before you were even born was of *future* Travis, streaming down the field after the ball is, naturally, passed to you, crossing into the end zone, and performing your own personal celebration dance as the crowd holds up pre-made signs with a yet unknown nickname like "BEAST MODE!" or "CADILLAC!"

And while I think you never made a touchdown once in your short football career, I did go to 90% of your football, basketball, soccer, and baseball games, and I never wanted anything more than to sit there and watch you enjoying yourself.

In reality, *that* was my grandiose dream for you.

Love, Dad

PS: I had to use Wikipedia in order to use the proper wording and usage for "touchdown." And I own that.

Dear Travis,

1. The word is "a lot" not "alot."
2. Never use "&" as a substitute for "and."
3. And 99% of the time, the punctuation goes *inside* the quotes, not outside. You're not British.

Love, Dad

Dear Travis,

Things for me got slightly better once I was in college: one, I had more freedom, and two, I became really involved in my new church, Fair Oaks First Christian. I never really took to college; I did enough work to pass with decent grades and never really involved myself in campus activities. Not only that, but I bounced from college to college, a mix of several junior colleges and two universities, until I graduated from Azusa Pacific University—wasn't sure if you knew that.

Even though college was not my thing, Fair Oaks was the place I cared most about. I loved it—I loved my friends who I served alongside, I loved the youth pastor and his wife, I loved the gospel and the intimacy that came with having a relationship with Jesus—one that was now a relationship based on personal choice rather than a religion that was handed down to me from my parents. Everyone has to come to a relationship with God that has not been created and defined by one's parents.

The same goes for you, Travis.

Azusa Pacific had a two or three day mandatory chapel attendance each week, and I used to skip them all the time so I could drive back home and hang out with my friends from Fair Oaks. One day I got called in by a dean to discuss my chronic chapel absences, so before I went in, I messed up my hair a little bit and took pencil lead and lightly shaded in dark circles under my eyes. When I told him that I was going through some really difficult personal problems and had a hard time making it to chapel and classes—used to skip those all the time too—he didn't chastise me but instead referred me to the counseling center at the school.

Now even though I was hamming up the toll the psychological battles were taking on my physical health, my junior and senior years at Azusa were some of the most difficult. In light of my involvement in church, you would think that since I was growing closer to God that the inner turmoil that was *never* letting up would have…tapered off a little bit. If the Holy Spirit was truly taking over my own spirit and crucifying my flesh, shouldn't I feel more "high on Jesus" and less consumed with the ever-growing desire to give in to my homosexuality? Shouldn't the struggle have been less of a *struggle* when I was filled with the Holy Spirit more than I ever had before?

But I came to the conclusion that drawing closer to God just meant His light exposed more clearly the sickness that was in my soul, and the pervasive guilt that weighed me down the older I became was also mixed with a resentment toward Him for having me struggle from a sin He had called "abominable" yet did nothing to fix. To me it was equivalent to a police officer putting up cones on three freeway lanes during a rainstorm and then giving you a ticket for driving too slowly. It didn't seem fair.

Consequently, instead of feeling God's love as my relationship with Him skyrocketed as I prayed and read my Bible more than I had been doing in the past, I felt His *anger* much more prominently. I was certain that since I was now turning to Him more throughout my day, it was just giving Him more opportunities to lash out at my disgusting, perverted desires that I just couldn't seem to pray away no matter how many hours I devoted myself to the task. No matter how truly sincere I was, He just would not take the thoughts and feelings and confusion away.

Now, if I had shared what I was feeling with a pastor or church leader, they would have told me quite the opposite: they would have shown me scripture that God treated each sin the same, and no matter what the sin *was*, God would, once confessed, would remember it no more. Only *then* would I no longer feel His judgment.

But I couldn't tell a pastor that! These were the same pastors that always laid a special emphasis on homosexuality in their sermons on sexual impurity, and while sexual sins were judged as no worse than others, their tone and body language proved otherwise as their voices would rise a couple octaves and their eyes would widen when the "Sodomites" were mentioned.

Dude, I know this Christian guy who is vehemently opposed to homosexuality, and, at the time, we also both knew a Christian couple who were having sex before marriage. My friend and I discussed it, but he eventually waved it away saying, "Eh, once they're married God will forgive it."

But in the Christian worldview, this "easily solved" sin issue could never be applied to homosexuality, and besides the blinding hypocrisy and ignorance of his conclusion, the flippancy in the manner in which he was misusing grace was as abhorrent.

So even though it is never said, everyone in at least 65% of modern evangelical churches subliminally understands that non-sanctioned, heterosexual sin ranks about a "4" on the 1-10 scale of "bad" sins while homosexual definitely runs at a 9.5.

Right under abortion.

It's abortion then homosexuality.

(I'm shaking my head) Aaaah...these two polarizing issues that suck up more of the spotlight in modern evangelicalism than Jesus Himself. Living in and among a truly suffering, unjust world, I just do not understand the prominent placement these two theological dilemmas have been given by the church in lieu of the hundreds of other issues that we face. It's like American evangelicalism went to university, and while they enrolled in the general education courses like everyone else, their major was in abortion and homosexuality, sadly only taking one or two unit classes on local on local and global poverty, immigration, evangelism, greed, consumerism, mental health, racism, and "A Biblical Response to the Covid Crisis 101."

But I digress.

By spring of my junior year, I was at the point where I was becoming so numb and yet simultaneously feeling so much pain that I knew I finally had to do something about it. So, I took the dean up on his suggestion and visited my first Christian counselor in a school setting. It was also the first time I had been to any sort of therapy as an adult. And it was the first time I admitted to a single person that I was attracted to men.

Another first: it was around this time that someone in my family flat out asked me if I was gay. And it was Papa. Grammy was there for that occasion as well.

Here's the story: about a month before that inevitable question was asked, I had bleached my hair and while Papa didn't like it, he didn't say anything.

But then later I somehow let it slip out that I regularly shaved my chest.

I think for your Papa, an ex-Marine and veteran police officer, detective, and, later, sergeant, that was the tipping point, and the three of us were in the kitchen a few days later and the conversation went something like this:

Papa: Greg, are you a homosexual?

Greg: No.

Papa: You've been struggling with depression for years. You bleached your hair, and now you're shaving your chest.

Greg: Dad, a lot of guys bleach their hair. And I told you a couple of days ago that I shave my chest because all bodybuilders do that; it defines the muscle more.

(Travis: I was 6'4 and I weighed probably 165 pounds. There were no muscles.)

Papa: Who told you that?

Greg: Brett Stamps from church does it.

Papa: Is *he* gay?

Greg: No. He has a girlfriend.

Papa: Well, I asked Joe Alfaro, another policeman at the station. He's into working out, and he said that bodybuilders don't shave their chest.

Greg: Yeah—women bodybuilders don't.

Ok, I didn't say that for obvious reasons: Papa would have knocked me across the room. But it's such a great response, I should have just taken the risk.

Alternatively, I *do* remember immediately wanting to meet Joe Alfaro the bodybuilder.

Sorry. I know that's a bit much.

Back to the college counselor: I don't think much was accomplished with this particular therapist because I only attended a few sessions—probably skipped those like I did chapel and classes—but it did put me on a path that I walked on for another twenty-five years or so as I sought various therapeutic means to get rid of what I labeled as my "broken sexuality."

Hey, do me a favor: go in and give your mother a hug and tell her you love her. She's been pulling double-duty for quite some time now and knowing her the way I do, she would really welcome that.

Love, Dad

Dear Travis,

To rewind a little bit, I'm going to take you back to my freshmen year when I was attending a local junior college, my first of several junior colleges, actually. I was eighteen and right out of high school, and I was just starting to take advantage of the freedom that driving was offering. I had a truck, two accidents behind me, and I was ready to explore the world within a twenty-mile radius.

It was a literature class and on that first day, like I always did, your mom and I both chose seats in the back. I still do that to this day.

Here is the best way I can describe your mom in those early days. Naturally, none of you boys had been born yet, so I will be using the future to describe the way I saw her then. Make sense?

This is easy: your mother is a 100% combination of you, Andrew, and Christopher.

Physically, although she's a woman, she looked exactly like Christopher would years later. While not particularly small overall, both Christopher and your mom have elfish-like facial structures. Hands too. Both have the same eyes—a fierce, crystal blue that even I was jealous of, and I *always* got compliments on my blue eyes. Like Christopher, they would be eyes that don't hold a lingering look for too long, her eyes usually dropping before mine—neither Christopher nor your mom will ever want to play "chicken" with someone else's gaze.

They are both sensitive, absorbing other people's feelings, and withdrawing when they are hurt. Both incredibly compassionate people, your mom and Christopher do not wear their hearts on their sleeves like I do, but as a result, they "feel" emotions and then tuck them away more than the average person does.

Within a couple of classes, I could see the personality that would be attributed to Andrew. Hard-working and stubborn and focused, your mom, like your oldest brother, are very shy when someone is first getting to know them. They say very few words and in a one-on-one setting tend to gravitate toward those who'll do most of the talking. They are content to step back, preferring to surround themselves with extroverts, letting them take "center-stage." And like most introverts, it isn't that they go out of their way to not speak in group settings, it's that they will only speak when they have something to say.

That's an excellent quality to have.

Andrew and your mom are better at expressing themselves through actions rather than words.

And they are both very loyal.

Now you.

Once your mom gets comfortable around a small group of people, there is a visible shift, and if she feels safe, her goofy side is on full display. In the thirty years that I've known her, we truly did have a lot of fun together, and not only did she have her own sense of humor, evolving over time, she could always see and find the comedy in types of humor that was different from hers; appreciating various levels and forms of comedy is, in my view, a sign of intelligence.

All I have to do is go back to that paragraph and replace the words "your mom" with "Travis"—that's how alike the two of you are: wry and comical and oh so sarcastic when it calls for it...and it called for it quite a bit when living with someone like your dad.

And you could both be so engaging. Out of all three of my children, you could come to me and take an ordinary event in your day and talk about it for so long that the TV I had put on pause would often go past the screen saver and get close to shutting itself down.

Now I love *Dateline* and *48 Hours* and *20/20*, and while I tend to bypass the celebrity interviews and political episodes, I always watch the true crime ones. And since I've been watching these shows for a good couple of decades, I have heard people claiming many a victim as one who "lit up a room whenever they walked in." Now as a writer, I hate clichés and try to avoid them as much as possible, but Travis, I really have no other way to describe the atmosphere of a room when you walk in.

You really do light it up.

It's like throwing a Smurf into an Ansel Adams photo.

You also get your sense of justice, directness, and black-and-white German worldview from your mom. Outside of your mother, I have never argued with someone as much as I've argued with you. I've even argued with you over the *way* we should argue. Sometimes I think you would argue as a hobby, examining ways to hone your debate skills like you do with your carpentry work.

There have been so many incidents where you've answered a question with a question—and then I likewise follow—that neither of us could remember the original question.

You are intense, heated, zealous, and everything you do is at 110%. When you find something you enjoy, you work at it 110%. And you *love* at 110%.

I need you now to apply that same standard to our relationship. No matter what you think I've done to you, it's only fair that I get to be the recipient of that intense passion you have for the things you value.

And I know at some level you value what we've had together. And I miss you. Life with you is like eating a McDonald's Quarter Pounder and large fries out of a bag on a long drive, or like drinking a Coke with ice instead of straight from the can. No one can explain why, but they just taste better. Life is just better for me with you in it.

Finally, Travis, the best way I describe you to people who don't know you is to tell them that you are unique, courageous, determined, and that one kid who can always open the window on a school bus.

Don't change.

Love, Dad

Dear Travis,

Your mom and I dated on and off six times for over five years before we married. Like I said, she was loyal, so when it was time, I was always the one who did the breaking up.

Now that we all look back, *everyone* knows why we were on and off again. I've always believed that was why your Uncle John, your mom's brother, didn't come to our wedding: even though nothing was said to Mom's family, I think he knew what I was, and it was his way of politely and quietly protesting.

I cannot remember at what point I told your mom that I found myself attracted to men, but I do remember I had just finished my shift (that was during my private investigator days), and we were sitting on the floor of her bedroom. I also can't remember if we broke up that same night, and I also can't recall if it were the 2nd, 3rd, etc. breakup, but when I gave her the "it's not you, it's me" speech, it could not have been closer to the truth.

Constantly breaking up with your mom had never been my intention when we first met and became exclusive back in 1990. Travis, I cannot emphasize enough how much I wanted to make things work with your mom—and from the very beginning.

After all, she embodied all those qualities I talked about in my last letter, *and* she was a Christian *and* we shared similar values and morals. And the topper? She was beautiful. She looked exactly like an 80s Kirstie Alley with light brown hair.

Probably most importantly: she liked me.

Well, not overnight, but I was persistent, and I think it was just a matter of weeks before I had asked her to dinner and a movie where we saw a great black comedy you need to watch called *I Love You to Death*.

Watch that movie one night and know that it is a part of your history.

But ultimately, my thoughts that this was the most perfect woman in the world for me could not overcome what had amounted to an internal war between my flesh and my soul—that's the church's labeling, not mine. The romantics will say love is enough, but that's not reality. A cliché for sure, but *romantic* love is complicated and since it's a noun that falls under the category of an "idea" and not a concrete one like "flagpole," it's fluid and can only be defined by each person who chooses to give it a shot. And once chosen, only that person can decide if they are experiencing "true love" since the criteria comes from a combination of an individual's mind and soul.

And if we were to push this issue further, we'd have to start debating as to what the soul is in the first place. No thanks.

In the case of your mom and me, love just wasn't enough. And I *did* love your mom. It's true that I loved the idea of *wanting* to be in love with your mom more than experiencing the natural feeling of love itself, but in some ways, wasn't my being with her—wanting to love her as she deserved—a stronger example of true love as the best of the philosophers and biblical authors have defined it?

When people describe being in love, they always use terms that imply their love is somewhat uncontrollable: they are "head over heels" which suggests they are stumbling, unable to control their actions. They "fall" in love, which also implies an accident to which a person has no control over.

For me, I was *choosing* to be in love with your mom even though I wasn't *feeling* like I was told I would feel when it happened with the right woman. But how dangerous is it if we walk around in life always guided by our feelings? Choosing your mother based on the person she was and *desiring* to love her, while still yet not having the feelings of romantic love that we allow literature and art to interpret for us, well, I think my love for her was more real. It was sacrificial since I was unable to let my soul naturally choose for me. I chose to use my head over my heart, and I think that exhibits some character.

So we can let the argument die here and now: I loved your mother, and since it wasn't like we really fought much while we were dating, the reason why we continued a pattern of two months on, eleven months off, is obvious. We hadn't talked about it at length, but while we had talked about my sexual orientation issues using language like "struggles" "desires" and "temptations," clear, concise language was also used occasionally. Since homosexuality was just barely creeping out from the dark recesses of the mind of conservative America, it still wasn't a mainstream issue like it is today—especially in Christian circles. In Christian circles, these types of sinful nature discussions were always talked about behind closed doors.

Or at the pulpit at the end of a church service where the pastor could come whisper with you.

Or in prayer circles where the leader would ask who needed prayer and people would speak about sick relatives…struggles with fear and doubt…even depression. But the gays would always raise their hands and say "unspoken."

It was hidden and shameful, and a gay person would know they would be looked at differently once that prayer request was offered.

But your mom and I *did* talk about it; we both understood the problem that kept breaking us up.

We were young when we married; I was 23, your mom was 27, and in some respects we were still kids, not physically maybe but certainly emotionally. To this day I believe our intentions were honorable and were created out of a sincere desire to *want* something to happen for both of us so badly. And we *did* want to have a marriage and kids.

For me, I also knew I really didn't have a choice. Based on how the church had spoken about the homosexual issue, I knew the consequences. I knew I would lose my family if I came out. I knew I would probably never experience the love of a spouse or children, and I just *knew* that I would lose God and He would send me to hell. So, it wasn't like I ever sat down and said to myself, "Greg, you need to make a decision here. Which direction do you want to take with your life?"

No, for me, that discussion wasn't even an option because there were no options.

I know your mom prayed on her own that God would miraculously take away these desires from me like He sometimes does cancerous tumors, and while we really never prayed about them *together*, we did carry on discussions about how God *could* "heal" me. So, we married in faith and trusted that over time—the therapy, prayer, church involvement, Christian friends and family, and, most especially, *the marriage itself*—could banish these unwanted fleshly desires once and for all.

So I decided to hunker down and wait them out.

Before I go for today, I have something to challenge you with and I think it is relevant and timely: most kids at your age are desperately waiting to turn 18, graduate, and become a recognized adult. Then they anxiously look forward to graduating college so they can start a career. From there, they dream about the spouse and the kids. Then, wealth. Then they look forward to retirement and grandkids.

Remember something: *you are right in the middle of what you used to look forward to*. Shut out all the noise, Travis, and enjoy the great parts of this particular moment in your life.

Love, Dad

Dear Travis,

In a past letter, I talked to you about the word "brokenness" and how it is a popular term used to apply to *all* gay people's "skewed" sexual "disorders,"

68

Christian or not. I gave you a list of books you could check out and receive a one-perspective view of homosexuality as seen through a Christian lens.

However, while I raised you in a pretty strict, socially and fiscally conservative, Christian household, I always taught you boys to see all religious, moral, ethical, and legal issues from multiple sides. I wanted you to listen to and examine all ideas and evidence, even if they ran contrary to what you were taught. Only then should you form your own opinions.

So in light of that, I would like to offer you some books that will help you look at this polarizing topic and maybe give you a different perspective.

Here is the list.

1. *Changing Our Minds*: by David Gushee. If you only read one, please make it this one.
2. *Hiding from Myself*: Bryan Christopher. This guy's story was so similar to mine that my mouth literally dropped open at several points throughout the autobiography that includes several instances of the author breaking down in the closets of Hugh Hefner's bedroom. Since Christopher is a much more competent writer and can deconstruct the psychological struggles of gay Christians in a far more adept way than I'm able to, there is no need for me to write my memoirs; I could just hand his book to people and save me the hours of back and neck pain.
3. *Crisis: 40 Stories Revealing the Personal, Social, and Religious Pain and Trauma of Growing Up Gay in America* by Mitchell Gold and Mindy Drucker.
4. *Boy Erased* by Garrard Conley. Good movie too.
5. *A Letter to My Congregation* by Ken Wilson
6. *Unclobber* by Colby Martin
7. *The Lie* by William Dameron

Love, Dad

Dear Travis,

Ok, maybe there was one small temporary moment before I was married that I considered what life might be like if I had...options. I was twenty or twenty-one, and although I couldn't really let my mind conjure up specific details as to what that life might look like, occasionally little pictures of certain possibilities began to peek out of my subconscious like a groundhog in February. Or is it March?

A little off subject, but speaking of groundhogs, did I ever tell you how my dad would get rid of gophers—nasty little groundhog-like things without the fluffy tails—when I was growing up?

Whenever Papa found a fresh gopher hole in the backyard, he would take us outside where he would grab the hose and shove it down the hole as far as it would go. Then he would turn on the hose, make sure the shovel was nearby, and we would wait. Now, I'd always stay way beyond the action somewhere on the cement because if the hole was truly fresh, indicating the gopher hadn't moved on to someone else's backyard, a small gathering flood would start to puddle up somewhere in the grass, typically within ten feet of the original hole. If that happened, I knew what would follow, which is why I chose to stay on the cement—I was never a fan of jack-in-the-boxes as a kid, and I wasn't a fan of this either.

As expected, the backed-up water and a soaking wet gopher would explode out of a new hole, and before the thing could recover from nearly drowning, your Papa would casually walk over and beat the gopher to death with the back of the shovel.

He'd do the same thing with the fruit rats that would run across the telephone wires in our backyard. He'd borrow our neighbor's extra-long avocado picker and wait for the rats to head for the fruit tree next door, usually at dusk. Avocado picker goes up, wire is jiggled, rat falls, and another one gone and another one gone and another one bites the dust.

Yes, kind of an odd family thing to do on a Saturday night, but you have to understand that in those days our TV had only seven channels, and we accepted our entertainment options without complaint.

To be fair, we didn't just murder random animals—we actually owned a few that we also killed. Papa went through a chicken phase (so did we, do you remember?), and we'd eat the eggs, and once the hens were past their hatching days, Papa would cut their heads off on a stump in the backyard where'd they run around for thirty seconds before dropping dead. That would be dinner that night.

It was in elementary school that I first heard the true story of Mike the chicken who in the 1940s had his head cut off...but refused to die. By God's miraculous hand, Mike lived for another two years without a head and his owners took him on tour where they made enough money to pay off some major debts. A dropper would have to be used in order to suck out the mucus from the exposed neck, otherwise Mike would have choked to death, which, eventually he did.

I thought about Mike the chicken once or twice when Papa cut off our chickens' heads. Even though I dreaded Chicken Beheading Day, it was a mandatory life lesson my dad felt we must be exposed to, and I did like to watch a little bit, just in case another miracle occurred. I've always had visions of being famous, even from an early age, and if that's what it took, then that's what it took.

We had some rabbits a couple of times too, and there is a family legend that we ate one of them as well, even though we had been told it was chicken.

However, I was allowed to have my own rabbits without fear of having to eat them at some point in the future. I was in junior high, only a year before I purposely rubbed my forehead on some kid's arm at school so I could get his diminishing chicken pox. In those days, I'd do anything to stay home from school.

Sound familiar?

Anyway, my parents bought me two European flop-eared rabbits in middle school, and to this day, any rabbit with ears that hang down is easily my favorite animal. They have the easiest poop to pick up; it's like picking up Coco Pebbles.

Anyway, the rabbits were in separate pens standing high off the ground, one-inch slats lining the floors making for easy evacuation of the Coco Pebbles. One morning before school I went to go feed them, and I noticed a half dozen or so tiny rats, their heads wedged between the slats of just one of the cages, their bodies dangling several feet off the ground. Once I processed what I was seeing and heard the rats screeching, some sort of paternal instinct came over me and I unfroze. Opening the cage, I took my finger and poked the top of each rat's head until every single one of them fell down into one large mass. I left them, screaming in the mud, and I went to get my dad.

"Dad, Dad—there's a bunch of rats trying to get up into the cage and eat *Flora*!"

Yes, her name was Flora. Don't ask.

"Rats?" he questioned. "Why would rats want to attack a rabbit?"

He followed me to the backyard—to the place that was soon getting the reputation for the being the most violent place in our home—and saw what I had tried to explain to him in the house. He looked at Flora and he crouched down to look at the rats, now dying in a mound of Coco Pebbles. He stood up.

"Greg, those aren't rats. They are her babies."

Whoops.

We didn't even know she was pregnant; after sitting with it for a while, we figured at some point she had gotten out of her cage. Or maybe Buckthorn had gotten in. I couldn't know anything for sure other than I had killed all her babies.

I'm pretty confident that the gophers…the chickens…the rabbit incident… didn't turn me gay, but they definitely played a role somewhere in my psyche because I talk about them to this day.

And those are my gopher, rat, chicken, and rabbit stories.

You'd have thought we'd lived on a farm instead of a two-bedroom home in a suburb of Los Angeles County.

Wow, did I get off topic in this letter.

Love, Dad

Dear Travis,

Today I'm back on track, hoping to get to the original point of the last letter. I had started telling you about that one fleeting moment early in my twenties where I entertained the idea of making certain life choices that would ignite a parallel universe for your dad (see *Sliding Doors* or *The Butterfly Effect*), one that I'm thankful I never experienced because in that universe there is no Andrew, Christopher, and Travis.

So here's the story, although I am quite aware you've heard it a few times. You just haven't heard *all* of it.

Midway through college, I started that private investigator job I told you about, but honestly, Travis, I was the worst employee. Most of the time I'd fall asleep in the back of my carpeted truck, tinted windows masking me and my video camera, crashing from the four or five Mountain Dews I'd drink each day only to wake up in a puddle of sweat, having no idea if the person I was supposed to stake out had left their home. I was as bad a P.I. as I was a first-year English teacher—standing in front of students and teaching *Hamlet* straight out of *Cliffs Notes* without shame.

But on my last day as a P.I. in training I made up for all that.

The guy I was hired to follow that day was the only client I could recall who was not trying to defraud his employer through a bogus insurance claim. His wife hired us because she thought her husband was having an affair.

Now *that's* the stuff of movies and TV.

So this sixty-something-year-old-man operated one of those catering trucks that parked outside large corporations and served burritos or hamburgers or churros during lunch hours. I wasn't on schedule to work that day, but John called me around 3pm that day and asked if I could drive to a near-by city where the suspect was working and follow him from there. The prevailing thought was that he'd drive to the girlfriend's house.

But here's the catch: I was supposed to have a performance at church that night; I was a high school youth leader at Fair Oaks First Christian, and I was in charge of the drama program. One of the high school girls in the skit we were performing, Summer, probably sixteen or so, had already asked me if I could pick her up on the way to church, and I had agreed before my boss, John, asked me asked me to do this job, a job he said I could do in under two hours.

Well, you know how I always find a way to take the easiest, most practical and time efficient routes in most everything I do? Keep that in mind before you judge me for deciding to pick Summer up before I did the job. It made sense: the plan was to follow the guy, take some video, and then go straight to church. It would be out of the way to pick her up after.

So, I did all that and got to the location on time and easily found the old man's catering truck. With Summer next to me, I followed him for about ten miles where he exited and headed onto a small side street. When we approached a round-about (or a "traffic circle" as we say on the West coast), he pulled over to the side and parked. Following protocol, I did the same and waited. Quickly, he took the round-about and headed back in my direction. I turned my engine back on and planned on doing the same—and that's when he jerked his wheel in my direction. Before I knew it, I was pinned in, the front bumper of the restaurant on wheels against mine.

I know it's cliché to say, "It happened so fast," but it really happened so fast.

Seconds later the old man was out of his truck and was at my open window before I could even think what to do next. Normally, if I was in a situation where I was caught by a suspect, I would leave the scene. In this situation, I would probably have just driven off, jumping over a curb or something, but since his gun was now through the window and against my left temple, I was stuck.

Now if my life had flashed before my eyes like it's supposed to, I cannot recall. What I do remember is this: Summer was screaming, but I remained very, very calm. At this juncture in my life, I was old enough to have faced one or two emergencies, but it was the first time an emergency had ever reached this level, and yet I don't think my heart rate, much less my breathing, changed one bit.

Only one other time did I ever feel that type of panic—and you were at the center of it. More on that later.

Oh, and let me interject to say that "holding it together" during a crisis is one of my strengths. This is something I feel I can brag about, and I think you'll agree with me when I say that while I lean melodramatic on an everyday basis, in an emergency, I will be the calmest person in the room.

Well, except that time I thought the dog was attacking you in the backyard. I never fully apologized for that incident either. I know in the past I've always defended my actions in that situation, but a person reflects a lot more when they get older, and I can acknowledge I overreacted. I apologize now.

Again, I'm *usually* effective under pressure: you were three or so when you pulled a Noah's Ark night light down from your dresser; the ark had some kind of steeple at the top, and it landed point down, puncturing the top of your head. I walked in seconds after, looked at you when you turned my way, and I saw flashes of Stephen King's Carrie minus the dress. I walked over, I didn't run, I picked you up, and I drove you to the ER with you on my lap the whole time.

It was like that on the one and only day in my life that I had a gun pressed to my head for five minutes or so. Summer kept screaming and the guy kept shouting at me "Why are you following me? Why are you FOLLOWING ME?" And I very evenly said, "Sir, can you please let this girl go? She has nothing to do with this."

"Why should I let her go?" (Or something like that). "You are the one following me!"

"Sir, I am not following you; we were driving and just pulled over for a minute."

Turns out Summer didn't need anyone's permission to leave; she opened the passenger door and took off.

Me and the old man went back and forth, gun still against my temple, me never giving up the lie that I wasn't following him. Something finally prompted me to reach into my wallet, however (with his consent of course), and I pulled out John's business card. I handed it to him and told him he would need to call my boss. For some reason that was all it took because he withdrew his gun, got back in his roach coach, and left. Anti-climactic sure, but that really was it.

So, long story short—

Too late, Dad

—Summer had found a phone and called the cops. They took a report, and we left, with plenty of time remaining to practice before the church performance.

That night, my boss called me, wanting to let me know that the police had gone to the old man's house for an interview. Turns out, because they carry so much cash, catering trucks are hotbeds for thievery, especially prone to "stick up robberies," and the old man figured I was following him to do just that. He had been a victim of robberies in the past, and he was hyper-sensitive to people following him. He said he knew I was behind him from the beginning. He also claimed there weren't any bullets in the gun.

Uh-huh.

The police left his home, no charges were filed, and after your Grammy found out what had happened, she begged me to quit. For me, that was not a problem; it was my excuse to get out of a job I was bored with. I did not see myself making a career out of the private detective business. To be honest, I actually *was* guilty of robbery, sleeping on the job and all that, ripping my boss off. I should have been fired. Three months later, I took my first teaching position at Fair Oaks First Christian School, and I've been teaching ever since.

Sometimes I sleep on that job too.

Summer was fine; we've since joked about it on Facebook. She claimed she wasn't too traumatized, and I didn't think I was either, but like I said earlier, while I was in the moment my life hadn't flashed before my eyes or anything romantic like that.

But it did a few days later.

Once the shock had worn off, a little PTSD caught up with me, and that's when I was confronted with little flashes of a life yet unknown, possibilities I had never allowed myself to consider...well, I now wondered if these possibilities weren't so impossible. I didn't understand then what I understand now: the shock of almost being killed triggered a natural retrospection of my life up until then, and once I took stock of who I was up to that point, I started to think about the future instead of focusing on life in its immediacy. Little unusual for a twenty-one-year-old, I guess. But I did think about how I had lived my life thus far and what it was going to look like post "gun to head," only this time I weighed two options instead of one.

It was the first time I wondered what it might be like to fall in love with someone like me. And to be loved back. Even with the gut-wrenching fear that followed, I gave myself permission to picture defying my parents' and the church's wishes to pursue a life that, while to others was "unnatural" and an "abomination," seemed perfectly normal to me.

Listen, don't presume that all of this reflection took place over a couple weeks...or even a couple of days for that matter. I literally entertained the idea for probably five minutes. Twenty-years of one-way, black-and-white thinking could not be undone in weeks or even months, so five minutes effectively did nothing. I didn't even have the time to consider that maybe what seems unnatural to billions of people across the world might seem natural to millions of others. I mean, we don't think it's odd when someone whips out their left hand to sign a document, and we certainly don't spend any time wondering if that person is *choosing* to use their left hand—we all just figure they're part of the 10% born with a dominant left hand. Even if someone switches between their right and their left, we don't turn it into an issue of choice—we understand that there are ambidextrous people in our world, just like there is a small portion of albinos in the world. Or those born with dwarfism. We don't call them "freaks" or "abominations," we recognize that there are small populations of people in society who differ from the norm, like the 2% of all humans around the world who are born with blonde hair. Are they "a distortion of God's vision for a world that is supposed to be living with brown, black, and red hair?"

So many Christians accuse gay men and woman of not living "God's best." Is that the case with all blondes?

I mean, you don't call Christopher a "sick, mentally ill" kid just because he was born with two preauricular pits do you?

Somehow I don't think so.

Why can't we accept the fact that a small portion of society was born with a different sexual orientation? Listen, if you'd like, you can still call homosexuality "abnormal" because LGTBQ+ folks' sexual identity and wiring *is* an abnormality: it runs against the norm. Like blonde hair does. And those with double-joints.

And it doesn't just stop with genetic anomalies either: why are some people born with natural talents that others don't possess? Why are some people born geniuses while most of us aren't? Why are some gifted at birth with an amazing amount of patience and yet a sibling can have the hottest head in the family?

When it comes to certain sects of Christianity in addition to some other religions, I started to understand that it is easy and acceptable for these groups to not only embrace but to celebrate the uniqueness of human beings—except when it comes to sexual identity.

I believe this hypocrisy can be compared to those who claim abortion is not only a sin because it's murder but have also labeled it as the ultimate social injustice we face in our current world…while these same folks vehemently support the death penalty.

I don't get it.

A lot went through my head in that five minutes, but I didn't have the life experience or maturity to question these things, or biblical tradition, or biblical study at it pertains to historical context.

No, those thoughts and questions were way off into the future, but it was a nice five minutes. One that I would revisit about twenty-six years later.

This was a long letter, and I need a break. I'm sure you do too. I think the last thing you read that was this long ended with "And he ate the green eggs and ham."

Bahahahahahaha…

Love, Dad

Dear Travis,

I truly hope that Walt Disney's head is not frozen in a cryonic chamber full of liquid, as the rumor goes, because while he played a huge part in shaping my childhood, stoking the imagination that serves me well to this day, his movies have also done a bit of…damage. Ok, maybe he didn't cause *major* damage like Nero or even the cast of *Full House,* but he used his influence in a more subtle way, as every true artist should.

Disney, the man and his empire, cannot take the entire blame for its role in the cultural shift that germinated and then took hold in the mid-twentieth century, but the Walt Disney Company was the trailblazer and then dominant leader in children's media from its inception, whether it was full-length feature films or television. To this day, at the heart of every Cartoon Network/ Nickelodeon/PBS program directed at children, Disney's shadowy influence hovers close by.

A Disney film is first recognizable not by their unique renditions on classic stories but for its habit of removing at least one parent in many of their films: see *Bambi, Beauty and the Beast, Snow White, Cinderella, Finding Nemo* and *Pinocchio*—you'll pick up the pattern. I'll even throw in *Peter Pan* because while the Darling children had two parents, their father was basically a useless moron.

Poor Tarzan saw *both* his parents killed off.

I'm not sure if *Cars* is a good example of missing parents because your mom and I took you and Andrew to see that when you were 3, and you choked on a soda and threw up on a girl and her brother in front of us. Too embarrassed or helpless to do nothing but offer a quick apology, I took you outside where we walked around the building until the movie was over.

Assembly line of dead parents aside, Disney productions are also recognizable for its love of pushing a theme I have unoriginally dubbed the "Follow Your Heart" message.

Here: instead of another straight lecture, let me provide for you an illustration by giving you the plot to the film *The Little Mermaid.* If you remember, it's an uncomplicated story: mermaid wants to find adventure outside of her home under the sea, and to the dismay of her father and a crab, and with the help of a fish, she rescues a drowning man only to fall in love with him immediately. She trades her voice for some legs and goes on a land quest to make her dream of finding this man so they can fall in love. Which they do. The end. Everything works out for the little mermaid.

But here's the real plot of the movie and a staple Disney mantra: "Children: follow your heart, disobey authority, and all your dreams will come true."

Pinocchio leaves his father, and he gets to be a real boy.

Mulan disobeys her father, and she gets the emperor's crest.

Nemo disobeys his father, and his father bails him out.

In *Fantasia*, Mickey disobeys his master, and his master bails *him* out too.

The subtle idea here is that the benefits of living by feelings, even at the expense of disobedience, is the greatest and noblest of values. The end always justifies the means.

We have been peddling this junk to kids for so many years now that we have created generations of people who put emotions and feelings ahead of logic and reason. The figurative heart, being the emotional center of our souls, certainly has a place in our actions, but our mind should take the *lead*. The Bible says the heart is deceitful above all things, but the scary part of that verse is what follows: "who can understand it?" Even non-religious people know that our heart has no ability to think rationally; we don't require our eyes to filter our body of toxins and waste—we leave that to the kidneys.

And we don't rely on the heart to guide us when confronted with the serious, more complicated issues of life.

Yeah, every-once-in-a-while we have to get up in the morning and give in to the *feeling* of not wanting to go to work or school. We get up, tell our employer we're taking the day off, and then we go to the beach. Or we take in a movie or two—just skip Disneyland. But these are not major life decisions; in these cases I mention we are letting our hearts lead us into momentary pleasures that truly have no long-term, life changing consequences.

Listen, take the following advice not as a lecture but as if I'm giving you "cheat codes" like the ones you use for *Call of Duty*...only these are more like "life cheat codes." It will soften the blow! Son, you, in particular, struggle with letting your heart and your emotions guide your actions. Maybe it was Disney's fault, maybe it was mine, but regardless, you are in for a world of hurt if you let your emotions run unchecked, dismissing the important role rational, logical thinking takes when decisions need to be made. Listen, since you were young you've had the uncanny ability to scrutinize and then process the world around you, examining all its precepts and instructions with healthy skepticism. From an early age, you proved to be an analytical kid; you asked "why" more than your brothers ever did, not out of obstinacy but because you were generally interested in making sure the things asked of you were reasonable.

But sometimes you dismiss objective thinking in lieu of living as a slave to your feelings. After all, giving in to your emotions is easier because releasing emotions doesn't require any sort of systematic process; the feelings that are innately inside each of us are already present, so letting them loose requires little effort, whereas logic requires energy. But when you get into the habit of letting your feelings routinely take the front seat while rational thinking is stuffed in the trunk, your mind doesn't have a chance to keep your heart in check.

Let me be very, very honest here: the worst battle you will ever fight is between what you know and what you feel. Store that somewhere; you're gonna need to remember it.

OK, I know you're thinking that I am the biggest hypocrite since I seemingly left our home so I could follow my own heart, but that cannot be further (farther?) from the truth. Over a period of months, not minutes, I resorted to praying and thinking logically before I finally agreed with my therapist that I would never have peace and be the dad and follower of Christ I've always wanted to be unless I made some drastic changes. Up until the day I gave up the struggle, I had primarily lived life with my emotions in the driver's seat, leaving all rational thought not in the trunk but back at a highway rest stop. In fact, I'd argue that for my entire life I had relied heavily on my emotions to get me from one day to the next, making decisions based on the nagging, fearful thought that God would not love me or consider me His child if I lived my life as a gay man.

The consequences of living a life led by feelings came to a head about a year before that day where our lives changed forever. You will remember the following, but it's important I write them down so you understand that I acknowledge the mistakes I made during that horrible year for our family.

1. While I firmly believe that overall I was an excellent father to you boys, I know that for all of 2018 I was "checked out." I was "there" but I wasn't actually "there" as I routinely gave in to my depression and anxiety. I lived a very self-centered life during that period.

2. Every night I was going to bed between 5:30 and 6:00, taking my sleeping pill earlier and earlier so I could sleep longer and not have to deal with the chronic depression that was getting worse with no signs of letting up. It's funny though, my psyche wouldn't allow me to get away with the continual denial and diversion by trying to sleep off the pain—I started having nightmares, mostly night terrors about being stabbed by either knives or swords. Some nights I'd wake up screaming even though I couldn't get a full scream out; the only way I can describe the sounds of my screams is to compare them to the grunts a rhinoceros makes while giving birth.

3. After the sleeping pill each night, I would often have a Xanax or a glass of wine or a beer before bed; some nights it was *two* glasses of wine or beer.

4. I would periodically break down in public places. Work…the gym…church. One night, your mom and I went to Lazy Dog, and I began sobbing right after we finished eating dinner. We packed up and left in a hurry.

5. Thoughts of death consumed much of my waking hours—the waking hours dwindling as 2018 continued. While I don't think I was suicidal at that point, I would entertain morbid scenarios, imagining what life would be like for your mom and you guys if I wasn't there. One day, I did cover my bases and called my insurance company to ask if my life insurance policy covered suicide. The poor Texan I talked to on the phone had *no* idea what to say. I kept apologizing to him.

6. I fought with you boys so much that year, especially with Andrew. I said many things that I will always regret, even if you and Andrew eventually forgive me for them.

All of these things were being discussed with my new Christian therapist, but after about a month, he told me he didn't think he'd be of much help with the things I listed above if I didn't start thinking rationally and confront and eventually accept my homosexuality as unchangeable and a permanent part of who I was.

So, using the Bible and 100% logic as my guide and moral compass, I objectively came to the conclusion that I no longer had to live in fear that God would send me to hell—trust and faith in Christ was the only requirement of salvation. Nowhere in the Bible does it say that I couldn't be a follower of Christ based on my sexual orientation.

Nowhere—and you can challenge me on that.

Back to you.

Travis, you gave in to your emotions the day you decided you didn't need me in your life anymore. That first initial emotional impulse is understandable, I probably would have done the same thing, but now is the time to free your mind and put your heart in the trunk for a while.

It's been almost two years since we've spoken face-to-face, and if your emotions led to the decision to punish me, please be assured that I have been punished. Even though you are the middle child, you seem to be the family spokesman, even more so than your mother, and you took it upon yourself to dole out the repercussions for my actions. Understand that I will live with the ramifications of this punishment for the rest of my life.

But here's an important question: am I the only one who is being punished with this "prison sentence?" Have you stopped to logically and rationally consider that you might be serving that sentence alongside me? Is the reasonable, objective idea that you need to have your dad in your life run contrary to what your broken heart is saying, the heart that is telling you to make me suffer?

If making me suffer was truly your goal, then Travis you've done your job—and you've done it well. I am missing out on everything in your life.

But remember: you're missing out on mine too.

Stop and think. Put your feelings on hold and stop and think.

By the way, Disney did redeem itself a bit with the first *Frozen* film. I think you were too old to have seen that by the time it was released, but early on in the movie, Elsa's sister, Anna, "falls in love" with a shady character named Hans. In this case, even though Hans is handsome and seemingly kind, Anna's infatuation with him puts roadblocks around all rational thinking. However, Elsa is one of the first Disney characters to stand up and warn her sister *not* to follow her heart—and as it turns out, she was right…handsome Hans has been plotting all along to use Anna to take the throne.

"Follow Your Heart" then becomes "Follow Your Mind."

Good for the writers of *Frozen*.

Be Elsa, Travis. Be Elsa.

Love, Dad

Dear Travis,

Around the time of the gun/hold-up incident I, ironically, tried to take my life a second time. This attempt was a little more drastic, the cry for help a little louder. The overdose that night was on a weekend my parents were gone and I was in the middle of a party with all of my friends around and a girl I was dating at the time, so I honestly don't know how serious I was about actually ending my life. What I can understand now is that I was subconsciously giving my closest friends an opportunity to help me without me telling them why I needed their help.

This time around I had graduated from aspirin to over-the-counter sleeping pills, hence the more serious nature of the attempt. I was at home, and even with all my friends present—and a girl I was dating at the time—I still took ten, fifteen pills, went into my parents' room and went to sleep. My frustration at God was at its peak; I still couldn't understand why He would create me to be attracted to members of my own sex yet deem it aberrant behavior and forbid me from finding the kind of love and companionship that most of my friends were experiencing.

Hold on: I can feel myself going off topic again.

The point needs to be made that when gay men and women use the term "attracted to the same sex," heterosexual folks have got to try and understand that while it's just as important to straight men and women, sex itself is not the driving force fueling our desires. Considering that, it is my belief that if our attractions were 100% just about the physical act of sex itself there would be less depression in the LGBTQ+ world, for sex can easily be attained by most anyone if they try hard enough. And if sexual needs could be regularly met, what's left to be depressed about?

No, sex is like one of the wedges on a Trivial Pursuit wheel: it's just one piece of a grander vision of a major human need. The need is not a necessity like food or water, but seeking out *the* partner who fulfills the desires of the *soul* like no other one person can is the implanted dream we all long for. And even if you aren't quite ready to experience this once-in-a-lifetime relationship that will connect the two of you in a way that not even the relationship with your children can emulate, your soul is already in love with the *idea* that its needs will someday be met.

I'm your dad, and I know it's hard to pull back and examine me as a fellow human being, but seriously, I'm no different than you, Travis. No different than your mom. Your teachers. The lady behind the glass counter at the Chevron station: we have a deep longing to connect and offer up our soul to one person in the short time we've been given.

So, with the vast experiences that two years brings with living as a gay man, I have now come to the conclusion that the deep depression the gay community experiences are a result of the societal and religious message that not only are we excluded from having sex, but we aren't even allowed to share a life with the one person who best suits our soul.

Everyone else can because their relationships are "natural."

And everyone else can because they are of a majority.

With that in mind, how fast do you think the church would get out their erasers and start making some changes to their doctrinal statements if all of a sudden 40% of the population were LGBTQ+?

That's what happened after World War 2: the divorce rate skyrocketed to that very same percentage in the years following that war, and church denominations everywhere came to the quick conclusion that some exceptions would have to be made because, after all, you can't lose 40% of your membership!

They figured, gotta start looking the other way on some things.

Oh well, not sure why we are even arguing these points: Christian homosexuals are not true homosexuals, according to many interpretations of the Bible, because their true identity is in Christ; however, heterosexual identities have nothing to do with their relationship with Christ, so they are allowed to keep these two things separate.

Aaanndd….we're back.

So, the girl I was dating, Maxine, quietly nicknamed Minor Maxine by my friends due to the awkward admission that there was an age gap between the two of us, was yet another victim in an ever-growing list of girls I had used to redirect my desires that, once again, I did *not want*. And even though it is a common thing for gay folks to try and make themselves straight by getting into "normal," "God and parent-approved" relationships, it is extremely unfair to rope the significant other into a situation that almost always ends badly. Dishonestly getting into a relationship with someone of the opposite sex to "ungay" yourself is just another way to use another human being like a pawn, completely for selfish reasons, and is no different than marrying someone for their money.

After I took that handful of pills and went to sleep in my parents' bedroom, my friends dragged me not to the hospital, but to Fair Oaks where we met with the youth pastor. Have no idea what was said. Then the emergency room was next, where the doctor and nurses put a long tube down my throat, injecting me with some sort of charcoal substance. I guess stomach pumping is an old-school way of dealing with overdoses, and the activated charcoal, a less invasive treatment, binds to the chemicals in the ingested pills or poison, thus decreasing the amount of the pills I normally would have absorbed into the body.

Walking to the parking lot is the next snapshot left in my memory, and I took that moment to read the hospital bill…which was over a thousand dollars. A thousand bucks I had no way of paying since I couldn't go through my parents' insurance. There was no way I could tell them I had tried suicide a second time.

I did later consider borrowing money from your Uncle Jim, but when I asked him if I could tell him something without telling our parents, he said "as long as it has nothing to do with another suicide attempt."

Somehow I paid that bill off myself.

Have you ever heard the term "white knuckling?" It's a broad, usually non-literal term for when a person has to take a stressful situation, one in which they must have complete control over, and they squeeze their hands and fingers so tight that blood from the capillaries is forced out.

Addicts often use this term when they are trying to quit drugs or alcohol; for some in recovery, the desire to use their drug of choice is such a powerful drive, they are metaphorically "gripping" their hands tightly until the desire has lessened to a manageable level.

Up until the time of my second suicide attempt, I was white knuckling it myself, using the last of my willpower to keep from killing myself. As expected, the desires were growing as my body matured but up until then I had so much hope that God would take these feelings away because I was *praying* that way. I figured it was just a matter of time in which the feeling of being in limbo between the Christian I was and the Christian I wanted to be would disappear. But something unexpected hit me hard the months leading up to that night at my party.

I fell in love with a friend.

A good friend who loved Jesus like I did.

Man, I thought I felt such shame and guilt before, but now I truly felt like a monster. What kind of Christian falls in love with another Christian? It was one thing to have certain "shameful" feelings for strangers at school or men on magazine covers, but this crossed a line. This was someone who loved God; a person who strived to live a holy life as I did. It felt like a form of blasphemy, and I figured God's anger at me, even though I never gave into any improper thoughts or actions in regard to my friend, had to have been stoked. The inappropriateness of my feelings had crossed such a line, was so utterly taboo, that I might as well had fallen in love with the pastor. Or the pastor's kid.

How could I be so wretched by bringing shame to His name by falling in love with one of His children? Couldn't I have found an *atheist* at least?

I started asking myself a lot of questions.

Maybe I'd become too hardened to sin over the last couple of years by letting my eyes wander in certain situations or allowing my mind to conjure up questionable images that were abhorrent to God and because I'd grieved the Holy Spirit, God had let me fall in love with someone I had once loved just as a friend and for whom I still wanted to have a healthy relationship.

Now this heavenly punishment would require me to see my friend all the time. The torture would no longer just stay in my mind, I would be confronted by it day after day after day.

I thought I was worse than a pedophile.

Granted, before this point in my life, the developing feelings I had for men were based purely on outward appearances and were something I considered as a temporary struggle; this was different: I had love for my friend based on the person he was *inside,* not the way he looked outside. The thoughts I had for him were completely based on an attachment to the soul that had never happened with the girls I had dated for any length of time.

However, I finally understood what the books, the movies, and the actual *experiences* of people around me were talking about when they described what it meant to be in love.

Mine were the same and yet they were different.

Love or not, it was unbearable; the guilt and torment and confusion reached its peak that night, and I really did think I was better off in heaven where I wouldn't struggle with this sin anymore. So, I took the pills.

Afterward, acknowledging that suicide didn't seem to be working, I decided a more aggressive, consistent form of therapy would be required to beat this, so I found a therapist outside of a college setting. A real therapist with a lot of initials behind her name.

And I started reading books.

Love, Dad

PS: I am grateful to God for never again putting someone into my life who I found myself attracted to; honestly, throughout all of this chaos, that was one of the most difficult periods I faced. I have been careful in choosing my friends ever since I went through that ordeal, and I am thankful that God helped me choose wisely.

Dear Travis,

For some reason, struggling with your absence today was especially difficult. Not sure why; it's only a Tuesday, and it's not your birthday. It's not Father's Day or Christmas or even my birthday. Other than the picture of you on my desk, I haven't looked at any pictures or videos of you today; of course, I really don't look at them any other time either.

A co-worker told me that whenever my sadness over our falling-out is "sharper" than the other days, I'm to remember that you are healthy, you have a roof over your head, food to eat, and love from so many people around you. And the potential for a prolific, fulfilling future ahead.

I have a feeling you're going to be a millionaire someday, so I really do hope we start talking soon.

These thoughts do bring a measure of peace. Unlike my situation, some parents have to go through an actual death of a child, and even the fraction of the pain I am going through doesn't compare to a parent having to bury a child. For me, I have the anticipation of seeing you again someday; thousands of parents around the country cannot cling to that hope.

I suppose once we're in heaven we'll be reunited, but that just feels so far off.

Most days, I have to keep an attitude of self-preservation in mind as I go about my day; basically I have to keep uber-busy, focusing my mind on my job, the house, and my relationships with others.

As much as I'd like to lay around and watch TV all day, I have discovered that television doesn't act as a distraction anymore; it's more of a trap, waiting to hook me in for a few minutes until I'm well-relaxed—then the mind starts to wander to the three of you. Next thing you know, I've watched two episodes of a new show and will have little knowledge of what the show was about.

And forget shows and movies about the relationships between parents and their children; can't sit through those anymore. Not fun to pay for a movie and suffer all the way through it. I went through something similar when Andrew was born, where I was unable to watch movies in which kids were in any sort of serious danger, especially if it dealt with kidnapping or a murder plot.

I can still watch *Cujo* and *It* though. Haha, I remember showing you those movies, and *Misery* among several others, when you were about six. It's weird to think about it now, huh? I always thought I was being a good parent when I'd show you violent, R rated movies but then cough loudly through the cuss words and fast forward through the sex and nudity, leaving you guys to watch dogs rip throats apart and clowns pull arms off children.

Aaah, we're such Americans. This is why the British think we're ridiculous.

So, I keep busy in order to keep myself sane, trying not to give in to the self-pity and constant thoughts and worries about you and your brother. Don't misunderstand, it's not like you guys aren't always on my mind…it's just sometimes I have to let you stay put in the *back* of my mind.

Just like you, we all have to learn to cope somehow.

However, I will indulge myself often by allowing myself to think of the Disneyland story. One you've heard a thousand times, but one I will put down in print so you will have it forever in ink. I suppose I'm doing it for me as well; I'm almost 50 years old, and even *I* notice my memory is slipping a tad. Hopefully, someday *way* in the future, I'll be able to return to these letters and relive memories that may be gone.

In fact, treat some of these rehashed recollections like you would a baby book: you may have been present in many of them, but like a magnet does to a credit card strip, when it comes to memories, time scrambles them at best and erases them at worst.

Speaking of baby books, please try to find your baby book and go through it; I wrote probably 80% of the memories and experiences you had those first couple of years, and I'd like you to understand just how much I loved you from the very beginning. I also wrote some funny things in there that you would appreciate.

So, Disneyland. You were eight, and we had just finished a long, arduous day at the park, the most hellish place on earth. Seriously…truly…no lie…those Disneyland years were not only expensive ones—we bought four passes a year once you hit 2—but once both you boys had experienced the park for the first time, the "Disney magic" disappeared only to be replaced by a different magic: one in which time slowed down and a ten-hour day supernaturally became a twenty-hour one.

If you're starting to think I harbor some antagonism against all things Disney, well, you'd be right. I'm sorry, but I can think of better ways to spend the day rather than dragging two strollers, endless snacks, diapers (depending on the age), water bottles, a change of clothes, more snacks, jackets, and wipes, just to stand in an hour-long line for a five-minute ride, all the while making sure your brother didn't try to beat you to death every single time you tried to bite him.

At least, there were $1.30 churros selling for $15 that we could rely on when the snacks ran out.

Well, that particular night the park wasn't closing yet, but we were heading down Main Street to go home anyway.

By the way, if you start at the very entrance of Main Street and look at the store fronts to your left and right, you'll notice the roofs get smaller and smaller as you progress down the street. The Disney architects did this to create the illusion of height—the trick makes the castle in front of you seem larger than it is.

OK, I'm not quite sure this urban legend is true since I never had the time to actually check this out myself—when I was with you and Andrew I was always on "bite duty." But I have heard this rumor somewhere.

Main Street was overly crowded that night, shoulder-to-shoulder, and we were kind of gathering ourselves to leave; I think your mom or grandma were finishing up in a store or something. By the time we had regrouped, you were missing.

No immediate alarms were raised since it was difficult for me to see even beyond the people I was smashed against, but I was concerned about two minutes later.

Paranoid by four minutes.

Panicked by ten.

Outright fear by fifteen. Remember that "calm, assured demeanor in the middle of a crisis" I bragged about in a past letter? Gone. Not the fear I had for my father, not a gun to the head, not the fear of going to hell for the unholy feelings that I kept repressing and repressing—nothing could compare to this type of terror. I had never experienced it before and I haven't since.

I ran into some shops while your mom stayed with Andrew and Christopher, who was just a baby, and you weren't in any of them, nor had anyone seen you.

The next thing I did was run down Main Street toward the exit, rooftops growing larger from one store to the next. Panicked or not, I was still thinking pretty clearly, and I knew the first thing that needed to be done was cover the exits. Morbid thoughts of someone coaxing you out of the park by dangling one of those hideous, gaudy Disneyland lollipops in front of your eight-year-old-self kept me running faster and faster, and as soon as I got there, I planted myself in the middle of the exit turnstiles, where I could see every single person leave the park. I grabbed my phone and dialed 911.

The dispatcher put me through to "the police," and I filled her in, still keeping myself together, composure intact, as I explained that by then it had been almost thirty minutes since we had last seen you.

The dispatcher was helpful and calm herself, and even though I knew Anaheim police dealt with these type of calls at least *weekly*, she validated my concern and wasn't condescending as if I were just "one of those parents."

I, however, did not return the courtesy but *did* turn condescending as soon as she told me she wasn't from the *Anaheim* police department but *Disneyland's* police department.

Holy freakin' zip a dee doo dah, the Mouse even had its own police force.

I balked for a second before I lost it altogether and asked to be transferred to an *actual* police officer and not to a security guard wearing Goofy ears and packing a Mickey Mouse cake pop for a gun.

Turns out, that was my only option. The DPD takes all calls made from within the park. Same as their fire department too. By the time I was done arguing, an actual police officer, stationed at Disneyland, was next to me, and when I noticed his badge wasn't a shiny brass sticker, I relaxed. Some.

It was around forty-five minutes by the time another officer radioed in saying a man had found a little kid wandering around the parking structure.

The *parking structure*, Travis. Can you someday please tell me, if you can remember, what was going through your mind when you left us, walked down Main Street, exited, hopped on a tram, went to the parking structure, took an elevator to "Donald 4"…only to get lost trying to find our mini-van?

And from what I understood from the police was that this man was *alone* when he walked up to you and asked if you were lost.

A strange man, apparently visiting Disneyland by himself, came up to you in a darkly lit parking structure, not a lollipop or a mouse ears ice cream sandwich in sight, to talk to you and you didn't *run*?

However, I did.

Quick disclaimer: again, I accept the fact that I tend toward the dramatic, but when I bolted out of those turnstiles it wasn't to play hero, it was out of genuine relief and fear—fear that while you were now safely with a police officer, you still weren't with me.

Getting on the tram would take too long, and I was in decent aerobic shape, so I opted to run the path that took me out of the park, across a major street, and to the bottom of the escalator where you were waiting.

In less than eight minutes.

I Google mapped the route: it was 1.1 miles.

Eat it, junior high PE teachers.

Now that I properly framed the story, you will appreciate what was going on inside me when I got down on my knees and hugged you. I could literally feel the love, relief, fear, and joy in my arms. Illustration: you know how you can taste fried chicken in your mouth even when you aren't eating it or feel real pain when you're dreaming of your leg being chopped off with a sickle by your 2nd grade teacher?

Well, to this day, at will, my conscious can conjure up and replicate the exact feeling of that hug.

I can feel it in my arms, along with a little carpal tunnel, as I'm typing this.

And scary as the whole ordeal was, I wouldn't change a thing because that hug goes down as the fifth favorite moment of my entire life, and I'm a very lucky dad because I can summon up that feeling whenever I need it.

So that's the story, and now I have to end this here because at this particular time of my life, this was a hard one to spend a couple hours thinking about.

But there's another reason I have to close this letter, and, as a mediocre writer, I might not do my thoughts justice. But I'll make an attempt.

Writers, poets, lyricists, and moms and dads everywhere have tried for centuries to accurately describe the love they have for their children. The Bible, Shakespeare, Nicholas Sparks, and Danielle Steele were/are able to use their words to give us a very close idea as to what romantic love feels like so that when it hits us, we are able to recognize it right away.

But parental love is different; we can use figurative language, draw pictures, or share stories and experiences, but these have always fallen short, for *all* world languages throughout *all* time have yet to come up with the adjectives it would take to convey what this love *feels* like. It's the only type of love that cannot be explained using words. It is 100% experiential.

On the flip side, the same can be said regarding the feelings and emotions that parents experience when losing a child, either through estrangement or death. It is a pain that the most horrible words in the English language cannot accurately define.

That is why I'm ending this letter now instead of rambling on with words and sentiments that you do not yet have the experience to first absorb and then turn into empathy.

But someday you will be a father and feel this love—then you will understand. But I pray that you never have to feel this pain.

I love you so much. Right now, I wish that I could just hug you. We don't have to talk…I just want five minutes to hold my son.

Love, Dad

Dear Travis,

As you well know, I am famous for my ever-growing list of pet peeves. I was going through an old journal yesterday and discovered that at some point I had actually taken the time to *write them down.*

With that in mind, today I thought I'd take a break from the advice and our history, and transfer the list to you, hoping that when you come across the behaviors—and words and colors—below, you will take a second to think of your dad.

1. When driving, people who don't offer the "thank you wave" when you let them over.
2. People who chew with their mouths open.
3. Farting and blaming it on an animal.
4. The words "pristine," "delectable," "dollop," and "chunked."
5. Clapping at movies.
6. Speaking of clapping, at theatre productions I just can't deal with the people who stand and clap immediately upon Curtain Call.
   a. This is why the British think we're ridiculous.
7. When people say the "www" first.
8. Men who use the words, "yummy," "tummy," "giggle," or "cuddle."
9. In movies and on TV, when characters wrap presents but they wrap the box and the top separately.
10. When people purposely emphasize the "K" in any word.
11. The color orange. Sometimes yellow.
12. Friends who haven't talked to you in years then contact you on Facebook to see how you've been doing. Then they MLM you.
13. People and companies who don't cash a check within three days.
14. People and companies who still make me write checks.

Reading that list brought back so many good memories, so I took that journal and decided to give it an update. I still feel the way I do about the list above, but as I've gotten older, the list has grown.

1. Cell phone dead zones. There are shops I refuse to go to because I know they are in a dead zone; this is why I don't get my hair cut at Great Clips anymore.
2. Instagram "followers" to "following" ratios. I think it is highly arrogant when someone has 15 thousand followers…but follow 3. My friends say this is the dumbest on my list, but it is what it is.
3. Clichés like "it is what it is."
4. Paid, professional news anchors who say "at the end of the day."
5. Putting on underwear or socks right after you get out of the shower.
6. People who announce it's their birthday on social media.
7. The mechanical pencil.

8. Commercials and sitcoms with out-of-shape, "dumb as rock dads" and their beautiful wives. Sitcoms with smart kids but dumb parents, too.
9. People who text "K" for "Ok."
10. The sound of Nicolas Cage breathing through his deviated septum.
11. Those who can't stop hitting "Reply to All," especially those who, when asked by the boss in an employee email to stop hitting "Reply to All," reply to all saying "sorry."
12. While at the gym, people who listen to their music on portable speakers.
13. Showing people brush their teeth in movies and on TV.
14. Showing people brush their teeth in movie and on TV but without obvious toothpaste.
15. People who stand on the left side of an escalator.
16. Apologies that aren't really apologies, like, "I'm sorry if you took it the wrong way."
17. The words "succulent" and "decadent."
18. Dog parents who call themselves "Mommy" and "Daddy."
19. Elevators in big buildings that don't have a "13th floor" button.
20. When you can barely hear the TV show, but the commercials are deafening.
21. *Full House*
22. *Full House*
23. *Fuller House*

Oh, Travis, I can think of so many more; I'll keep writing them down when they come my way. Probably tomorrow.

Love, Dad

Dear Travis,

I was having a text conversation with a co-worker recently…well, co-worker/friend.

Actually: never refer to a co-worker as a "co-worker or work-friend" if you have *any* sort of friendly relationship with them—always call them a "friend." Several years ago, I really hurt the feelings of someone I worked with when I introduced her as my "work-friend." Don't compartmentalize your relationships.

So, I was having a text discussion with my friend, and he pointed out something that not *one* of my many therapists over the years had ever picked up on. We were talking about time management, and he said, "You're one of the best teachers when it comes to managing your time because you always get things done quickly."

I took the compliment, and he followed that up with, "But that's because you cut a lot of corners."

Hmmm. Wasn't sure how to take that at the time he said it. In my understanding, cutting corners can be an efficient way to get a job done, if it's done correctly; however, I still don't know if he meant that positively or negatively because I wasn't exactly sure how he defined "cutting corners."

But last week, when I was sitting on my couch and didn't want to get up to go get the floss to pick something out of my teeth, I took the blanket next to me and pulled out a string, using that to do what the floss would have done.

Hear me out: in this case, I had saved time by not getting up, knowing that one string off a blanket won't unravel the whole thing.

That's when I understood what my friend said, and as I started thinking about it, I realized he was pretty accurate: I'm the "as the crow flies" kind of person, meaning if there's a quicker way to get something done without compromising the quality of the task, then I will gladly do just that.

I've taken Amazon packages and punctured holes in the tape with my keys or my fingers instead of taking the five steps to the kitchen to grab the scissors, since it would have taken, round trip, an extra fifteen seconds.

When going out to eat, I've asked the waiter to bring the check once I've ordered because then I save a little time between finishing my meal and leaving.

Things like that.

When I began reading the "ex-gay books" and started cognitive therapy back in my early twenties, I treated my homosexuality as I was used to handling everything else: by chasing after the fastest, most efficient, time-saving methods to get rid of it.

A huge fan of books that start with "8" or "9" or "10 Easy Steps to…" I naively thought that in order to eradicate all homosexual tendencies I just had to follow some structured guidelines like I had with books such as *5 Easy Steps for a Bigger Chest* and *7 Ways to Get People to Like You*.

For the first several sessions, all my early therapists wanted to do was focus on my childhood, and that is why I quit going almost immediately. No steps were offered, no addressing the gay issue right away, and so, early on, I knew I wouldn't be able to cut corners with this particular battle, and I really didn't have the patience. Every day I grew more convinced that I wasn't just a struggling Christian with unwanted desires but that I was truly *mentally ill*.

The books weren't better. There was so much exposition about gays and their relationships with their fathers and a rejection of all things male, including basic masculinity, that I ended up skimming the first one or two.

The one that stated that the homosexual man or woman first needed to be anointed with oil was the first of its kind that seemingly offered an easy way out, and that one, *The Broken Image,* I finished. I had to make a cover out of a paper sack so no one could see what I was reading when I was out in public though. I also remember taking it to the beach with me. Strange beach reading.

It was also the first time I had heard homosexuality referred to as "brokenness," a term that would do more damage than any one word in my life. To this day, I still have the habit of separating myself from others by saying I'm "broken" instead of a "sinner."

The third or fourth therapist during my college years—remember, I'm lumping pastoral counseling into this group—was an actual, licensed counselor (perhaps MFT or psychotherapist) close to Azusa Pacific University where I was currently a junior, with English as my major.

The therapist and her office were right out of an "80s Cybill Shepherd" style guide, splattered in soft, halo lighting and pink and blue pastels. While never a fashion guy, even *I* knew what straight up gaudy looked like.

Turns out her office should have been draped in "red flags" instead of Motel 6 paintings of vases and ships.

About a month in, as usual, I was about ready to bail when I decided to bring up the idea of her assigning me some homework that included specific tasks that might contribute to the reduction of my homosexual desires. I could do that during my downtime and then focus on my childhood during our weekly sessions.

Keep this in mind: I asked for it.

That was when my therapist, whose name I wish hasn't permanently escaped my memory, wondered if I had ever heard of a particular therapy called "aversion therapy," explaining that sometimes it was referred to as "conversion therapy" when specifically working with gay folks who wanted to change their sexual orientation. I hadn't, and since Ask Jeeves was still several years into the future, and Google even further, I couldn't do my own research. She was my only source, and she had a degree, so I trusted her.

Once she covered the basics, I told her that Uncle Jim had once had an elementary school teacher who went through a similar type of therapy. This 4th grade teacher was a bigger gal and had gone to a clinic in order to lose weight. The clinician took a survey, making a list of the favorite junk foods the teacher was prone to eating and thus sabotaging her weight loss. Doughnuts was on her list, and so they took condiments like ketchup and mustard and pickle juice, mixing it in with a fresh doughnut. They had her smell it and then eat it so it would make her nauseous, even to the point of throwing up. This same thing was repeated every week with the doughnuts and other favorite foods, the hope being that she would associate doughnuts, cake, etc. with repulsion. This would turn her away from that food.

I just thought of something: when I was a kid, Papa would take us to get doughnuts on Saturday mornings. As soon as we pulled into the shop's parking lot, I'd get nervous, my stomach twisting and making weird sounds, because I knew I wanted and would order the rainbow sprinkled doughnuts. See, some time in my childhood I had come to believe there was something wrong with me for wanting colored sprinkles on my doughnuts. I didn't know exactly why, I just knew it made me "different." However, once I was an adult and you boys came to the doughnut shop with me, I would order them because I figured anyone who might question my choice of rainbow sprinkled doughnuts would think I was buying them for you guys.

Sometimes you guys were the best beards, I swear.

Even within the last decade, if the doughnut shop was crowded and I was by myself, I have opted for the chocolate sprinkled doughnuts instead of the rainbow because I didn't want people to think I was gay. These days when I go to Randy's Doughnuts, I get slightly uncomfortable when I order the Froot Loops doughnut, basically a big, bright, dime-sized rainbow sprinkled hunk of fat and sugar, but I do it anyway because the thought of a Cinnamon Toast Crunch doughnut is just disgusting.

I don't know if the aversion therapy practiced on Uncle Jim's teacher worked or not, but I was instantly attracted to the idea of it because it would give me the opportunity to do something besides read books or write down thoughts about my dad or the male bullies that picked on me all throughout elementary and middle school. It would also provide me a sense of control over my own therapy, and I could move quickly through the homework, thereby reversing my sexual and spiritual disfigurement at my own pace.

The following is a skit roughly recreating that session when I was first introduced to conversion therapy. We'll call her Cybill.

ME. So how am I supposed to make it so I'm physically disgusted at my homosexuality?

CYBILL. Well, there can be two faces to conversion therapy, and we'll have you explore both. Listen, it's not enough to turn your unwanted sexual feelings into *undesirable* feelings by experiencing images and associations that are repulsive—we have to create *wanted* sexual desires by exposing you to images and associations that are attractive.

That didn't make sense because that seems like Uncle Jim's teacher would've needed to add sugar to green beans, defeating the purpose.

ME. How…exactly?

CYBILL. In your case, we can start with pictures and combine them with your imagination.

ME. What kind of pictures?

CYBILL. Well, are you sexually attracted to women at all?

ME. Not really. No. I mean, I find some types of art, like, beautiful to look at, but I don't want to, like, make-out with them or anything.

CYBILL. What are your percentages do you think? Compare your attraction to men vs. women. 80/20? 70/30?

ME. Um.

To this day, I hate this question. Why the flip does this matter? Do some people automatically think that the more equal the percentage the easier it would be for me to swing permanently back to women? If it were 60% women and 40% men, would the advice be to just give in and choose women because at least my feelings for them are above average?

I can hear it now, "You know, Greg, a D- is at least passing…"

I never answer this question anymore.

ME. 90/10?

CYBILL. Ok, let's concentrate on that 10%: what kind of women fit into that percentage?

ME. You mean, what kind of women do I find attractive?

CYBILL. Yes. It's easier if you pick a couple of celebrities. I'll explain why in a bit.

ME. I've always liked Kathleen Turner. Kirstie Alley.

CYBILL. Ok, both brunettes. Any blondes?

ME. Uh…Rebecca De Mornay.

CYBILL. Great. Can you get pictures of them?

Me: Yeah, most likely.

Pre-internet days, remember.

CYBILL. And you can get some pictures of different men you find attractive?

ME. Ok.

CYBILL. Good. You're going to spend equal time with both the pictures of men and women.

I'll stop and fast-forward here, just like I did with the R-rated movies I used to show you boys, because I'm not going to go into details with my child about what the therapist wanted me to do with the pictures of women. But I will say this: part of the assignment threw me off, and it was the first time I started to question the integrity of Cybill Shepherd the therapist—how was it that a Christian counselor was recommending I get rid of what I thought was a sin by essentially asking me to substitute it with another sin?

Lust over men, bad. Lust over women, good.

Once that part of the conversation was out of the way, my mouth began to dry on the left side like it always does when I get nervous. I knew what was coming was not something I would enjoy.

CYBILL. The way repulsion is generally acquired is to consistently, even daily, introduce something to humans that produce something so revolting that a person can actually vomit.

This I knew, but with my limited time and resources, how was I going to find myself at a church potluck every single day?

ME. Like making me eat doughnuts with barbecue sauce on them while looking at pictures of guys?

CYBILL. Well, probably not. I'm not sure that's strong enough to provide the results you're looking for. I was thinking you could use feces.

ME. Feces?

Wait. What?

ME. As in poop?

CYBILL. Yes.

ME. Whose? I mean, how do…like, I use my own?

CYBILL. You could…unless that's too personal.

It *was* too personal, but I had no idea whose poop I could use where issues of personal boundaries wouldn't be crossed because I just assume that when you start digging around *anyone's* toilet asking for handouts, you're breaching all sort of rules of privacy, not to mention etiquette. And basic hygiene.

ME. I'm not sure I could put my hand…

CYBILL. I understand. Do you have a dog?

ME. Um, well…

So, at that time, I was living with my best friend, Alex; I lived with him and his parents in a large, two-story home close to where I had grown up.

Those years in that house were the best of times…and the *best* of times. It was my first time living on my own where I had my own room, paid rent, and was accountable only to my boss and myself. Not only that, but I got to live with my best friend and his family, mom, dad, brother, and sister, who I loved. Still love those people to this day.

Living with the Trumans offered me a distinctive change from the only living environment I had ever known. Both my family and the Trumans were deeply Christian and conservative, but the way their household was run was unlike anything I had ever experienced, and I think that's why I wanted to move into their house instead of finding a place on my own…which worked out since I wasn't ready to be financially independent anyway. I also didn't want to go from living with a family to getting a small apartment by myself, so the house acted like a young adult "half-way house," a place to be on my own without being on my own.

In a way, my time at the Trumans gave me my first foray into living amongst a community of people where the customs, food, mannerisms, priorities, and values were foreign. It was not unlike a relocation to a country on the other side of the world, and this move into their home couldn't be compared to spending time with extended family or going to a friend's home for a day or two; no, I had immersed myself into an environment where I wasn't just a visitor. Like ex-pats have to do, for example, I had to adapt and then adopt portions of their lifestyle in order to feel a sense of belonging, and even though I wasn't cognizant of it yet, I got my first lesson in realizing that the rest of the world did not run their lives as Greg Elsasser thought they should.

Sounds pretty basic, I know, but until you're out on your own, you don't understand that you are subconsciously putting yourself into this bubble of thought where your life choices, your ideals, and your principles are the model for what is true and right, because you, Travis, like the rest of us, use your experience, as modeled to you by your parents, as the ultimate righteous standard in determining how to live. You know what "normal" is because *you've* set the standard for normality. Anything that falls outside *your* understanding is *abnormal.*

I've always explained to my students that while it might be difficult for us to understand why some people around the world would choose to live in polygamous marriages with each family having upward of ten, fifteen children, they, on the flipside, are looking at the rest of us and thinking the same thing: to them, *we* are those weird people with just one mother and a couple of siblings.

How lonely they must be, they probably think.

For them, our lives are strange because *that's all they've ever known.*

Now I'm not making a case for plural marriages, nor am I playing with questions or philosophies that reject moral absolutes, but until you become independent, your own man so to speak, the way people run their lives and go about their business will no doubt seem foreign to you because *your* experiences are *all you've ever known.*

So Alex's parents, Peter and Sherry: they are best described as hippies without the acid and directionless passion, both becoming Christians around the same time and at the tail end of the Jesus movement of the 70s. Easily the most down-to-earth, stress-free people I've ever lived with, someone in that house was always playing the guitar or coming back from the beach, and their front door was never locked, even at night; friends, family, neighbors, and relatives were always walking in and out. No one ever knocked.

But while the house was loud, gratingly so when I was trying to sleep, I never once heard them yell at any of their kids—not even at Samantha, the youngest of the siblings and the only girl, who, in retrospect, might have benefited from a little yelling. She was always in trouble. Coincidentally, she was in my freshman English class at Fair Oaks Christian School the same year I was living at the house, and one night she went into my room, opened my briefcase, and stuck a maxi-pad to my Bible.

It wasn't funny when I pulled out the Bible in first period the next day. It's kind of funny now.

The Truman kitchen was in a state of abandoned renovation, dents and holes in the drywall, and I never saw anyone attempt to finish the job; instead, phone numbers and messages were scratched in with pens that always seemed to be running out of ink. Drawings, messages, and fragmented sentences started from the cabinets and ran to the back door. Peter was in construction, and one of his long-term jobs was working on the parking structure at Disneyland, the same one I'd find you wandering around in almost twenty years later.

Sherry worked a variety of jobs and side jobs—she was a hustler let me tell you—and she taught me more than a few practical things that I've since folded into my life, like cooking tortillas straight on a burner. She was also the first Christian I knew who used beer in her chili and sauces, which, at the time floored me because what would have happened if someone from church saw her at the store buying beer?

The family had a dog, and she was very, *very* old…and this is where I pick up the story from where I left off. She was Chelsie or Bessie or Patty or something and was so old that on the day I finally got the nerve to go outside to collect a piece of her poop, I noticed many of her droppings had gone gray.

You know a dog is old when even their poop has gray in it.

Obviously when no one was around—which was hardly ever—I went into the kitchen to take a Mason jar from the cabinet that had no glass remaining because Alex and I were goofing around one day, and he picked me up and slammed me backwards through that same cabinet door.

He threw me down the stairs once too and even did that to your *brother* Andrew years later when Andrew was around six—Alex was playing with him and kind of just picked him up and body slammed him to the grass in our backyard.

That was Alex. If he wasn't slamming grass down my throat that would cause little, tiny pimples that to this day occasionally appear on the back of my throat, he was throwing me through the metallic blinds covering the living room window.

Like I said, they were the best of times.

With just a couple samples inside it, I took the Mason jar back to my room. Six people lived in that house, so I couldn't just put a jar of dog feces on a shelf inside my closet to be found by anyone who needed to borrow a t-shirt.

Or maybe try to hunt out a weird smell coming from my bedroom.

Since people were in and out of my room all the time, my beat-up JanSport was big enough to hide a notebook, a couple of good-sized books, some pens, my checkbook, and a Mason jar, so I hid it in there. Then I placed the whole thing in the closet. And putting it in a backpack would not only hide the poop, I could take the backpack with me to do my "homework" whenever I was out of the house since the plan was for me to work on the aversion/conversion therapy a couple times a day—it would be convenient if I could go to the library to work on an assignment for *The Canterbury Tales* while ducking into the bathroom once in a while for some feces sniffing.

Turns out, there was no way I could look at pictures of good-looking men while taking five or six deep breaths of the dog poop a couple times a day. It was proving difficult to do it even once a day.

The end goal was to keep my nose in the jar and my eyes on the pictures until the retching became full-blown vomiting. Then I would be done. For that session.

But I never once threw up. It would make for a better story, true, but I couldn't make it past the retching, although I think the retching is worse than vomiting. At least, when you throw up, you get a release; I just got a bad case of nausea that sometimes lasted a while because I could *always* smell the poop for hours after.

Most of the time, I was able to complete the therapy from my bedroom, but there were times I had to do it while out and about, which means that at any given time, I was carrying a jar of dog feces. To school. To church. To get my oil changed.

Consistency was the key, but I was only able to do it for about a month. Go to class, come home, look at black-and-white pictures of men advertising cologne, unscrew the lid, and sniff for several minutes—that was pretty much my routine for those very long thirty days or so. In order for it to be totally effective, I'd had to exchange feces every few days, and there were times I would have to wait until everyone was asleep to go outside to get new samples.

About halfway through the therapy, the humiliation set in. Sitting on my carpet floor with pictures propped up at various places against my closet door while holding a jar of dog poop on my lap brought on literal warm flushes to my cheeks. At the time, I chalked it up to the nervousness of unscrewing that lid and knowing what was coming, but I think I really understood that what I was doing, and what I must have looked like, was deeply shameful, albeit stupid.

Honestly, if I had ever forgotten to lock my door and someone would have walked in, I'm pretty sure another suicide attempt would have followed. How do you even explain something like that to people? How would I have explained that not only was I inhaling dog poop, but the poop had come from *their* dog?

Worse yet, the guilt I was already feeling increased ten-fold because now I was not only making a willful decision to try and trigger a lust for women, but I was purposefully engaging my desires for men. Sure, the whole "the ends justify the means" was a powerful defense while I gave in to what I whole-heartedly perceived as sin, but at least before I was able to keep any illicit thoughts stored tightly into my subconscious. Now I was forcing myself to entertain them. How could that possibly be godly? Was God pleased with me for taking action, or was my sin count piling up, God's rising anger just fueling hell flames? Sound melodramatic? It wasn't. I had read *Sinners in the Hands of an Angry God*, so I considered that a real scenario.

None of it worked anyway, of course, and from then until now, I have never felt the expected accompanying nausea when I see a good-looking man, whether it be in an article in *Men's Health,* a cologne advertisement, or in person; blame can be placed on the therapy for my aversion to Drakkar Noir and Polo, however, but then again, maybe I just have good taste.

Today the general and scientific consensus is that trying to "cure" homosexuality by aversion, reparative, reorientation, or gender identity therapies is impossible. All prominent mental health organizations in our country have stated that any therapeutic attempt to change someone's sexual orientation is not only problematic but can cause lasting psychological damage.

Now whether a person believes a gay man or woman should reign in their desires and remain celibate is a different argument altogether, but any sort of therapy that can trace some of its roots back to the imprisonment of homosexuals in Nazi Germany and its subsequent sexual orientation reversal experimentations should be of great concern.

On the spiritual side of the matter, reading the Bible and praying more doesn't work either. Doing so may create opportunities to get out of one's head for a bit, temporarily blocking out *all* identity issues, not just sexual ones. It can even bring the seeking gay man or woman to a much deeper, closer relationship to God. But it will not reverse a person's sexuality.

For me, not once did I ever feel that my attractions to men were waning. Over time I may have told people I was healing from my "skewed" sexual affliction, but in reality, I had just become a master at burying them.

Lastly, while my little experiment did produce some permanent, negative repercussions, I got off easy, for my experience was minor compared to what thousands of gay men and women before me have had to endure, either voluntarily or involuntarily, in order to reverse their sexual orientation. Yes, I may grimace inside whenever we go to Lucille's and watch them approach my table, serving me my water or lemonade in a Mason jar, but that doesn't equate to electroshock therapy, sterilizations, castrations, nausea inducing drugs and pharmacological waterboarding, lobotomies, or boot camp survival months. Conversion camps. Literal beatings with Bibles.

What's a little smelling of some dog dung when you hear stories of young men like Mark who took a razor blade to his genitals and poured drain cleaner on the slashes in order to punish himself for giving in to his sexual desires?

Ever hear of that kind of behavior when single, straight people give in to their desires and have sex before marriage?

Today, even the current evangelical thought aligns closely with that of the American Psychiatric Association, the American Psychological Association, the AMA, etc. by acknowledging that any type of therapy, religious or not, is unlikely to change a person's sexual orientation. But more on that later.

Much, much more.

For now, the next time you see a Mason jar, think of your dad and try to understand the lengths I went to please you and your brothers, years before you boys were even born.

Love, Dad

Dear Travis,

After the aforementioned therapy didn't work, I quit going to that wacko counselor, and while I continued to read a few books from authors in the ex-gay movement, I needed a break from talk therapy.

This time I had a different plan to deal with my sexual issue, a different form of behavior modification that might finally get rid of all homosexual inclinations, and it had far more promise than sniffing dog feces.

I graduated from Azusa Pacific University in 1993 but had already begun my teaching career at Fair Oaks First Christian as a junior high and high school teacher a year or so earlier. While English was my major, I was also asked to teach drama, health, PE…and driver's ed. All of that was fine with me; I was just happy to have a teaching job when other people my age were still working retail. At night, I was taking classes for my teaching credential at Azusa, the hope being that I would eventually teach at a public school where the pay was much better.

Your mom and I had met in junior college back in my spring semester of 1990, and like I said earlier, we had a series of break-ups by the time we married in May of 1995.

By the time of our engagement, Mom and I were both working at Fair Oaks, although she was on the elementary side of the school teaching kindergarten. We had become good friends before we decided to get married, and while the confusion and doubt still reigned supreme, I knew I wanted your mom in my life. We had so much in common, she was stunningly beautiful, and she was quickly becoming my closest friend.

Travis, there is no debate: I loved your mom. I loved her the whole time we were married. People can debate the meaning of love all they want, but when it all comes down to it, each individual person gets to define for themselves what love looks and feels like.

Yes, I did love your mother, and I had nothing but godly, honorable intentions when I asked her to marry me. Since I loved your mother, and I wanted to please God and my family by embracing a normative, heterosexual lifestyle, I figured marrying her was the ultimate way to repair my sexual attractions. I honestly believed that if I married a woman, my feelings for men would slack off and then eventually disappear altogether.

Now since marriage was my goal, why *wouldn't* I choose your mom? Besides what I've already mentioned about her and our relationship, she was kind, she put up with my neurosis and depression, my indecisiveness and obsessiveness. All of those character flaws she willingly looked past, hoping and praying, as I did, that we'd be able to have a wonderful life together despite the major obstacles in our way.

And while we didn't speak of it anymore for many, many years, the unspoken fears about my sexuality were the quintessential elephant in the room. At least, it was for me.

We were young and very naïve, if not blindly optimistic, but we were also both stubborn and knew we wouldn't give up easily. Looking back now, I could very well lay the blame on others, claiming we were victims of some misunderstood Christian dogma, but when you strip it all down, we were adults making adult decisions. We were not foolish teenagers with little to no life experience that could act as guides or counsel.

No one put a gun to our heads. We both knew what we were taking on, even if that elephant was no longer a discussion between the two of us.

All that being said, I do not regret the decision to marry your mother. In so many ways, she made me a better man, and I hope she also sees that our relationship was never a mistake. Today many people ask me if I would do things over if I could, and my answer is always quick and sure: no way. No way would I trade those years in, difficult as they were, because out of those decades your mom and I brought into this world three people that I'm proud to have helped create, mold, and influence.

And my love for all three of you goes without saying.

There were problems from the beginning. Listen, marriage, especially that first year, is hard on *anyone*. In it, you are taking two people with their own insecurities, habits, preferences, quirks, etc., and throwing them into a situation where both people are required to set aside a great portion of their wants, dreams, and goals in order to make space for that other person's wants, dreams, and goals.

Not only was I struggling with issues that no marriage counselor could have fixed—and we did try once—your mom faced her own challenges with living apart from her parents. From what I have witnessed, girls seem to have a harder time leaving their childhood home upon marriage, and your mom was no different. She was very close to both of her parents, and that challenge aside, she was now living with a man who, as she was quickly figuring out, was not emotionally or mentally invested in the relationship as she'd hoped. As both of us had hoped.

It's tough. That first year can be a shock to the system, and with the burden of both partners embracing a life of selflessness, disillusionment can creep in as expectations step aside and reality takes over.

Straight…gay…whatever: marriage is not for the unprepared.

Within the first month, we were fighting so vigorously—and publicly—that Uncle Jim and Aunt Lori came to our apartment unannounced; we had just returned from a miserable weekend in Sacramento, and I was in the bathtub reading *The Joy Luck Club*. How I can remember that specific detail but not one of my old phone numbers is beyond me.

Anyway, your uncle and aunt felt an "intervention" should take place, and the gist of the advice given was to end our marriage if we were going to be that miserable. The confrontation that night was one of the most embarrassing moments of my entire life, and this is coming from a guy who purposefully sniffed dog poop.

But like I said, your mom and I were stubborn, and we kept working on it.

Within a year or so, we had moved to the home we would live in together for the next twenty-three years. I had a public-school job, and I was back in counseling. I was also re-reading gay reparative books, but this time, my heart wasn't in it. Talk about *disillusionment*: none of the work I had put into changing my sexuality had made a difference, and now that I could see that *marriage* wasn't changing anything either, the hope I had carried with me since I was a kid was fading away.

I found myself at Genesis counseling with Joe Dallas. Now, if you look Joe up, you will discover rather quickly that he is a very prominent figure in ex-gay circles. Like Michael Jackson was the King of Pop, Joe was the King of the ex-gay movement. Still is to this day.

And to be fair, neither Joe, nor most of the evangelical Christian ex-gay authors I was reading, were supporters of *aversion* therapy. Reparative or conversion therapy, yes, but I think a good many therapists saw the ridiculousness and futility of aversion therapy by the time I was seeking help. Certainly, my previous experience was not something Joe thought was a valid way to rid someone of their homosexual desires, and not once did he ask me to do anything that I would consider a violation of my conscience.

Again, my therapy didn't last long; once I saw that nothing was making a difference, and my relationship with God was souring as a result, I quit.

Jeesh, if the King of the ex-gays couldn't even fix me, why even bother anymore?

Although my time with him didn't last long, I still consider Joe as one of the more compassionate therapists I've worked with. For a man with such strongly worded opinions, heavily scattered throughout the ten plus books he's written, he is remarkably soft-spoken and warm. I thought so highly of him that I even turned to him years later when your brother, Andrew, was around three. Andrew was sitting watching TV one day in what I ridiculously thought was a…suspect…position, and I reached out to Joe, worried that your brother might grow up to be gay.

He basically told me to get over myself and stop projecting my own fears onto my kid.

All that panic because your brother sat with his legs behind him instead of in front.

However, I did *not* call him when you watched the entire *Annie* movie with me without complaint—this coming from my kid who couldn't sit still for *any* movie longer than fifteen minutes, and based on that event, I wondered for all of about five seconds if *you* might be gay. It was a musical after all.

I got over myself that time too.

Next up was another female therapist, whose name also escapes me. She was in Whittier, a red flag right away because Whittier is not close to any major freeways, and you know how lazy I am about driving.

That aside, I liked her at first because she was one of those counselors whose role it was to validate my feelings and ideas instead of challenging them. When I told her I was angry at God—a first for me—she told me I *should* be angry at Him. But when she told me to go outside, look at the sky, and yell out "F*** you, God," I knew our time had come and gone.

Aside from a few phone calls to various pastors in my area, my time of one-on-one counseling was coming to a close, and instead of continuing the work to reset my sexual orientation, I alternately decided to ignore it and throw myself into a state of continual distraction instead. The plan, understood at the moment or not, was to keep myself so busy that I didn't even have the time— or the desire—to focus on anything to do with my sexuality. I was so sick of the subject by that point, I wanted to move on.

I had lived in denial for so many years, I could do it again.

Ok, writing is starting to take a toll on my body; my upper, middle, and lower back can no longer handle marathon writing sessions, no matter how many ergonomic chairs I buy. Ug, my shoulders hurt too.

I apologize I've been so self-focused in these last couple letters; I wish I could talk to you in person and let you ramble on instead.

Love, Dad

Dear Travis,

"Your heart broke in pieces. It will heal in pieces too." Najwa Zebian.

For the last several days, I have read that saying over and over again, absorbing it as I am attempting to strip away all self-righteousness, trying to see our situation through the eyes of you and your brothers. There has been so much damage, much of it precipitated by me, the one person whose job it is to keep you from as much calamity as possible. Like it is with all parents, I can no longer make life easy for you as I might want to, but because of our situation, I can't even dull the sharp edges a bit.

You know what a helicopter parent is, right? It's an overbearing parent who hovers too close to their children as they monitor and micromanage every activity and every decision, each choice the child makes supervised and approved by said parent.

You and I both know parents like that, don't we?

There's also the "lawnmower" parent, that one parent who mows down every obstacle in their child's path so when the branches and weeds of adversity begin to tangle together and block the way, the kid has a clear route in front of him.

As I see it, in and of itself, a modicum of helicoptering and lawn mowing isn't as damaging as many will claim they are as long as it's applied rationally, keeping balance and the age of the child in mind and with the understanding that this method of parenting does need to dissipate at some point.

All this week, however, I just kept wishing I would have had the opportunity to helicopter or lawnmower you these last two years, even if it would have made you crazy. Damaging or not, I wish I could have been there to clear the path ahead of you of all problems. I could have made your route smooth for miles ahead of you, or at least gave it my best shot, but instead, I looked at the encroaching weeds, lining up around the lawn that is metaphorically your life, and instead of cutting them down, I gave them water and fertilizer instead. Then I walked away altogether.

When it came to yours and your brothers' troubles, those last couple years that we were together as a family, your mom and I had a habit of pulling you out of the river instead of going upstream to find out why you guys were always falling in. There was plenty of yelling and lecturing about specific *actions* but not enough digging into what might have been the real issues all three of you were going through.

I was too blinded to see that I wasn't the only one troubled, and I wish I would have taken more time to dig a little deeper with you.

What I would now give to just pull you out of the river one more time…clear your path…hover too closely…whatever it would take, just to be in the same room as you.

This won't surprise you, but once I came to grips with who I was, over the months after I had moved out, and once I resigned myself to the revelation that neither I nor God was *ever* going to make myself straight, I threw myself into the subject of all things gay and all thoughts and theologies about being gay and Christian. Within a few months, I had read five or six books and had scores of conversations with gay men and women, some religious, some not, some newly "out," and some "old timers."

In fact, these discussions with the older folks were the most helpful for they had plenty of stories and wisdom they were willing to share with me; most weren't just open to sharing but downright eager to talk with someone who took an interest in their histories.

A common theme I picked up from those I grilled—and I don't exaggerate when I use that term—was the raw pain that accompanied many of the coming out stories. Naturally, the older the person the more traumatic the experiences as progressive attitudes toward homosexual acceptance didn't even take hold until the 90s, after the world had been given a decade to witness the thousands of gay men who had lost their lives as a result of the AIDS devastation. Gay or straight, when people are dying in a most horrific, public way, a rational society will take note and suddenly discover their collective sense of compassion and sympathy.

As cynical as I tend to be, this is my belief about the majority of mankind.

Story after story had the same plot: the gay man came out, the family disowned them. Teenagers…thirty-somethings…middle-agers—no one was exempt from familial disassociation. One man had come out to his parents in his mid-fifties, and his parents disowned him. At fifty-five years old.

Of course, that wasn't the experience with everyone I talked with, but after a while it was enough to become a cliché.

Most of the stories didn't end badly, however; human beings have a natural desire to have their own people no matter how they have to get them, and gay folk are no different as the creation of substitute families, sometimes forming bonds that are stronger than that of blood relatives, become a lifeline. No one I talked to who had been kicked out of their original families seemed to be alone. Everyone had someone.

During those interviews, I often had an opportunity to share my own story, and that was the advice many well-meaning people gave me: lose your family, Greg, make another. Find your people, and *they* will be the ones to whom you will commit yourself. They will be your support system as you will be theirs. They will be the ones you share weekends, holidays, special occasions, and personal accomplishments with as you leave your old life behind and celebrate the new.

I understood the reason for the advice, for having a society of one's own is really just another form of survival.

However, I was not, and I *still* am not, in a place to form a new family because I am not done with the old one. And I'll never be done with them. You. Your brothers. Now, my situation was different than everyone I talked to because my parents, brother, and extended family didn't disown me.

Instead, as a result of my coming out, I had lost my children.

But the advice was the same: I was still encouraged to create a new family, find kids that need parenting, which, since I work with kids every day who are going through familial situations not unlike ours, would be easy. But although I understand the sentiment, I have since decided to keep the kids I have, broken as the relationship may be.

Now, this experience *has* opened some doors, giving me a few opportunities to help kids who are struggling with *their* sexuality, both teenage girls and boys. I've had a few kids who go to Marshall High reach out through Instagram, all three of them using anonymous names for fear of anyone knowing their situation—although I made it clear from the beginning that I wouldn't betray their confidence over something like this.

One young man was bold enough to come talk to me after class, and since he comes from a very conservative Catholic Hispanic household, he doesn't have many options.

Yet.

But I'll be there for him when it's the right time.

There will be more opportunities, and I especially look forward to helping those who are questioning their sexuality as it relates to their relationship with Jesus. But no matter how many hundreds of kids…or adults…I counsel in my remaining years, none of them will replace the loss of not being able to sit down with my son and help guide him through the remaining years of *his* life.

Gay dads and moms can swap out parents and sibling and friends, but children are irreplaceable. *My* kids are irreplaceable, flaws and all. No kid will ever be Travis, and no matter how lonely I get, I wouldn't allow another kid to come in and fill that spot I carved out in my heart the day your yellowish little body came into this world.

And even if I was inclined to do so, who realistically could replace *you*, the kid who, if in the situation, will always be the first person to drive his car around the broken and flashing railroad crossing gates when it's obvious that no train is coming?

Yes, you're *that* guy, for you take steps that everyone else is too afraid to take, and once you've led the way, everyone follows you.

Love, Dad

Dear Travis,

I thought of you today when I went into the liquor store and got an energy drink, recalling that time I gave you your first Monster on the way to the rehabilitation center to visit my dad. You'd never had anything stronger than a regular soda, and once that overload of caffeine absorbed into your body, you kept pointing out how the colors on freeway signs were extra bright, like they "were sticking out at you." You kept turning around in your seat like a dog on the way to the park.

Then for some reason, on that same visit to the liquor store, I remembered when you were about four, and we were at Target, and you told a lady she was fat…

And I probably never told you this, but one year you were so sick with a stomach virus that you threw up multiple times a day for almost a week—and then repeated it twice more that same season. By the third round, I was convinced it wasn't a regular illness but stomach cancer, and I spent a lot of time diagnosing you on WebMd.

You'll do that as a parent. Your kid will have the flu or a weird rash or a bloody nose, and you'll automatically go online to research leukemia. Overthinking and paranoia are unfortunate byproducts of parenting. Don't try and fight it.

When it came to getting sick, out of all three of you boys, I worried a little more about you because you were ill the most often, at least three or four times a year. You would always turn bone white. Remember how we'd lay you on the couch, towel underneath, with the popcorn bowl right by your head so you could still watch TV while you were throwing up? Still don't understand how I could continue to eat popcorn out of that bowl for all those years.

Along those lines, I still don't understand how I, up until recently, could use the same sponge to clean the bathroom and then the dishes in the kitchen sink.

Incidentally, did you notice I said "stomach virus" above and not the stomach flu? That's because there is no such thing as a stomach flu—the flu is strictly an upper respiratory illness, so calling any stomach ailment the "flu" is a misnomer and an example of the "Mandela Effect."

The Mandela Effect: I want you to look that up.

Also look up "misnomer" if you need to.

Here's another untruth, a favorite of parents and grandparents everywhere: going outside when it's cold does not and cannot make you sick. The only thing that can make you sick are germs. The only thing a jacket or sweater does is warm you up.

One more: don't insist your kids drink juice, even if it's *100%* juice. Making sure children drink their fruits was something the juice companies drummed up to make money, and all it did was pump kids full of sugar, almost as much sugar as what's in a can of soda. The only liquid a person needs is water…maybe milk…so when you're a dad, give your kid water and make them eat an orange. They'll get the vitamins and all that fiber while taking in less calories.

Well, this was not what I was going to talk about in this letter, but it was fun anyway.

Love, Dad

Dear Travis,

Once again I found myself, just this morning, in the liquor store buying an energy drink, having moved on from *Monsters* to join the *Bang* and *Reign* craze. When I reached in to grab a Cotton Candy flavored Bang, I stopped myself because two college-aged guys were waiting behind me to grab something out of the same refrigerator. Reflectively, I grabbed the Purple Haze flavor instead, a flavor I hate.

When I got back in my car, I thought about the doughnut story I told you about, the one where I spent years ordering colored-sprinkled doughnuts only when I deemed it "safe," where there weren't people around to connect me and a doughnut with being a guy who likes other guys.

The doughnuts sparked other childhood and teenage memories, and I thought of other ways in which I used to try and hide my growing sexual confusion, a staple in the "Gay Teenage Survival" tactical book. I thought about how I'd be careful with what type of music I listened to, switching the radio or CDs when people came into my car so they wouldn't find out I was gay when exposed to my music preferences.

Watching my hand movements when I talked so I wouldn't look so "flighty."

Deeping my voice and walking "heavy," like a man would.

Reading the *Flowers in the Attic* series and the book to the movie *Romancing the Stone,* followed by its sequel, only at home in the privacy of my bedroom.

Then there was the whole sports "thing" which needs no deep explanation since many, many gay men have had a hate/hate relationship with anything that requires a ball and simple athletic ability. It's a stereotype, sure, but again—there are reasons for stereotypes.

If any one thing tipped people off that I wasn't just feminine but straight out gay, it was the way I played any sports that required even a small amount of coordination.

As a kid, I was so bad at baseball, my dad had to make a special request to have me put on a T-ball team, even though I was at least a year past the age eligibility regulations. Bad hitter for sure, but as an infielder/outfielder I was worse, and I found myself placed in left field almost immediately. When I failed at that, I was put into right field. When that didn't work, they just pushed me back to the parking lot of the liquor store next door.

I was made fun of all the time, but thankfully, my baseball career ended after only two seasons. There were no further encouragements to get me involved in football or basketball.

In middle school, I made my first and only touchdown. For the wrong team.

In high school, I hadn't yet grown into my body, stuck with zero athletic prowess, and like many kids—straight or gay—I was the last to be picked when choosing for any team sport. Sometimes I wasn't picked at all which, actually, was fine by me. If I sat on the bench, the teacher would just have me run the track, which again was fine by me because I never thought I "ran" gay, and it kept me from failing PE every semester.

By college, I was at my tallest, 6'4, and although team sporting requirements were a small trauma buried in the past, I still found myself having to engage in *some* sports once in a while. Extended family gatherings or church events like softball leagues—which were universally understood to be a requirement for church membership—always created some anxiety.

Jeesh, I was even bad at indoor broom hockey.

One time I was with a friend when I was about nineteen, and he wanted to play basketball at the local park with a bunch of random high schoolers. Usually prepared with a variety of excuses, I couldn't think of any reason to get out of it that afternoon. When it came time to choose up, my height made me an immediate favor among these strangers…but then we had to actually play, and in less than ten minutes I was done with them, and they were definitely done with me. I was humiliated, but not wanting to relive my high school gym experiences I decided to save face, so I told those guys that I was not physically at my best since I had recently gotten out of a wheelchair.

That is a true story, Travis.

But eventually I found myself blessed with three boys, so when it came time to put you and Andrew in sports, I made sure you were *encouraged* to participate but never forced. I did the same when Christopher became of age, and when he nixed the sport option year after year, I let it go.

So how I was going to teach you two older boys how to throw and catch a ball when I could do neither? And I'm just talking about a *baseball* here. I didn't even bother with a football. Do you recall *any* of this?

In case you don't remember, let me explain.

For visualization purposes, please imagine what it would look like if your left arm was taken off only to be replaced by your right…and vice versa.

Side note: it's never "viSA versa." Nor is it "for all intensive purposes."

So, picture both of your arms switched and now you have to get the ball from right field to the catcher, but you look and feel as if your body has been replaced by Dr. Frankenstein's monster whose legs and arms were sewn together after they were taken from different bodies.

With this image in your mind, you'll have an idea as to the range of my sporting abilities.

Another side note: the green creature with the big head, flat top, and neck bolt? Not Frankenstein. He's just "the monster." This is another example of the Mandela effect, where everyone thinks the monster is actually the doctor who created him. The monster was never given a name. It's all symbolic and blah, blah, blah. Read the book.

But I was a good dad, and I was going to teach you regardless of my lack of talent. Perfecting your throw was never the goal of tossing a ball around with you anyway, so I decided I would work with you guys and then your coach could correct all the mistakes. You were young and didn't know any better, and, because up until that time I was the first person to throw a ball with you, you probably thought I was at Hall of Fame level.

But I knew better, and I also decided I would never again throw a ball in front of other human beings like I'd been required to do all my life, so the only option I had was to teach you in the backyard, and as a result, to this day, I have never been made fun of my throwing or catching abilities because *no one* has seen me do it.

I don't throw balls of paper into a trash can. I don't catch a pen when someone tosses it to me. When we have a staff development day at work and we engage in "team building" exercises, I take the day off in case we have to make a deeper, more meaningful relationship with an art teacher—who, incidentally, I never see because they teach in classrooms about a half mile away—with the expectation we will bond over a game of Pickle or kickball or something equally abhorrent.

Except once.

It was baseball season and either you or Andrew were playing that day, and I was sitting in the stands, probably scrolling through Facebook until you were up to bat. Now I know it wasn't you, but some kid on your team hit the ball, chipping it at just the right spot (see, I don't even know the lingo), and the ball sailed up and over the backstop. When it landed into my hands by mere chance, hands that were now free since I foresaw an incoming ball smashing my iPhone, any gratification I would have had for "catching" it was replaced by a sudden realization and fear that I would somehow have to get that ball back to the umpire.

Just like in the movies, everything went slowly. The whole thing went down in less than two minutes, but time really does slow down the moment you don't want it to.

Naturally, the expectation was for me to throw the ball back over the backstop like a normal "butch" father, but I'm just not your average "butch" father, and, again, I had made a personal vow not to throw in public, and I wasn't about to break it over a little league game. So, I got up from the stands, walked all the way around the dugout, stepped onto the infield, walked past the batter, and handed the ball to the umpire. Then I went and sat down.

Everyone was staring at me.

Outside of our backyard "trainings," for lack of a better word, that day was my one time as an adult that I had actually caught a ball, purposefully or not; however, I still have never *thrown* one. Never participated in an after-Thanksgiving game of touch football. Never dodged a dodge ball or even kicked a soccer ball.

Yikes—kicking balls. That's not pretty either.

But here comes inevitable small print. A disclaimer. Once, when I was in my late twenties, I did participate in a very awkward basketball…league…and that story is coming very, very soon.

So back to yesterday. After I left the liquor store, sitting in my car with my dark purple drink, the taste of it only slightly better than radiator fluid, was the day I thought of sports and energy drinks and doughnuts. And of certain bright or shiny or tight clothes I've worn in the past that lifted people's eyebrows. Even *cars* I have purchased (remember the bright green Volkswagen Beetle with the silver lightning bolt stripes?), spoke volumes about who I was even before I had figured that out myself.

Even as an adult, I still fight my stereotypical gay insecurities like rainbow desserts and finely shaped eyebrows, but it's progressed to stupid *energy drinks* now, for a Cotton Candy *Bang* has two strikes against it: it's called "Cotton Candy" and it comes in a pink can!

This is something I might deal with for some time yet, for acceptance didn't immediately change the manner in which I was used to internalizing and expressing my emotions. Saying to myself, "Ok, I'm gay" didn't eliminate habits and patterns I've grown accustomed to for fifty years because it doesn't really affect the *soul* of a person, I suppose.

But if I could figure out how to turn this neuroticism around and take my experiences and humiliations and see if they could benefit you and Andrew and Christopher, then at least I can feel there was a reason for all of it. See, no matter the sexual orientation, *no* parent wants their kids to struggle with the same things they did, so while major insecurities at my age are probably lifetime companions, you are young enough to combat negative or harmful ways of working through your own "demons" and establish new patterns. You're still impressionable. You're still "fixable."

So here's the takeaway; here's what I want you to do differently: Travis, you aren't too old to stop putting *too* much stock into the thoughts of others and to their opinions as to how you should live your life. Seems like throw away, standard advice straight from the self-esteem lectures received in school and on TV, but living a life where the decisions are made only after you've received input from others is a ridiculous way to live a life. It has left me at an unhealthy place where I've only been able to have peace if I know I've pleased someone else by following their ideas for *my* life. This way of living has now become habit but has brought me nothing but grief and anxiety and has heightened my neuroticism to new levels year after year. It is a subtle form of narcissism in which I was so concerned with concentrating on what others thought about *me* that I would change and adapt my lifestyle and beliefs, not because I was this altruistic, selfless son, friend, and employee, but because I wanted to receive affirmation from *everyone* in my circle. On the surface, it may seem like I was gracious, humbly deferring to others, but it was really self-focused, and it has *never* made me a better man.

Which, in turn, has affected you. Your mom and your brothers.

I do *not* want the same for you, and it won't as long as you remember that no matter what you do with your life, some people will like you, and no matter what you do with your life, some people will *never* like you. It really is that simple. Don't waste your time making sure *all* people are happy with you *all* the time. It's fruitless and exhausting, and, frankly, it makes you look weak.

I didn't go back into the store to trade my *Bang* in yesterday, and to be fair, in the future, it'll take a concerted effort to buy a pink drink in front of people. Some progress has been made: in a few restaurants I've managed to order neon colored drinks instead of "manly" smoky colored ones a few times. In clear glasses too.

But I'm always cognizant of what I'm doing.

Don't do this to yourself. Fitting into society and obeying laws are important yes, of course, but sometimes the photographer will ask you to tilt your head when taking studio pictures for school or staff IDs, but if you don't want to, don't. You tell him you're gonna keep it straight.

For the most part, and until you are married, focus primarily on what God thinks and the person who pays your bills. That's it.

Love, Dad

Dear Travis,

Months after your mom and I married, I started to question the likelihood that marriage was not going to "cure" me. Both of us were frustrated, not really understanding the gravity of the situation we had put ourselves in, but over time, we slowly started to adapt to our unusual circumstances.

We both continued to work at Fair Oaks, but it would be my last year. In hindsight, that was probably best both for the students and administration but also for me. My relationship with God was beginning to wane as disillusionment overcame the passion I once had in following Him. Nothing was changing with my sexuality and the self-condemnation was weighing. Our pastor had always preached that Christianity wasn't a life filled with happiness but one of joy. And I had gone years without either.

Travis, I'd like you to find a life that consists of both.

While I refused to give up the battle, I wasn't ready to fight it with the same…fervor as before. My communication with God was sparse, and when I did pray or read my Bible, I came away empty. I was coming down from the religious "high" I had been on for so long, but surprisingly enough, the emptiness remained the same; now it was just a different "empty." Before the empty hole, I walked around living a life filled with hope, just *convinced* that healing was right around the corner, but that hope was now almost gone, and the following disappointment had put me into this really weird place where I figured living was just a short obstacle I had to overcome until I died and received the good things that were waiting for me in an after-life.

However, I couldn't just sit around. Most definitely I was making Mom unhappy and facing the issues in our marriage that I knew were just going to get worse didn't seem like a viable option.

So, I began searching for what psychiatry has labeled "coping mechanisms," a fancier term for any action where an individual attempts to replace pain by engaging in something that brings pleasure. This can be achieved with something healthy like exercising, but of course, drugs and alcohol are straight shots to masking deeply-rooted trauma, and they deliver a *quick* relief, a relief that is so strong, *temporarily* strong, that nothing can match its efficacy.

Now I don't think at the time that I was consciously muffling pain and running away from myself by seeking out personal coping mechanisms. I was still a Christian, so outside of the occasional alcohol use, drinking and drugs weren't an option. The pursuit of my *passions* became my drugs and alcohol, and I found myself diving into them with 100% focus. Living only for the promise of an afterlife loses its appeal rather quickly, so I abandoned the idea of sitting around until death and sought ways to distract myself with… well…distractions.

Practically speaking, there was plenty of time to poke about and look into different activities that peaked my interests; we didn't have any kids yet, and once I became a public-school teacher in 1996, money suddenly wasn't an issue.

For starters, I put together an acting troupe, *The In-Between Work Players,* and we got together on Saturdays to rehearse different plays and perform them in Hollywood and Orange County. I won't bore you too much with the details; overall it was a fun two years, and after investing my own money into the productions, I ultimately disbanded the group and walked away with a $1,000 profit. One of the actors that performed in one of the plays was a gay man whose sexuality I didn't discover until the whole cast went to his and his "roommate's" house for some sort of after-production party. Curtis was an odd guy who would cut his own hair which came out looking as if someone had prepped him for surgery. We didn't get along too well, our actor egos clashing over the most random production details, and I'm sure we didn't miss each other one bit once that play closed. But at the cast party that night, he took us on a tour of his two-story Orange County home, and when he showed us the bedroom, even I instantly noticed the two bedside tables with two lamps, books stacked on both. A coaster on each one.

Aaaaahhhh…Curtis's roommate wasn't just the "roommate."

Here's my point though: although it may seem odd now, it was 1997 at the time, and while I had seen and interacted with many a gay man and woman over the years, I had never encountered any type of gay domestic household, much less walked into one. I don't think I had even seen one in a film or on TV yet—*Will and Grace* were still about a year away, and I don't think even *Will and Grace* showed gay couples living together for at least a couple of seasons.

So, until that night, any images I might have had of gay couples who lived together like any other married heterosexuals didn't exist; instead, my worldview was limited to mental images of men running around in various states of undress while donning feather boas and dusting furniture, Bette Midler on the CD player…brought to you by the evangelical Christian community.

No, my stereotypes didn't have room for gay couples who make dinner together after they've both had a long day at work, each one giving an account of their day while cooking and then cleaning up the kitchen before falling asleep together in front of the TV by 8pm.

Looking around the rest of their house, the leather and oversexualized visions I had previously figured were just a part of the lives of all gay men didn't seem to mesh with the way Curtis and his boyfriend were living, and my previously held perceptions were instantly challenged. For the remainder of the evening, the two of them interacted with us like all the other actors and their partners. Curtis and his boyfriend never told us they were gay, but even more importantly no one else in the room acted like it was anything but a normal relationship. They didn't show any more physical affection with each other than the rest of the partygoers had.

They took turns serving everyone like any good co-hosts would and not taking turns going into the bathroom to snort cocaine or smoke crystal meth, which, as I was always led to believe, was part of the package when choosing to adopt a gay lifestyle.

It was all so ordinary, it bordered on appearing rather…dull.

Although I didn't know it at the time, this whole domesticated situation made a serious impression, and I would think about Curtis and his boyfriend whenever someone would make the point that healthy gay relationships were an impossibility. Gay men were "already broken as it is," so "throwing two broken people into a relationship is as disastrous as two recovering addicts setting up a life together."

While doing plays, I of course was still working, and the middle school where you would go to school twenty years later, was my first public-school job where I scored a drama/English teacher gig. Coming from a private school, the pay was incredible, and, again, your mom and I now had financial freedom to where we could relax and not have to worry too much about the money we spent.

I *threw* myself into that drama job, doing three productions a year that required hours and hours of commitment after school and on weekends and holidays. During the summer, *The In-Between Work Players* did a couple productions at the school to raise money for the drama program, so I was very busy year-round where there was very little time to think about anything else. If work had been my alcohol, I would have been drunk most of any 24-hour period.

There were a couple occasions where I relapsed and re-visited efforts to try and engage in healing methods to rid me from my homosexuality. The internet had exploded by then and I was doing research, reading testimonials from people, asking questions—anonymously of course—in group chat rooms. Apparently that little hope I had been holding onto wasn't completely gone.

Exodus International was the largest ex-gay ministry, and they had more resources on the internet than any other organization. With the support of Focus on the Family, Exodus's popularity skyrocketed, and for the first time, families who had gay and lesbian children and relatives had real hope that their loved ones *could* reverse their sexual orientation. Once the "evidence" and testimonials began, people claiming they were healed and no longer had sexual feelings for members of the same sex, Exodus' went international, spreading all over the world and their promise was *complete change*, not just the *possibility* of change.

A little more on Exodus later, but as large as they were, I didn't find any ministry chapters in my area. A smaller ex-gay ministry founded by one of the authors I had read, Andy Comiskey, Desert Streams sprouted up around the same time Exodus did and while there were different approaches, both ministries took to assist in healing the gay or lesbian…close your eyes and the curriculum sounded exactly the same. There was a chapter not too far from our house, so I signed up for that one.

As was the case at group therapy over at that megachurch in Orange County, my time there didn't last long. Frankly, I was tired of hearing the same message over and over again, *applying* that message, but getting nowhere.

In my last meeting, I vividly remember something the leader said that didn't sit well with me at the time, and it *really* bugs me now. One of the "curing" methods he encouraged us to apply consisted of a specific prayer to God whenever we ran into a straight person, especially a straight person of whom we found ourselves attracted. First, we were to subtly figure out if they were straight and once that was confirmed, we were to silently pray to God, giving Him thanks that the person was a heterosexual. That there was no brokenness in his or her sexuality. We weren't to be jealous but to be grateful.

By once again using that word "broken," my personal "sin" portrayed me as inferior in light of other peoples' sins. In the Christian worldview, a guy who steals gets branded a thief. If someone cheats on their spouse, they're an adulterer.

See the obese guy in the church pew next to you? Well, he's just a sinner like the rest of us.

In the minds of many churches, gay people aren't even "normal" enough to be called a sinner, a difficult label in and of itself, and some Christians need to make sure that everyone understands that homosexuals are *abnormal* sinners—not even on the same level as drug or porn addicts.

The church loves nouns like "adulterers" and "coveters," but they reserve the adjectives for the gay folks.

A friend of Mom's recommended I visit a pastor at a local church where he ran an uber secret men's group that dealt with my "particular issue"—

although I don't know how "uber secret" the men's group was if Mom's friend knew about it. For anonymity reasons, I guess it wouldn't be fair of me to mention the name of the church, but we met after the second service, at night, in a small office tucked away from the main church building.

Bill was the pastor and leader of this strictly gay men's group, and I did stick with it for several months. I really warmed to Bill immediately; there was never condemnation in his voice, and I truly believed, even with his limited study on the issue, that he wanted to do whatever was in his power to help the men in front of him who he considered not *broken* but profoundly depressed, wrestling with the struggle within. According to him and the majority of clergy around the world, gay men were depressed because we wanted *out*; it never occurred to them that maybe we were depressed for other reasons. In truth, we were men who just wanted to follow Jesus as we also accepted our sexuality, but the church made the unilateral decision that it was impossible to do both. Maybe *that's* why we were depressed.

Agree with everything I've said or not, but just imagine telling a person who follows Christ on a daily basis that he or she is horribly deceived, fooling themselves into thinking that being gay and living for Christ is nothing short of being a fraud. An "anti-Christ" if you're gonna be truthful about it. Show me the pastor or priest that has the power to *do* that!

In a past letter, I briefly laid out one of the now debunked theories from ex-gay Christian thought. This theory relied on the idea that adolescent boys eventually find themselves struggling with their sexual identity when their masculine needs aren't met from the primary male in their life which, for the most part, would be the father. Now I don't need a book from a psychologist to tear that argument to shreds because over the last two years I have engaged in many discussions with gay men who many claim they've had nothing but positive experiences growing up with their dads. There were many accounts of dominating mothers, yes, but there were just as many stories of warm, loving ones as well. Many men attested they didn't grow up with weak or perhaps verbally or physically abusive fathers. According to what I've been hearing, there are many gay men who grew up in healthy, normal households. Not perfect, naturally, but very standard upbringings.

Pastor Bill had a son, and he had worried at some time in his son's life, like I had, that his boy might be gay. The kid didn't like sports, was somewhat artistic, and hadn't seem to bond with his dad as much as his dad thought he should. So, Pastor Bill did some quick research, relied on the theory above and the solutions they proposed and decided to do his best to reverse his son's apparent lack of masculine characteristics, just like the books and articles and ex-gay seminars claimed was possible.

Of course, how do most fathers in the Western world bond with their sons? Sports of course.

On a consistent basis, Pastor Bill began taking his reluctant son outside to play basketball, and after many months of patiently working with him on a one-on-one basis, the pastor claimed his son and he had most definitely bonded—a claim I don't deny in the least—and that any traces of supposed femininity were disappearing—a claim for which I am skeptical.

And since it worked for him and his boy, he started to wonder if maybe the grown, gay men in his group could reverse the damage their childhoods had done to their masculinity.

The idea was for us guys to bond ourselves together through healthy physical contact while receiving affirmations from the other men.

While playing basketball.

Let me break the ex-gay theories down for you: if you're gay and you play basketball with other men, preferably straight men, the masculine needs that were never received in childhood will be met through the power of osmosis and the outcome will be heterosexuality.

So each meeting night, after we had prayed and shared with the other men the struggles we had faced over the past week, we went into the church's gym where Pastor Bill reintroduced us to basketball fundamentals, followed by one or two quick games.

Shirts and skins weren't an option for thirsty gay men like us, so trying to figure out who was on whose team took some work.

Of course, that was the least of our problems.

Travis, I wish you could have been a witness to the six or seven Frankenstein monsters lumbering around on a basketball court, each of us forced to relive our childhood's worst nightmare, recalling past insults only so we could turn them around and revert them into positives. The old and familiar, "You shoot like a fag, Elsasser," could now be turned into "You shoot like you were born with a basketball in your hand, Pete!" "You dribble like a girl, Elsasser" becomes "you dribble just like a real man, Fred, the kind that likes women and fixing things with tools!"

And there was plenty of healthy and appropriate touching like high fives and pats-on-the-shoulders. An occasional mid-pat on the back was also acceptable as long as the hand went no lower—this wasn't baseball after all.

After a couple of weeks, Pastor Bill nixed the bonding activities. Not sure if he figured out this experimental exercise was working or not, but based on the theory, it wouldn't: the whole idea was to have straight men bond with gay men so gay men could become straight men. Granted while none of this makes *any* sense, this line of thinking is especially bizarre because it defeats the purpose of trying to have gay men attempt to become straight men by bonding with other *gay* men since an infusion of heterosexuality was an impossibility. The attempt was as useless as the fire department in Bikini Bottom.

Basketball season over, we went back to our normal weekly whining sessions, and over time we saw the writing on the wall: if we didn't miraculously find ourselves having sexual feelings for women, we were destined to be alone forever. The thought became depressing, and after the failed male bonding activities, I think Bill had come to the realization that sexual orientation change was a nice spiritual idea but not a very practical one, and soon after the groups' focus went from trying to change our desires to learning how to live with them.

And I was done. Any relationship I had with God was dimming like the headlights in a mafioso's car submerged in water, and I decided the whole subject was getting tiresome; I was also finished trying to please a God who seemed very apathetic to all the work I was putting in. Even rats get the cheese once they get through the maze.

Four years into our marriage, I told your mom I couldn't be married any longer, and I moved out of the house. It wasn't an easy decision to make, but it paled in comparison to the one I would make years later.

Love, Dad

Dear Travis,

I polled my students recently, asking them to anonymously write down one of two things: what piece of advice they wished their parents had given them or what practical skill they thought their parents should have taught them up to this point.

Going through the list, the "mental regret" pile I created the moment me and your mom separated increased as I watched these kids list so many important life tips, tricks, and essentials, life navigations that I never got to share with you. Now I'm sure Mom has come behind me and picked up where I had left off, but there are just some things you need to hear from your dad. I'm not exactly sure *why* they need to come from your dad and not your mom, but they just seem like "Dad" things.

The following are missed opportunities, life requirements, and hacks I regret not guiding you through earlier. Alternatively, I'm going to list them here, and then I have an idea to follow.

1. Budgeting your money. When I gave you allowance, the only requirement I had was that you give a portion of it to our church; how much was up to you. However, I wish I would have advised you more on the issue of saving in general…how to spend wisely…the 50-30-20 rule is a good basic savings goal (Google that), but leave some money to give to charitable or non-profit causes.

2. How to change your tire. This is about the only mechanical thing I could do. It would be easier to teach you how to call AAA, which is the way I do it, but you never know when you're in a situation in which you have to change it yourself.

3. How to say "no" to people.

4. Understanding credit card interest fees.

5. We should have had you start an IRA account from birth. We could have taken a quarter of the money you earned every birthday, and, if you would have continued to deposit money into that account, by the time you were my age you would have been very well off. You could have cashed that in and bought investment property.

6. You need to know how to acknowledge and accept your feelings and emotions while learning an efficient way to rope them in when necessary.

7. I should have instilled the idea into your head that college may not be right for you. And that's ok.

8. Expectations versus reality while maintaining a sense of adventure and hope.

9. I wish I had focused less on God's anger and focused more on His love.
10. Mental health should be treated like our physical health—with no embarrassment and an understanding that psychological therapy should be a routine part of everyone's life.
11. How to invest in the stock market.
12. The importance of forgiveness even when someone doesn't ask for it.

This, of course, is not an exhaustive list. As I get older there will undoubtedly be more fragments of wisdom I want to share with you, especially as you become a husband and a father. And with my advice, you never have to worry about qualifiers, and I will always recognize and respect your adult autonomy because there are no expectations when I give you counsel—I offer it and then you do what you need to do. No matter what decisions you make in life, big or small, I will love and treat you the same way I always have, even if you turn your life in a direction that I figure will only lead to disaster or heartbreak.

These are *your* victories and mistakes to make. My job is to support you when you go through both.

However, the reality is that you and I are at extreme odds at the moment, but regardless, my job is not over. Legally and morally, it is still my responsibility to guide you through the potential pitfalls you'll face between now and dead—I brought you into this world, and no matter the method, I will make sure to fulfill my end of the bargain.

So, as promised, here is what I suggest: during this estrangement, I think it is extremely important that you find yourself a surrogate father.

Hear me out: from the rumors that I'm hearing, you've insulated yourself, and since your mom's brother lives several states away, and you aren't speaking to my side of the family, you are only surrounded by an older brother—who could use some guidance himself—and your mom and grandmother.

But when it comes to the various issues that the burgeoning male adult will most certainly face, a male perspective can be valuable, if not necessary, and although I don't have much of a choice here, I am willing to temporarily relegate my fatherly responsibilities, handing them over to another man of your choosing as long as he walks alongside you with the sole purpose of steering you into becoming the man you need to be for yourself, for God, and for your family.

Please do not misunderstand my intentions: I am not relinquishing the certain rights I have as your dad. This is a temporary solution to a problem that we just don't seem to have the answers for at this particular moment. You need a male figure, and since it is my job to *be* that male figure, I should provide a substitute since I'm unavailable.

Travis, your job as a father is to always try and do what is best for your children even if it brings you personal pain. While I have not always done that for you boys, that does not get you out of your obligation to consider what I'm saying.

Ok, so before you go "father figure shopping" I'm going to lay out some parameters since I should still have some input when it comes to choosing the man my kid is going to look to for guidance. That being said, the man you choose should meet the following criteria:

1. He should be at least thirty years old or older.
2. A man who makes God his priority. He needs to understand that there are many ways to interpret the Bible and press upon you that not one specific sect of Christianity has all the right answers.
3. He should be a dedicated, hard-working employee *somewhere*. I don't care what he does for a living, but he must have a clear vision when it comes to his career.
4. He's open minded. Whatever the issue, he should teach you to look at all sides before making a judgment.
5. He challenges you. He should be supportive of your goals, but he also needs to give you a kick in the pants when needed. He should never allow you to be satisfied with where you are at that moment.
6. He should listen first and talk after.
7. The chance to make mistakes without having to face consequences every time is something we all need. He should apply grace generously but judiciously.
8. As a man growing into an adult, you will butt heads with the adult figure you spend the most time with: this man needs to teach you to always respect your mother even as you become less dependent on her.

9. He shouldn't be the dragon from *Pete's Dragon*, the kind of man who helps a kid and moves on to the next one. He should always check on you in perpetuity.
10. He should do whatever is in his power to reconcile you and I.

Get started.

Love, Dad

Dear Travis,

In our family, your sense of humor has always been the sharpest. While I lean toward the easy gag, you are the king of the snarky one-liners. Spontaneous and original. You work best off the top of your head; my jokes are sensed by others, seconds before I make them.

Look up the works of Neil Simon, especially his play *Rumors*. You could be his heir if you spent more time writing.

So, you've had a lot of great lines, but the best came when you were about 9 or 10. I had the Prius in those days, and you guys were always so cramped in the back, remember? Horrible vehicle choice for someone as big as I am with two pre-teen boys smashed in the back, inches from the driver's seat.

Within seconds of leaving our house one day, you and Andrew were already fighting. Now I must have already been on the edge because I flipped out only blocks away from the house, and I yelled, "You'd better knock it off NOW because you don't want me to stop this car and come into that backseat!"

Without hesitation you threw back, "This is a Prius! You ARE in the backseat!"

There was no punishment that day; I always had a hard time punishing you when you were clever.

Love, Dad

Dear Travis,

When I separated from your mom back in 1999, I packed a few things and drove to my brother's house, where my parents were visiting at the time. I needed a place to live, and looking back, I don't know why I thought your grandparents would consider letting me live with them while I had decided to divorce my wife in order to live as a gay man.

When I asked, it didn't go well.

From there, I went to Alex's house where his family asked little questions but let me move back in. Of course, I talked it over extensively with Alex, and when I told him exactly why I had left, he said, "It doesn't matter. I love you anyway."

That was a pivotal moment in my life. Regardless of his personal convictions or thoughts about what I was doing, Alex chose to love me as he had before. He highlighted unconditional love, and I never forgot that. While many of my memories of the past are shaded with fuzzy gray colors, that day I remember perfectly. He is the reason I have always taught you boys to love people no matter how they choose to live their lives. Disagree, sure. Love anyway. And get rid of the phrase "love the sinner, hate the sin." It's not in the Bible any more than "ask Jesus into your heart" is.

The only thing Jesus said that comes close to "love the sinner, hate the sin" is "Love Others. Hate your own sin." When you say you love the sinner but hate the sin, the hatred will nevertheless spread to your feelings about the person…and they will feel it. Let's stop hating. Disagree. Debate. Fine. But always love.

Here: how about we change it to "Love the sinner, let God deal with the sin"?

The two months that I spent living apart from your mom was a mix of relief and fear like I had never experienced before. I was sure that what I was doing would eventually send me to hell, and it was the first time I had made a serious decision that went against every religious mandate that I had been taught. This wasn't me deciding to go to a secular college instead of a Christian one. It wasn't me only giving 5% of my income instead of the recommended 10%.

This was me living a lifestyle that the church and the Moral Majority was saying was partly responsible for the destruction of America—it was that serious.

I'm going to spare you any details concerning my behavior over the two months I was living on my own, but I wasn't proud of my actions then and I'm not proud of them now. Look up the word "hedonist" in the dictionary, and it will give you a brief overview of those eight weeks. Truly unleashed for the first time in my life, I pretty much decided there wasn't anything I wouldn't do, and I lived for my own pleasure and thought of nothing but doing just that. And I think that it was why, after two months of solid partying, I came up empty, finding no solace in the shallowness that goes along with just living for the flesh. Instead of addressing the deep identity issues I had struggled with for almost as long as I could remember, I chose to *entertain* my flesh instead, the result leaving me more confused than I was before I had become what was quickly labeled "The Prodigal."

A moniker I am slapped with quite a bit these days.

I couldn't figure out why I was still not happy.

I didn't understand why my mind was stuck in full battle mode. I thought I had accepted who I was, I wasn't running from the person I knew I had always been. So why was I still struggling?

Because I *wasn't* embracing who I was. That was the problem at its core, for I was dealing with the symptoms instead of the cause. I was like a guy with a chronic back injury who just uses narcotics to deal with the pain instead of getting himself to a chiropractor or surgeon.

In between the days of partying, I spent a lot of time praying. Begging for healing. Repenting. Repenting for not repenting enough.

Smack dab in the middle of all of this, I got pretty sick. For two weeks, I laid in bed; there were times I was too weak to even go brush my teeth. Through my illness, God was definitely punishing me—there was no doubt in my mind. Like Jonathan Edwards had preached over two hundred years ago, my "guilt" was "constantly increasing," and I was "every day treasuring up more wrath; the waters are constantly rising and waxing more and more mighty."

Combine that fear with an overwhelming sense of panic that I would lose all the people I valued the most, and I decided my only choice was to go back to your mom where, if she would have me, we could try again.

This time, we would pray harder for healing.

This time I would even stop eating for a day...maybe two...since fasting was a biblical practice I had always avoided, so *now* I was wondering if refusing to submit to God in this particular manner of devotion was the reason He had chosen not to heal me so far. Months later I did attempt a fast. I fasted for almost an entire day, but it didn't do anything to quell my sexual desires; all it did was make me a hungry gay guy.

Your mom was gracious and welcomed me home without hesitation. She asked very few questions…but she knew I had not been faithful during this time. Putting that aside, she allowed me to resume my role as her husband, and we decided to start over. Things would be different.

And in a sense, they were, for a little over a year later we were pregnant with your brother. Six months after we found out Mom was pregnant, I was a dad.

And my identity did change as promised. And *this* identity was one I fully embraced.

I was a *dad*.

Love, Dad

Dear Travis,

Right before Marion Crane is murdered by Norman Bates in *Psycho*, she sits down with him in a back room of his hotel office where stuffed birds and other animals lined the walls. Norman was a taxidermist of the extreme kind and right before Marion commented on the oddity of stuffing dead animals, she said, "A man should have a hobby."

A "tongue-in-cheek" line for sure, but when I teach the movie during my Film as Literature unit in my English 11 class, the line always stands out to me, as much as other memorable lines such as "A man's best friend is his mother" and "we all go a little mad sometimes."

The line resonates with me because I've always put great stock, even a little obsessively, into my hobbies. I don't know if it's more of a "man" thing or the results of a particular personality trait, but I pointed out earlier that when I find something that piques my interest, I throw myself in to it with nothing less than my full concentration. I did that with my relationship with God and my church, with acting, writing, teaching, reading, working out, etc. I tend to give my passions my full concentration until I am ready to move on to the next one.

When Andrew was finally born, I found the ultimate uber-hobby quite unlike anything else that came before it. A human being became my passion. A four-pound little preemie, warming and tanning for six weeks in a fancy heated Tupperware within the NICU unit became my latest obsession.

I dug in even deeper years later when you joined your brother. Finally, I found something I could not only throw my time and energy into but my heart as well. I joke when I say you guys were a "hobby" because I know *you* know that you guys were more than just the center of my world…universe…but you were the very reason I felt like staying alive for the immediate and not so immediate future. The three of you became the reason I got up in the morning. I was a dad with purpose, a plan, and a huge responsibility that exceeded far beyond writing a play or immersing myself into British history and literature.

I often said at that point that God had finally "cured me of my homosexuality," and I clearly told that to the men in the secret group that I led Tuesday nights at church for those who struggled with their sexuality.

Yeah, I was taking the basic curriculum of the ex-gay movement that had done nothing for me and I began foisting it onto others. I shared the same ideas and strategies (minus the aversion therapy), and secretly thought that if any of the men in my group were to find actual healing, maybe there was still hope for me. I spoke with authority when I told them healing was possible, even though I had yet to meet or talk with anyone who had experienced a switch of sexual identity that lasted.

Mostly I met men who were white knuckling it, holding on to their celibacy and avoiding relationships that might lead into monogamous, loving partnerships.

For almost four years, I met and counseled with men after men, listening to their struggles, taking on the role of priest as I heard confessions of "backsliding," urging them to continue down the path of celibacy, always emphasizing hope for change. The average man came for no more than three sessions, each hoping, as I had once done, for a quick fix—a five steps to a straight sexual orientation.

However, those meetings only took place once a week, and outside of work and spending time with friends once in a while, all my energy and focus went into raising the three boys that, growing up, I used to fear I would never have if God didn't change my sexual desires. All I had ever truly wanted was a normal marriage and family experience like everyone in my world. And now here I was, a secret gay man who had not just been given one child but three.

Most likely, and because he was the firstborn, I had bonded with Andrew pretty quickly; most nights watching TV while he was laying on my chest, many nights falling asleep with him. All three of you were pretty easy babies.

As toddlers, you and Andrew were horrible.

I'm serious, I loved you both, but the two of you were *awful* toddlers.

Andrew was also big into imaginative play and movies and TV, so the time we spent together was easy. A lot of lightsaber fighting. A lot of pirate themed movies.

Then you came along. A preemie as well, you were too stubborn to stay in the hospital longer than the required one day, and the doctor felt it was ok to send you home immediately, sparing your mom and I another experience with a pseudo igloo uterus.

The bonding between you and I didn't happen as naturally as it had with Andrew. You were far more interested in playing with balls than toys—and we know how inept I was with any object that was round and could be thrown—and you could never sit through a movie…although you did press the Pay-Per-View button on the remote control one afternoon and watched at least twenty minutes of Mel Gibson's *Apocalypto*.

By the time you were almost five, I was so concerned that we hadn't seemed to bond in the same way that your brother and I had that I sought out a parenting class instructor to get her advice. Basically, she said all parents have unique, individual relationships with each one of their children, and, in the end, she couldn't have been more accurate.

As feisty as your brother, the two of you challenged each other, your mom, me, and your grandmother from the second you could say your first words. Andrew would smack you around whenever our backs were turned, and we'd find you defending yourself the only way you knew how: chasing him around on your knees, mouth opening and closing, a sort of crazed Pac Man looking to chomp down on your brother's leg or arm. Or the side of his face. I can still picture the bite marks on your brother—tiny, bright red pebble marks bubbling up on his already sensitive skin, a drop of blood or two around the edges if you got a good enough hold on him.

When Christopher came around six years later, the Lord decided to give your mom and me a break because that child hardly said a word, and in all honesty *never* had to be disciplined. I don't think I ever even spanked him or grounded him. You guys would get furious with me for the disparity when doling out corporal punishment, and I used to yell back, "Do you want me to smack him around for something he didn't do just so you can feel I'm being fair?!?"

You both were ok with that proposal.

So, for the next sixteen, seventeen years or so, I threw myself into the lives of my kids. Not as a hobby. Not as a distraction. There were now three people I loved just as much as myself—and let's face it: all people love themselves more than any other person—and it was the closest I had ever had to experiencing happiness.

Happiness, joy, whatever you want to call it, I had "it" for the first time in my life. And while your mom got stuck with doing all the "unfun" and "responsible" part of parenting, I got to do the fun, play stuff. She made sure you were fed, clean, and had ironed clothes, and you, Andrew, me, and later, Christopher, sat around and played video games and watched TV hour after hour after hour.

It was as close to the idyllic life that I had wanted for so long, and even though I was still battling internally, I was so busy chasing you guys around, taking you to practices, riding bikes, and basically taking advantage of this part of my life, I could not care less about sex or attractions. My priorities had shifted, and my kids' very existence was enough to fill the void that I had been *promised* I would receive each and every time I asked Jesus to "come into my heart." Don't get me wrong: I still feared God and wanted an afterlife with Him, but you guys met a need that trumped all others. An unhealthy burden to put on children, sure, but I was not about to go back to the dark place I had been stuck in for so long, so I used my love for the three of you as the ultimate numbing agent of all time, and for many, many wonderful years I was able to function without much pain.

Unhealthy or not, I'd do it all over again.

And you know what? You and I did eventually bond, so I was able to put those worries aside. But the force that attached us wasn't in commonalities and shared interests, it was a natural bonding based on nothing other than your existence. You still wanted to use your scooter while I half-read/half-watched you race down the street, and I would try to get you to sit through at least twenty minutes of a movie only to lose you to something round that could be thrown, but regardless, our connection was as solid as the one between your brother and me, and in some ways it was stronger because it was based on a love we had for each other that existed for no reason other than I was your dad and you were my son.

We were always close, and that's why I took our estrangement so personally. Relationships that are manufactured can easily be ended or replaced altogether, but relationships that exist organically can never be broken, neither through time or distance.

It doesn't matter how many years you and I may be separated—our bonding is something that not even death can dissolve. It exists because you exist.

Love, Dad

Dear Travis,

In the early years, during the period I was counseling men at Fair Oaks First Christian to "pray away the gay," I took a stab at the internet one final time, a "hail Mary," to see if there were any new groups in my area that could help me fix the same sex "affliction" I was telling everyone had no longer any stranglehold on my life. My sexual brokenness was now under control; I was "free."

But I was lying. 100%.

It was during that search that I inadvertently stumbled onto a website that would change the direction of my life for the next good ten years or so.

Living Waters was a same-sex addiction umbrella group of Exodus International, and, as I found out, a popular name given to churches started by millennials with names like Chance and Mandible. Later, when I dug a little deeper, I found out Living Waters also went by the name Desert Stream Ministries which was the ministry I talked about in an earlier letter. But I didn't know all that then because when I clicked on the first Living Waters link, it took me to livingwaters.com, and within seconds I knew this was no SSA outreach program.

The first thing that cleared up any confusion that the ministry I had stumbled onto wasn't catering to "broken" men and women was because the website wasn't saturated with images of the typical "lost," and "depressed," homosexual figure, looking as if they had recently received a bad blood report from the doctor. No dark colors filled out the site's template. No cloud and rain jpegs hovered over a pasty-gray gay guy who stared at a colorful man, woman, and child standing inches away under streams of sunlight.

Instead, on the opening page was a picture of a man I wasn't familiar with and another man I easily recognized: Kirk Cameron.

Kirk Cameron was the ex-Hollywood star of one of the most popular 80s sitcoms of all time who had, in recent years, become a rock star in the Christian community, starring in Christian films like the *Left Behind* series and speaking about his faith to churches throughout the world.

For evangelical Christians, Kirk's conversion was a big win, for whether or not they are cognizant of the fact, the evangelical community had been looking for a celebrity spokesperson for years. Someone people could look to in order to legitimize Christianity as if 2,000 years of impacting the world and changing the course and direction of millions of lives weren't enough. History has its place and is all good and fine, but if we could just get that one Brad Pitt or Taylor Swift to stand up and openly confess to being an evangelical, red letter, King James only Bible reading Christian, they argue, then the rest of the Christian community could proudly pronounce, "See? Even celebrities endorse our beliefs. *Now* we can be taken seriously."

I hope I'm not disparaging Kirk when I highlight his fame within the evangelical community. Over the next ten years, my involvement with Living Waters afforded me opportunities to meet and speak with Kirk several times, and he never came across as anything but a genuine Christian who did his best to stay out of the spotlight, only to step in front of the camera to take advantage of his celebrity status so it might bring more people to Christ. He was definitely guarded around people he didn't know well, like myself, but I didn't pick up anything from him other than a sincere desire to serve God.

I would find out soon enough that the other guy on the website was the founder of Living Waters, a missionary, New Zealander transplant named Ray Comfort. And as you are well aware, Ray and his ministry had more of a direct effect on my spiritual journey than thirty years of church attendance, Bible camps, and cross-country ministry trips combined.

You were pretty young by the time I began volunteering and running around with the team at Living Waters, and I don't know how much you remember, but what you *should* know is that my lagging spirituality received a boost from a five-year energy drink called Living Waters, and a new understanding of God and His relationship with me kept me focused and learning, diving into the religion of my youth in a way I had never experienced before. And like I've pointed out, I either do things at zero percent or 100, and my work with Living Waters, combined with my devotion to you boys and my teaching responsibilities, catapulted my ambitious drive to find some sliver of joy amongst the living hell that was still raging within my soul. Dramatics aside, I was engaged in a spiritual war of despair and anxiety of despair and anxiety that would only be tempered when I kept my mind surrounded by a variety of responsibilities; the more spiritual, the better.

So, I figured this new spiritual awakening within would certainly squash the sexual attractions I had been fighting against; God would certainly act this time, especially when I began to realize the immense influence Living Waters had throughout the evangelical community, locally and abroad.

After all, a ministry that was handpicked by Kirk Cameron, the most celebrated Christian of the modern era, would give me a more direct access to God. Sounds ridiculous, but I really hung on to the idea that if I aligned myself with the closest thing to the *correct* version of true, classic, biblical Christianity, I would have a better chance of enjoying a more intimate relationship with God. A "get in front of the line" mentality, in my mind, was not out of the question.

And the more I learned about Ray Comfort and Kirk's ministry and its focus on evangelism, instead of, let's say, homeless outreaches or drug and alcohol rehabilitation centers, the more I wanted to be a part of it. When I first visited the Bellflower ministry shortly after stumbling onto the website, I met Ray and walked away with a ton of materials and a few free books. And a couple of new jokes. Ray is like me in his humor—he only has ten jokes but a thousand ways to say them. I got home that afternoon and dove into all the new material.

For the next year, I went through a personal "evangelism bootcamp," training myself in the particular style of evangelism and biblical understanding that was at the center of all of Ray's books and sermons. While I'm certainly not suggesting "Ray's God" is a separate God, I did *understand* Ray's "God" a little better than the God of my youth.

While all mainstream Protestant churches share the same basic view of the gospel and salvation, denominational churches and the distinctions and creeds that set them apart are not unlike that black and white drawing of the old woman with a big mouth and jaw. If you know what I'm referring to. When staring directly at the drawing in front of you, it clearly shows an old woman, but if you adjust your eyes a little or come at it from a completely different angle, the old woman disappears only to be replaced by the profile of a very young lady. Tilt it again and back comes the old woman. Have a couple drinks and it's a macaw holding a plunger and handful of lilies.

So, is the picture technically a picture of a young woman or an old woman? Well…it's both. Depending on your focus, your eyes will favor one image over the other. Most people don't see both at the same time.

It might be a poor analogy, but each Protestant denomination tends to place "focus" on certain aspects of God and the Christian faith in favor of others.

I had been solidly planted into Fair Oaks First Christian's distinctive theology where the overarching takeaway was that Jesus was a God of love Whose desire was to show His grace and mercy for every person by dying on the cross for their sins. The theology relied heavily on a loving Father who wants to be reunited with us in heaven.

In this illustration, Fair Oaks is the picture of the old lady.

Ray's ministry, Living Waters—an "umbrella ministry" rather than a church—represents the young, profiled lady in our black and white picture example. Again, while his ministry and other mainline Christian denominations are in line with the basic tenets of Christianity, the team at Living Waters primarily focused on the *consequences* of a person not putting their faith and trust in Christ and Christ alone, so there was a lot of talk about sin and damnation versus love and heaven. Ray felt it was important that people give their lives over to Christ not because of what He could *give* them but what He is *saving* them from.

Which is an eternity in Hell.

Therefore, Christian churches or umbrella ministries generally favor and adopt one of the following overarching themes and gospel presentations for their doctrinal statements. It's either:

1. God loves you and wants to save you in order to join Him in heaven.

Or

2. God loves you and wants to save you from going to hell after you die.

Fair Oaks leans toward #1.
Living Waters leans toward #2.

Now to be fair, Christian ministries make a concerted effort to find a healthy balance between the two, but a particular preference for one over the other becomes evident to even the casual church goer.

And I believe *that* is why I committed myself to Ray and Kirk's ministry with such evangelistic fervor. They presented an angry God who hates sin and is just waiting to throw people into Hell for the crimes that they continuously commit. Break one of the Ten Commandments? Then you've broken them all and you deserve hell. Told one lie? Judgment and then hell awaits you immediately upon death.

Now *that* was a God I could get behind. *That* was a God I could understand. I had been *living* with *that* God my whole life—a God who was so angry with me for the abnormal, unnatural thoughts that ran through my malformed mind despite the efforts to distract myself in a thousand different ways. Often, I gave in to those thoughts and desires, but I understood my particular offense was not just a sin within the context of a religious ordinance but was considered a societal taboo as well.

In my estimation, I was an immoral human being inside and outside the church, and that classic picture of God high above the clouds, thunderbolt in a hand that rose high above His shoulder, ran continually through my head like a Spotify playlist put on repeat.

I wasn't comfortable with the God of love, peace, and mercy. Sure, I had heard about Him enough to have a solid, biblical head knowledge of Him, but the God who was angry at sin and ready, at any moment, to cast me into Hell, where the eternal darkness and bottomless pit were waiting for all sinners, was the One I was most acquainted with. As a kid, the threat of punishment for disobeying any rule was a far more effective method than enticing me to obey for the rewards that would surely follow.

As a consequence of being raised in this way, as a grown man I likened all authority figures, especially males, as having the very nature and character of God: pissed off and hungry to punish.

I remember I had opened up these thoughts with a casual friend at church right about the time I began my years at Living Waters, and he felt the need to let me know that since I had adopted a skewed version of the God in the Bible, I was guilty of breaking the 2nd Commandment as dictated to Moses and recorded by him in Exodus 20:4 "you shall not make for yourself an image in the form of anything in heaven above or on the earth beneath or in the waters below."

Now I was guilty of another sin.

They certainly were piling up.

To make my life even more interesting I had, of late, been obsessing for years over the passage in Luke 20:47 where Jesus made clear that different sins have different degrees of consequences. In the verse, Jesus was going after the scribes, calling out their religious hypocrisy, which, in turn, completely freaked me out because if the greatest condemnation was saved for hypocrites like Luke reported, how much worse would it be for the sexual deviant? The deformed pervert like the ones God wiped out in Sodom some 5,000 years ago?

So, the God who emphasized the obedience to the Ten Commandments—who would then punish those who broke them—was someone I was familiar with, and I ate those books up. Ironically, I fell in love with God more during this time period than when I had a relationship with the "God of love" Himself.

I'll spare you a summation of the ten years I volunteered with Living Waters; after all, you were there for most of them. I used to drag you guys with me on some of the evangelism outreaches, and you were witnesses to the first couple of months where I stood on a box and preached the gospel to sometimes hundreds of people in public places.

Man, I was an awful street preacher. My mouth works faster than my thoughts so I would stumble constantly and speak at an accelerated rate if only to talk so fast that no one in the crowd had a chance to challenge what I was claiming—again, primarily, that they've broken the Ten Commandments and the price to pay was hell. Jesus was the only solution.

Upon reflection, even as I write this, I think part of the plain dreadfulness of my street preaching was the subconscious awareness that I was a fraud. Yeah, I had been taught that since I wasn't "acting" on my homosexual impulses that I was "clear" from sin, but the Bible was also clear that even if my *thoughts* were impure, I was committing adultery in my heart and that was a breach of the 7th Commandment. Like most men I know, *any* sexual thoughts were a struggle.

I was also aware that in the eyes of the non-Christian, those of the world, street preachers of *any* sort were indistinguishable from the preachers of the "God Hates Fags" folks. Look up the Westboro Baptist "church," and you'll know what I'm referring to.

Although Ray was known in Christian circles for his street preaching, and sometimes even unfairly equated with the Westboro ilk by other Christian communities, he never carried signs, and we were all under strict guidelines to never give people an opportunity to mix us up with the aforementioned hate groups. We did speak in public, we did stand on boxes to elevate ourselves above our surroundings, and we did raise our voices—if only to reach the maximum amount of people in our vicinity. But that's where the similarities ended. Christians and non-Christians alike can say what they want about Ray and Kirk's overall ministry and mission, but it was never one of hate, even when we spoke of issues like abortion and homosexuality.

And I did talk about homosexuality many, many times.

I explained it was clearly defined as a sin in the Bible and while there wasn't anything wrong with *struggling* with this particular temptation, it would be a sin to give in to it. I equated homosexuality with the struggle heterosexuals have with the desire to have sex outside of marriage. I compared it to the desire to steal from others. To the desire to murder someone when angry.

No, it wasn't necessarily a message of *hate,* but if you were in the audience and you were a homosexual having to hear me preach at a considerable volume that loving someone of the same sex is not unlike wanting to steal someone's wallet…well, you get the idea.

But I simultaneously believed that I might be "cured" since sexual thoughts for men had started to dissipate to the extent where I hardly thought of sex in any form at *all*. I was too busy running around with you guys, working full time as an English teacher—having quit teaching theatre so I could spend more time with you and your brother—preaching on the streets with old friends and with the new ones I had made from Living Waters, and just generally consuming myself with so many different "life wants" and desires that I didn't have space for the sexual ones.

It worked. And it worked for a long time.

Early on, Ray had asked me to act in a couple short films/sketches for the ministry and for their evangelism and apologetic TV series that he co-hosted with Kirk. I remember thinking, "I'm going to be on a TV series with the most successful Christian actor of all time." By the time my tenure with Living Waters had ended, I had been a featured "actor" in a dozen or more of Ray's projects, had helped edit one or two of his books, and had narrated one of his fiction books, *Jake's Fortune,* for the audio market. I had also been a "script consultant" on his short film, *Audacity*, a fictional movie about a gay guy who needs Jesus because he's gay. Not only did I assist with early script development, I acted in the film, playing a *very* butch cop who arrested some guy for holding up a liquor store. Honestly, I don't recall anything about the film since I hardly ever watch anything I've acted in; all I remember about the shoot was that Robin Williams died the same day I was "arresting" the liquor store robber.

Today that film has almost 1.4 million views on YouTube, and I carry some regret that I was a part of a film whose message has undoubtedly hurt many of the LGBTQ Christian community around the world. Ray had good intentions when making the film, as did I, but I'm sure the thousands of young gay men and women didn't care about intentions. Once again, through this film and hundreds like it, gay Christians were being told *yet again* they couldn't have a relationship with Jesus based on a sexual preference they have no control over.

There was one guy who worked for the ministry who would have a profound, lasting impact on my overall philosophy and understanding of salvation, even more so than my parents or any pastor I had sat under. I would get introduced to Valentino before he had started working at Living Waters but after he had retired from the Los Angeles County Sherriff's Department. When I first met Valentino, he was a full-time private evangelist, but once he began volunteering with Living Waters, the man's intellect, talent for debate, and solid "hermeneutical" grip was on full display when he stood on a box to preach, and I'm sure Ray felt Valentino could be an asset to the ministry. He was hired to head up Living Waters newly "Ambassador Alliance" department, and I volunteered for two or three of his monthly evangelism training weekends.

As my own street preaching style was evolving, while I was observing and then stealing from other street preachers whose methods I admired, Valentino's methodology was one I discovered myself mirroring more than Ray or Kirk's, most likely because I spent more time "in the field" with him than anyone else. When me and three friends first had the idea for our own ministry, Last Words, I asked Valentino to be a co-host of the radio program we started under Last Words because the solid biblical exposition he would bring to the broadcast would help balance out the goofy, amateurish "hey everybody, not sure what I'm doing but let's get together and put on a show" feel to the radio program that I was co-hosting, writing, and producing. And even though I had been raised up in the church, any biblical insights I may have had did not develop beyond Christianity 101, making me hesitant to wade into the deep-end of the theological pool. It was also a live call-in show, and I would need to take advantage of Valentino's sharp wit and quick retorts to legitimize *Last Words,* the radio show, as a solid, evangelical program in line with 99.5 KKLA's other biblical broadcasts.

It was serious business, and I realized we hit the big time when I saw Stephen Baldwin walking past our recording booth one night.

Every Friday night before the show began at 10:00pm, we set up a box on Brand Blvd in Glendale, across the street from the *Americana* mall, and open-aired preached with the rest of the team. You may have memories of those nights; you boys would come down with me once in a great while, and we'd have ice cream before we drove to the station where you'd watch the show, resting your head on the desk next to me as I stuttered and stumbled through the hour, falling back on joke after joke to cover for a serious lack of any true biblical depth.

Unfortunately, my time with Valentino as co-host soured after about a year. As I had done with many a man before Valentino came along, I have a bad habit of elevating people, men especially, who embody all the elements and characteristics I feel I am lacking, and I did that with Valentino, bestowing upon him the burden of "super-Christian" hero status weeks upon meeting him.

Off topic a bit, but it's human nature to have heroes, especially celebrity heroes you've never met. It is as natural as breathing or for having a hatred for people who carry dogs in a handbag onto a plane. Even the quintessential heroes of the last 100 years like John Wayne and Harrison Ford have heroes. Now while there's nothing wrong with the idea of hero "worship," here's some advice: don't ever meet them. Part of the benefits of admiring someone from afar is that you usually aren't given the opportunity to get to know them beyond their appearance behind a screen, making it easy to romanticize and idealize the athlete...the actor...the YouTuber.

If you want someone to stay your hero, let them remain a mystery.

In the year that I worked with Valentino on the show or on the preacher's box, I went through a profound crisis of faith. True, I was always wrestling with my understanding of God's nature and His thoughts in regard to my homosexual struggles, but I never really doubted I was saved or not going to heaven after I died. After all, I was an obedient man who never permanently gave into his sexual impulses, so clearly, my Christianity wasn't tenuous.

Valentino was my first real introduction to the theology of Calvinism, and he was the first Christian to introduce me to the precepts and concepts of this theological branch of Protestantism that Fair Oaks had often referred to as "cult-like." My years with the Free Methodist church and Fair Oaks had made me come to think that Calvinists were to be put up on the shelf between the fundamental Mormon polygamists and the Moonies.

Go ahead and Google Calvinism; I'm afraid if I go into it too deeply, you'll skim it like you did *The Odyssey* in your 9th grade year.

While I don't want to besmirch the Calvinist movement as a whole or speak ill of those that would call themselves Calvinists, I can only wonder if Valentino's sheer cold and arrogant, ungraciousness condemnation of other Christians stemmed from his Calvinistic beliefs. But not unlike all sects of any religion, there are liberal folks for every extremist, as well as kind and unbending and staunch and intransigent people too, so I don't want to fall into the same trap of labeling a group of people like Valentino would. That would make me a hypocrite, right?

When Valentino would question people's salvation almost as often as I silently questioned my sexuality, when he would shake his head in disgust as I'd share Jesus with someone in a way he communicated to me by facial expression was "trite" or "damaging to the gospel," when he wrote a book about the sinfulness of women preaching the gospel to men and not exclusively to women or children, when he would declare most Arminians (folks like my mother…my pastor at the time…you…) as destined for hell, when he questioned the salvation of his own close family members, it made *me* question for the first time in my life if *I* really was a Christian. I can't tell you how many conversations we would have about someone else where he would say, and with such *authority*, "Well, they're not saved."

And while Valentino wasn't the same Calvinist friend who had once questioned the salvation of this sweet lady acquaintance, Sherry, the firm condemnation ran along the same vein. All Sherry did was confide in this other person that she was unsure as to whether or not she was truly a Christian. My buddy's response: if she isn't assured, then God hasn't given her that assurance which probably means she really *isn't* a Christian.

Now, it certainly is not Valentino's fault that I was so weak-minded and put so much stock into what he said as "gospel truth." I was the one who looked to him for validation. I was the one who gave him the power to determine or define my salvation. I ignored what the Bible was telling me in lieu of what Valentino was proclaiming.

I pronounced myself a Calvinist some months later, and when I did, I embraced a false sense of salvation security, as the accused became the accuser, as I became just another ungracious condemner and "sin sniffer" of those around me. However, in some ways I was worse: I had become a self-righteous, rigid, black-and-white Calvinist with little to no research or deep study, and where previously I had been blind, I now had *all* the knowledge of exactly what the Bible said and claimed about the gospel, knowledge that so many millions of people were flat out denying, ignorant and clueless about the *real* path to Jesus and everlasting life.

However, even though there was a safety in the new-found security of having finally adopted the whole *truth*, the large ball of doubt that was loosened the moment I sat under Valentino's teachings came rolling toward me…and it was not unlike the boulder that chased after Indiana Jones in *Raiders of the Lost Ark.*

Although in this case it wasn't a fiberglass creation but a solid peridotite rock.

Holy cow, I'm so dramatic. How does anyone put up with me?

Well, surprise, surprise, the secure feeling I had felt when I converted to Calvinism didn't last long; the honeymoon period was soon over and not long after I started asking myself, "Um…if I wasn't a Christian before I became a Calvinist, but I *thought* I had been a Christian, how can I be sure of it *now*?" What if I discover something about salvation later that I don't understand *now*? Will God declare me "saved" if I'm currently living in some ignorance that I won't be enlightened to until later, a "later" I won't have if I die before I am blessed with the knowledge I'm missing?

Listen, regardless of everything I just said in this letter, I don't want you to think that I burden Valentino with the responsibility for my crisis of faith. My time with him just sparked the musings that still roll around in my head to this day. Quiet little questions that had previously been simply seeds began to sprout. Questions like:

"Well…if after all this…if I'm still not really a Christian, then why am I trying so hard to *be good*?"

Love, Dad

Dear Travis,

I acknowledged then and I acknowledge now that celebrity and fame is a *huge* draw for me. From as early as I can recall, I had this fascination with wanting to be *someone* special, different and set apart from my family and friends, and I didn't care how that came about—although acting in Hollywood was the preference. The plan was to be an actor making secular movies in Hollywood without compromising my Christian beliefs. I would be lauded by my actor peers while respected for my personal beliefs.

Going through therapy these last couple of years, my therapist and I dealt with why I had this obsession with wanting to be famous…or special…or at the very least, *not ordinary.* Coincidently, on the internet one day soon after my therapist had first brought the subject up, I ran across this Oliver Wendall Holmes saying, "Nothing is so common as the wish to be remarkable."

That depressed me because not only had I *not* reached extraordinary status by the time I was 47, I discovered I was just as ordinary as everyone else in my desire to *become* extraordinary. It was one of those embarrassing "ah-ha" moments that I'm glad only my therapist found out about. Well, and now you.

But at the time I thought Living Waters and Kirk Cameron was the way to the fame I had been quietly searching for, even though the couple times I had met Kirk he was a bit standoffish and guarded, so, I figured, he was going to be no help. I don't hold this against him, naturally; after all, I was probably one of the thousands of people that came before me that wanted to use his celebrity to launch a career.

But after some time passed, and I still hadn't been offered some sort of path to Hollywood via the short, essentially skits I periodically filmed for them, I decided to find fame and recognition on my own.

And I figured *The Adventures of Roman and Jorge* would finally make that happen.

Love, Dad

Dear Travis,

I heard the song "Bad Day" by Daniel Powter earlier this week while I was clothes shopping. I hate Big Man/Tall Man stores: they only seem to make clothes for big men who are either "big" or big and tall men. Not very many of them consider the tall, thin man.

So, the song came on, and of course, my insides dropped like they do whenever I have to lead an English department meeting. Usually when "Bad Day" comes on my playlist, I just hit forward and move on to the next song; I don't listen to it but I'm not at the point where I can remove it altogether.

I think it's probably a pretty rare, if not odd, thing for a father and son to have their "own" song, but if ever there was a song I've mindfully associated with you and me, it's this one. Can't remember the exact details as to how this all came together, but somehow it's mine and yours. And it's a better choice than the song from that musical about the town who wasn't allowed to pee—that's the song that always makes me think of your oldest brother.

I haven't broken down in quite a while, which I haven't decided whether or not is a good or bad thing, but I've now most certainly stopped crying in public. No more awkward scenes at Lazy Dog, El Pollo Loco, or the bowling lanes on Florence Avenue. But the song had come up so quickly that I was more than just caught off guard, instead, my body felt out of *context*. The last time I had heard "Bad Day" was at some point when I lived with you guys, so now, standing between racks of XXX large polos and belts so long I could have used them to tie Christopher's bike to the top of my Kia, it kind of…"shoved" me back to a time where I could recall you and me either singing at the top of our voices in my Prius…or occasionally arguing at the top of our voices.

The emotions hit hard and fast, and I was unable to pull myself out of the past. But I didn't feel like walking out of the store either. And not unlike pushing down on a bruise, the memories felt good and bad simultaneously, and I gave in and let myself get emotional for the first time in a while. My nose was dripping even before my eyes were, and in the 8' x 34' mirror I could see that my face was getting all red and puffy, so I kind of hid my whole body behind a pair of hanging chinos.

Next week it'll be two years since we have officially spoken to each other with actual words, and it's been over a year since I've even seen your face. And while your face is imprinted in my mind, it's a face of the past, and I just have this obsession with needing to know what you look like. With no social media, no senior pictures, no snapshots on your brother's phones, and me not having the funds to pay for a private investigator who could grab a few pictures while you're outside mowing your grandmother's yard, I live with the old Travis that lives on through the images on my computers and on the walls of my home. So, while everyone you've allowed to stay in your circle gets to see you so regularly that they take for granted the changes your face and body and mind make as you transition from an adolescent into manhood, I have to learn to be content with "Travis of the Past." *That* is my burden and my joy and *that* is what I thought about last week while sitting alone in a dressing room the size of a condominium's kitchen, holding on to a shirt I had no intention of trying on, before I pulled myself together and walked out.

In the past, a triggered incident like the one could cause a sadness that would last all day, but instead of, once again, embracing the comfortable familiarity of the depression, leaping back onto that familiar rotating cycle where I would plan and scheme ways I could force some sort of meeting—if not an entire reconciliation—I just kept my thoughts on the song I had just heard…and on your humor…and on the way you used to flip the front part of your hair—even when it wasn't hanging in your face. Nope, I found that the 3:48 which composed the entirety of "Bad Day" was a long enough time to grieve that day, and by the time I was in my car, I was able to completely cut the cord on that pain and drive home.

I gotta wrap this letter up, but I feel the need to address something that maybe I should have addressed in an earlier letter, for if I had, maybe any misunderstanding of my perceived lack of focus on the lives of you and your brothers would have been cleared up right away. Then again, maybe there isn't anything I could have said or done at any point over the last two years that could have lessened the trauma I left in the wake of my leaving—only God and time has any real control over that.

There is no doubt you've heard stories of my activities over the past two years, and as you may have wished for, once I moved out of our home, I didn't sit around feeding pods to pigs like the Prodigal. I didn't lay on my bed *all* the time, crying and playing that futile game of "What If I Had…" over and over, drinking vodka and Sprite, eventually passing out to episodes of *Friends* which would run on a loop until early the next morning. Sure, I relied on that coping mechanism once in a while, but the melodrama loses its appeal when there is no one to witness it, and, pain or no pain, I found myself still needing to interact with people. I still had the desire to *live* even though I often wanted to end my life…if that makes any sense.

Now unlike yourself, I'm pretty active on social media, never the one to shy away from posting a gym selfie or a quick pic of me leaning against a fence at the James Dean crash site, but I'll admit something that you probably know already: I've left all my social media accounts on "public," secretly hoping you're cyber stalking me.

Which I know you are by the way.

However, while the social media activity, as shaded and colored a lens as the posted, filtered pictures themselves, will attest to the fact that I have no doubt moved *forward* with my life, I really need you to understand that I have not, under any circumstances, moved *on*. I'm a dad first, but I'm still a human with all the basic needs to love, experience, and *feel* as anyone else. Early after I moved out, I understood that Sprite and vodka…sometimes rum…and the occasional whiskey…could only get me only from the kitchen to my bedroom, and, to be frank, I wanted to finally start living life this time as truthfully as I could—even with the full knowledge that I couldn't have you as a part of it.

Do you remember how I trained for that triathlon a couple years back? Horrible experience, and I'd never do it again, but it was on my bucket list right next to breaking a bone and testifying in a jury trial.

To train for the swimming, I used the pool at LA Fitness, a cesspool mixture of urine and gym body sweat that I thought about every single time water flowed into my mouth—which was all the time since the swimming portion of the triathlon, which had to be done in an actual ocean, was the most challenging. To prepare for biking part, I decided against a stationary bike and trained with my real bike in the riverbed, which, by the way, is apparently an easy way to get washed away and die. I didn't realize until recently that people are actively encouraged to avoid a riverbed when riding bikes, playing hockey, or sitting around a pentagram doing witchcraft.

But when it came to the running part, I refused to train outside. I hate running on cement, and to be honest, I'm not too fond of running on grass either.

I used the treadmill to get into the best cardio shape of my life, but now I want to use the collective time I spent on the treadmill as a metaphor to help you understand something important.

When I first started training, I was able to run at 5.5 miles for ten minutes, and each day, or each cardio session, I added one minute and a .1 to the speed, so by the time of the triathlon, I was able to do 3 miles without too much effort.

Too much.

Not only did I see an increase in my cardio endurance, but my legs were stronger, I was able to sleep better, my urine was fantastic, and the energy levels needed to complete even normal activity shot up. Sure, I finished that tri in 129th place out 150th, but that is not the point I'm shooting for here.

I look back on those weeks on the treadmill, and by the time of the competition I had been training for a good four months. I'm not going to even try to do the math, but I figured I had logged in enough miles to get to San Diego and back. Went through two pair of running shoes too.

That's a lot of distance covered by a person who doesn't actually like to go anywhere.

Can you imagine the places, people, and things I could have seen if I'd actually taken to the streets to run those same miles instead of completing them on a treadmill? Each session I could have taken different routes…I could have driven to the beach and run there (although I refuse to run on sand) or run on the sidewalks in the expensive neighborhoods of Westwood or Palo Verdes. So many missed opportunities.

So while I consistently ran on the treadmill, I never actually really went anywhere.. I just ran and ran and ran but never really moved from one place to another. Every session I started with the same rows of TVs in front of me, and when I was finished, I found them where I had left them: still six feet ahead.

Always moving forward, but always ending at the same place I started.

The relationship between you and me, defunct as it may be, is still a relationship, not unlike the one I had with the treadmill, because while I am waiting patiently for a reconciliation that I now understand cannot be forced, I still have to move forward with my life. And while I have no regrets about moving *forward,* without you solidly planted back into my life, I will never be able to move *on.*

No matter what I do with my life between now and the day I take my final breath, I will always be waiting for you at the same place I started.

And it will have to do…for now.

Love, Dad

Dear Travis,

Barbara Cameron is the mother of Kirk as well as Candace Cameron, star of *Full House* and *Fuller House* and *The View*. Candace has also been in a Hallmark movie where she's a successful woman from the big city who throws away her career to move back to her small town. Now of course that's the plot of every Hallmark movie, but in her film, Candace wears a red hat.

Since Kirk worked with Ray, Barbara spent some of her time volunteering for the ministry. I think she had managed both her kids' careers as they rose to fame, so she knew the industry, and as a Christian and mother of two famous actors, she had written her own biography and published it with the help of Living Waters. I had met her and her husband a few times at a couple of functions, so I thought maybe she might be of some help to the career I had always wanted but had never materialized, and I didn't just need a leg up, I needed my whole body thrown over the Hollywood Christian fence where I would be the next Kirk Cameron. I'd act for a living, do some script writing, or maybe even produce either a wholesome TV show or create an exclusively Christian film that would actually "cross-over" into the mainstream Hollywood film industry.

It's extremely embarrassing to admit that some of my involvement with Living Waters was not as magnanimous as I had pretended it was. Much of it was self-serving, and I'm just being candid when I tell you that everything I did for the ministry was done for the sake of the gospel first and Greg Elsasser second, but I was always looking for a way to piggy-back on the message I was presenting, praying that the work I was doing would produce some fruit for those who didn't know Christ, but secretly hoping that some of that "fruit" might fall into my own basket.

Before the idea came for *The Adventures of Roman and Jorge*, I thought I might get my break-through the radio venue, and that's when the radio show I told you about, *Last Words,* was born. The show was broadcast on a popular Los Angeles FM Christian radio for one hour each Saturday night where we would debate all things having to do with Christianity and evangelism. We had live callers and everything. I wondered if this might be the "break" I was looking for.

The show was expensive and lasted two years, but no influential listener ever tuned in to the show and followed through with a call to the station owner screaming, "I must buy that evangelism show! Forget Saturday nights! I want them for a morning show! I need them on air Monday through Friday from 7-10am!"

A part of me really thought that might happen. Sincerely.

The Adventures of Roman and Jorge came next, and the episodes told the story of two Christian dudes who wanted to share the gospel on the streets, but their newbie status and inexperience ended up creating as many comedic moments as the dramatic ones. Simple. Funny. Low budget.

When we finished the first three episodes of *The Adventures of Roman and Jorge*, we asked Barbara Cameron to sit down and give us a critique of this show that I had acted in, produced, and written. A couple years and tons of personal money went into our Christian television show primarily about friendship and evangelism, and it was basically, up to that point, my third child. The show was created and shot as amateur pilot episodes in hopes that a larger Christian company might pick up the series and run with it.

Eventually, the show was aired on JCTV and produced on DVD and YouTube. By the 4th episode, the dream and excitement were fading and never fully came off the ground. The fourth episode was one of the worst scripts I've ever written.

Still wanted to give it to Barbara though. Maybe her "influence" would take the production value up a notch, even if I needed to step aside as producer. Or even writer.

We never met with Barbara, however. Once we read her critique, we knew it was over; we went ahead and finished that poorly written episode 4 and then we let *Roman and Jorge* die out. Although by the time of Barbara's review below I was losing the passion for the project, but *some* of the rhetoric she used in her review hammered in the final nail.

Without wasting any more time, here is the review of our show *The Adventures of Roman and* Jorge by Barbara Cameron, mother of actress Candance Cameron who, in an ironic twist, just happened to be a star in of one of the worst TV shows of all time:

"Hi Greg,

I have reviewed 'The Adventures of Roman and Jorge in its entirety. You have asked me to be honest with you and so here is my opinion and thoughts on your project'.

Greg there is a lot of work that needs to be done. I totally get your heart and passion in making this video series, however, it was difficult to come to any one thing that I felt was redeeming. On a whole, I felt it was boring and unadventurous and seemed outdated. I understood the humor thou it didn't come across as humorous but kinda corny. The editing was choppy and there were scenes that didn't flow.

Most of the acting was not good. I'm sure that many were family and friends that wanted to help you. And that is what came across. I found that Dru' s best scene was when he was evangelizing. He wasn't acting. He was in the moment of what he was doing and who he was.

He wasn't acting, he was being himself and sharing something that was a part of him. That's acting. Being the character and being so familiar with the character that he comes across natural and real.

Your character was colorful! I also felt that with a little coaching some of it would come across more real. Felt there was some elements of over acting.

In the beginning of the story, there needs to be a hook to the viewer! Something that grabs their attention to make them want to keep watching.

The title of your video is The Adventures of…. Greg I didn't feel any adventure. I was trying to figure out what I was looking for with that word and so I looked up the word adventure. I found that there are many different ideas and images on just what adventure means, because what some of us might think is adventurous might not be so adventurous to someone else.

With your character coming across as being humorous, I thought that we were going to see some really funny scenes and although there were some great ideas I felt they came across flat.

I think there needs to be more work done on the script, writing, then eventually, casting with an experienced director and editor.

All this to say that at this time, I'm not in a position to be able to help where help is needed right now.

God knows the desires of our hearts and I know that you have a heart for acting, evangelizing and making a project that will bring others to the Lord. I pray that the Lord will give you guidance and direction and hope that my thoughts were helpful.

This was difficult for me to critique because it is not my nature to critique other people's work or feel I am someone with that kind of experience. Thou you have asked my opinion I can only be honest and hope that it was constructive in helping you invest more of what I felt is needed to make it the best it can be.

God Bless,

Barbara"

OK, looking back, the review wasn't as awful as it seemed to be the first time I read it. I was a lot more vulnerable at that point because I was putting every last bit of talent I had into that show, but now I've had the benefit of time and perspective. Originally, I had panicked when I first read her review because I understood that I didn't have a store of extra talent buried within that I could draw from—this show was the *limit* of my ability and creativity. In the end, I had created an unexceptional passion project, and the disillusionment came with the knowledge that I truly couldn't do any better.

Maybe God was finally punishing me for having ulterior motives. Maybe the failure could be traced to my large ego, and as a consequence, God had finally saw fit to teach me a lesson in humility.

Or maybe it didn't lie in anything to do with the Divine—maybe I just had a mediocre talent of which I had romanticized into something that it really wasn't.

Whatever it was, I moved on. I'd find something else to throw my life into at 100%.

Next up, *The Field Trip*.

Love, Dad

Dear Travis,

When you get married, everyone will tell you that the success to a good marriage is the couple's ability to "communicate" effectively.

Bogus. That's secondary.

The number one path to a successful marriage is the couple's ability to practice *behavior modification*. Communicating your needs to your spouse is important, that goes without saying, but if no one does any changing once those needs are articulated, the marriage is in trouble.

Boom—I just saved you $150 a week in therapy bills.

Love, Dad

Dear Travis,

The Europe trips that you and I took together will remain my favorite memories of our time together, hands down. Never having the means to pay for trips to Europe, or even New York, myself, I began traveling with junior high and high school students overseas in the late 90s as a way to see the world myself without having to worry how I could afford it.

Once you and your brothers were old enough to travel—your first trip was at 9—I got to take both of us at no cost, and the work and stress dealing with 40-70 kids, getting them on multiple planes, moving from country-to-country and hotel-to-hotel, was something I was willing to do if I was able to bring you boys with me.

Remember in Paris when I left you with $6,000 in tour guide tip money inside a backpack while you sat in the center of the Louvre only to come back to find you asleep on the floor with the money laying on your lap?

Then there was that morning at our hotel in Germany where we were having breakfast. It had been a week of traveling with very little sleep at night, and that morning you broke down when I told you that the hotel didn't have any "normal" cereal. In much the same that you barf, you were very quiet when you cried that morning, little tears dropping into your empty bowl, and I can recall thinking of that scene from *Terms of Endearment,* and all I wanted to do was jump up and run around yelling, "GIVE MY SON SOME FREAKIN' FROOT LOOPS!"

I think you and I ended up doing two trips in total (not counting the trip to New York that was just you and me), but I have so many pictures of you from so many different European countries, I can't remember what year and even what country they were taken in.

With ten or so student trips under my belt by 2016, even I was getting bored seeing the same touristy spot or statue over and over. In fact, I have been known to say to people, "Uggg…I'm so tired of going to Paris. If I have to see the Eiffel Tower one more time…"

Yeah, I know how that comes across.

However, whenever I'm bored, my mind always wanders into creative mode, and, besides that fact, as a natural born storyteller, I'm always seeing potential stories wherever I go, especially when I'm in places outside of my normal…habitat? Does that sound right?

Anyway, one afternoon, in Venice I believe, the kids were to meet up with me and the other chaperones after having a couple hours of free time. Again, I can't remember if you were on that trip or not. Venice is the one with all the water and canals. We had that glass blowing demonstration? Ring any bells?

I arrived a little early to the meeting place at St. Mark's Square, but I didn't *know* I was arriving early. For one reason or another, I thought I was late and when I got there and no one else was there *either*, I started to worry. A little. And that worry morphed into a question which, eventually, turned into a book idea, which was: "what would I do if on one of these trips every single student just disappeared?" Besides the obvious lawsuits, can you imagine if I lost 30…40…50 kids in the middle of Copenhagen or someplace similar? What would be the first thing I would do? Who would I call first? And why in the heck would someone want to steal 40 high schoolers in the first place?

With that idea ruminating around in my head for a couple years, plotting and outlining, I eventually took two years to write what would become my very last artistic "distraction," *The Field Trip.* A novel of suspense and humor that finished at 144,000 words before it was trimmed to 119,000. A novel that took me to London for nine days of research and, from the constant hunching over while typing, created an upper back pain that I still struggle with to this day. I'm having that same pain right now just writing this letter.

When I had completed the novel, from start to finish, including editing, printing, and marketing costs, I spent $14,000 of our money to fulfill yet another dream I had—to become a working novelist. However, by the end of the second chapter, I knew I wasn't a strong enough writer to get a book contract from a publishing house that would pay me and incur all costs, but I just figured that with my Living Waters connections, I may be able to sell enough books to at least recoup my investment.

When it was all over, I had made $1,700, and not one of my "connections" at Living Waters had come through with a contract for a ten Christian novel series book deal.

I would *not* be writing the next *Left Behind* series.

Now since I had taken a job as an assistant principal for summer school we could afford the financial loss, but I couldn't take the emotional hit that something else I had created had failed. This loss was especially difficult because I spent two to three hours a night some evenings writing and editing over a two-year period—this wasn't some play I wrote and produced in three months—and my already super-inflated ego was bruised with the recent failure of the radio show and the TV series.

At this point, I could tell you something like, "little did I know that the failure of this book would be the domino at the head of a thousand other dominoes," but you know what? I *did* know. I remember telling your mom on a trip home from Northern California that if this book failed, I just had this feeling I was going to go through a depression unlike anything I had experienced since before you boys were born.

I had nothing left, creatively speaking, to keep my mind occupied anymore; I was empty of ideas or inspiration, and once I accepted the fact that the leftover thirty boxes of *The Field Trip* would most likely stay in the back shed, I started to inwardly panic. Consciously I thought, "What am I going to do to keep myself from being bored?"

Subconsciously I was thinking, "What am I going to do to keep the sexual frustrations in check?"

Even with the idea that the mind-numbing projects that have held my focus for so long might disappear, I at least had you two—and now Christopher—to fall back on and occupy any leftover space in my daily regimented schedule. I knew if I freed up too much time in my day, only to give myself to idle activities such as games on my phone or hours of Netflix, there was a hidden danger that I would start *contemplating things* like "well, what…if?" And, "Does the Bible *really* say…" But while I knew there was a real threat here, I began indulging anyway, slowly, over many months, giving in to periods of…*self-inspection*.

To my credit, I did try to busy myself with my kids like I had in the old days, before all the ministry work with Living Waters, and the TV show, and the book, but you and Andrew were teenagers now, and you simply did not need as much Dad in your life as you had before. Nor did you *desire* to have Dad hovering around like you wanted me to when you were a pre-teen, which was a natural and expected part of growing up. I didn't freak out as my control began to slip as you were in the process of becoming your own man, and around the time I began to get really depressed, you were thirteen and most parents of thirteen-year-olds can't compete with video games and phones. I understood that even as I still tried to insert myself into your lives as much as possible.

I used to ask you if I could at least sit down on your bed and watch as you played video games—a means to get some quality time in. You would always say, "No," and when one day your response went from "No," to "Eww, that's what pedophiles do," I stopped asking.

Side note here: to this day, the "pedophile" comment sticks with me; I give it more attention and time in my thoughts than what it deserves. Once my therapist asked me why I kept rehashing this scene in my therapy sessions, and I proceeded to tell him it plays in the forefront of my mind because when I came to terms with my homosexuality and had moved out of our home, a "concern" around your house was that when your brother Christopher came to my home during our time together, he might be molested by someone I might be dating. This comment was also made to my mother and father.

I cannot reiterate this enough: nothing upsets a gay man more than being told he's a child molester.

But here's another reason, a less traumatic reason, as to why the video game comment bugged me: I think one of my most brilliant parenting moves was the way I handled video games in our house. I work with over 150 students each year, and after hearing from them about their particular experiences, you had it easy with my "carte blanche" attitude toward your personal free time. My only rules were that you were to first spend some time with your family and made sure your homework was done. Once those requests were met, you were allowed to play video games or spend time on your phone for as many hours as you wanted. When you were older, I didn't even try to enforce a video game *curfew* on you. As long as you got up for school, you were allowed to stay up.

Yeah, ok, I wasn't a completely "rules free" parent. I did surprise "phone checks for inappropriate material" for a couple years, and I even put a useless phone blocker/accountability software onto all your devices. I may have drug tested you and your brother once in a great while, and my GOSH you were grounded all *the time*, but you had it so easy in comparison to other kids your age. I've talked to many parents who limit their kids "screen activity" to a certain amount of time a day. There are parents who make their kids get straight "A's" or take part in countless extra-curricular activities, or never, *ever* date or have a boyfriend/girlfriend, but when it came to the house rules, you had an easy gig.

So when it came to gaming, I was resentful that you had all that free time, and I couldn't even sit to watch you play a video game on a system that I had bought you with my own money.

Yeah, I'm not over that one yet.

I'll refocus.

Christopher was six years younger than you, and I admit that I could, and should, have focused my attention on him during the final years I was at home, recreating the same type of relationship I'd had with you and Andrew, but any normal seven-year-old would probably rather play video games with his older two brothers than put together Legos or go through the *Lost* series with his dad. So, I backed off a bit.

Well, to my discredit, I backed off a lot. Too much even.

My work hours fell from 7:30-2:45 every day, and outside of that, I found myself bored pretty quickly. I was still evangelizing with the Living Waters folks on Friday nights, occasionally, and we went to church on Sundays, occasionally, so there was so much empty time left. I'd get up and go to the gym before work, but from 3pm until the time I went to bed, the hours would drag on and on as I played Words with Friends and chess on my phone. Or watched British television and the occasional movie or series on Amazon, Netflix, Hulu, or DIRECTV. I subscribed to it all.

Note: watch more British television, Travis. In so many ways, they do it much better.

Eventually even my work with Living Waters—including the time I spent with Mike and Bryan, my two closest friends at the ministry—on Friday nights, time dwindled away to nothing. I had a lot of excuses, but it was hard to explain to all my friends and family that all I wanted to do after I got home from work every day was eat and watch TV until I fell asleep.

This went on for a good year, but it was such a slow progression, and you guys had homework and video games that I don't think you really noticed it. Or did you?

Soon enough, falling asleep at eight wasn't doing much for the depression. As a result, I started eating dinner earlier than you guys, using the excuse that I needed to eat in the late afternoon because I got up so early every morning and was on a different schedule than the rest of you. Some days I'd be done with dinner by 4, 4:30, and that would leave me at least three hours to lie in bed in what was becoming far more serious than just a depressive state.

I'd been taking a prescription sleeping pill before bed for at least fifteen years; the amount of daily dosages of caffeine through energy drinks and caffeine pills—at times up to 1,000 milligrams of caffeine a day—not to mention the anxiety I was carrying around would mess with any regular sleep pattern, and not only did I have a hard time falling asleep, I'd wake up several times a night. The sleeping pill would cut that down to about two times a night.

The nightmares started that final year before I left, which just added to the sleep disruptions. A doctor might have diagnosed them more accurately as "night terrors," but that could be a matter of semantics. All I know is that about every couple of months I would wake up, not from the nightmares themselves, which, 90% of the time included a scene in which I was stabbed repeatedly with a knife or a sword or, once, the leg of a chair, but from the sound of my own screaming. You'll have to ask Mom what that was like for her too; freaked her out as much as me, I would imagine.

Soon, the sleeping pill was followed by a beer, once I discovered my love of IPA's, which, someone told me recently, is the only beer gays will drink.

Of course it is.

Why is it that most things I am drawn to somehow has a stereotypical gay connection? It's not like my love for tank-tops and colorful martinis isn't enough.

Some nights beer was switched out with red wine, and as I stated earlier, one glass often became two. Typically starting my drinking around 7pm each night, the pill chaser that followed was scheduled at least an hour after. As time went on and the pressing sadness and hopelessness grew stronger, my will to wait until the evening to start drugging myself was staring to wane. I hated myself, and the sexual confusion that I had managed to suppress for so long was coming back, ten times as fast, twenty times its strength.

When I was young, I believed the old wives' tale that said if you ever got any kind of worm stuck in your intestines after consuming some bad water in a foreign country—an event which would *never* take place in one's own country, of course —you should take a piece of cooked meat, stick it on a fork, and stick it in your mouth. Then you would wait. Eventually that worm would smell the fragrance of the meat and begin its journey up through your intestines, through the esophagus until its head peeked over your tongue. That's when you're supposed to throw down your fork, grab the worm's head with your dominant hand, and keep pulling until the whole thing slid out.

In my case, that parasite was my sexual identity, and all the angst…the depression…the suicidal idealization…the hatred of self…the anger I directed at my father…had been buried so far into the lower intestines and for so *long* that the worm's journey was going to take some time. I think it began to move around winter of 2017, and by the time I was yanking it out, almost an entire year had gone by.

By the way, that whole thing was an extended metaphor. Not a great one, but an extended metaphor nonetheless.

Ok, so within months of binge watching and medicating myself, the time I had allotted to start drinking each night moved up an hour or so. My appointment with my sleeping pill, naturally, also moved up so that the buzz from the alcohol would strengthen the effect of the pill.

Sometimes I didn't wait to start drinking until I got home. I'd meet friends from work, and we'd go to happy hour, and more often or not, those "happy" hours weren't spent with friends or colleagues at all—I'd occasionally find myself sitting after work drinking by myself. One memorable afternoon, I had drunk so much at Bar Louie that I had started crying, and I needed to sit in my car for a while to sober up and collect myself. It wasn't even 5 o'clock. I sat there, my eyes all read and itchy, when your brother and his girlfriend walked up to my Jeep.

Not a proud moment. Not only did my *son* find me like this, but so did his girlfriend…who went to the same school he did where both of them were in my third period English 11 class.

Your tax dollars, folks.

A little off topic but let me tell you something: if someone tells you that alcohol and drugs doesn't take away emotional pain, they are flat out lying to you. Sure, you can make the argument that numbing substances really don't *take* away pain as much as *cover* it, but again, semantics. From the moment your drug of choice enters your system—which for me was quick because I would take the sleeping pill, stick it under my tongue and suck on it so it would get into the blood stream faster—that pain you are carrying around, consciously or unconsciously, is not only muffled, it begins to completely detach itself from your psyche. And if it *isn't* gone, you're so full of euphoria that your pain seems…reasonable.

It's no big deal.

The British polymath Bertrand Russell once said, "Drunkenness is temporary suicide," and when I read that in some fiction novel, I found myself comforted. When someone commits suicide, we tend to feel great sympathy, if not downright *empathy,* for the pain that person must have been experiencing before they took their life, but when someone's a drunk, well, we just proclaim them a drunk. But perhaps if we could look at people who use alcohol and drugs and dole out the same amount of compassion we would for someone who's *suicidal,* maybe it wouldn't be as hard to offer them help instead of the usual superiority and judgment.

After a couple drinks, thoughts like "Why am I so upset that I'm a fraud?" or "I don't understand why I'm so lonely when I have so many people around me who love me" seems trivial.

Once I permanently left your home, I'd often drunkenly question: "Why am I so upset about losing my children? Aaah, that's no big deal—they'll come back."

Being high is like getting an epidural and then stabbing yourself in the leg with a fork. Your pain sensors have been completely shut off and like an epidural, drugs and alcohol serve the same purpose: for that one to three hours you're "high," you are completely psychologically separated from whatever has been crushing you during the other twenty-one hours of the day, and for up to three hours or so you are liberated from the symbolic prison your mind has been stuck in.

However, when the epidural wears off, you are going to feel the effect of that fork.

But I didn't care about that fork when I was sucking on that sleeping pill and drinking my wine out of that steel goblet I got from the Renaissance Faire. If I drank and took my pill, not only would I be divorced from the depression, the alcohol and drug combination would knock me out, not to wake up until the next morning when it was time to get up and go to the gym.

Then to work.

Then home to eat my one chicken breast by 4pm. Then to bed to watch… whatever. Sometimes a lot of *Friends* and *Seinfeld* 'cause I'd seen them so many times there was no real reason to concentrate on a story.

While most people live for each two-day weekend, my 7pm drinking and pill start time was something I looked forward to from the moment I woke up that morning. The occasional Xanax or two would also bring me some extra joy during the day if I had gotten a recent prescription, which I tried not to do because Xanax was the "weed" of the new millennium, and I would *not* be associated with a drug that was surrounded by such negative connotations.

By the time fall began, you could often find me passed out by 5:30 in the afternoon.

I knew I needed some help.

But I was 47 years old and as far as I was concerned, I had tried *everything*. *Except*.

Except *maybe* I hadn't really given therapy a chance. Or perhaps I hadn't completely applied all of the suggestions that the books I had read and studied throughout the years had offered. Maybe I had missed steps along the way.

This time, I thought, I would not miss one step.

Love, Dad

Dear Travis,

Growth Into Manhood by Alan Medinger was the book I had read when I was in my twenties while deeply involved in the reparative therapy movement to eradicate all traces of my homosexual impulses. Out of all the material I had read, I returned to this one because I remember the concepts laid out in the book, which would lead to a reversal of my twisted sexuality, were not only doable, but there would be no weird aversion practices, nor would I have to spend a lot of time examining my relationship with my father.

Medinger's basic theory was that some heterosexuals, not just homosexuals like me, have missed out on acquiring a basic masculinity that came naturally for most boys as they "grew into manhood." The book spent some time detailing steps to take to reclaim that missed masculinity, and like a nice "To-Do" list, I gravitated to its simplicity. Follow these steps, and I'd be healed.

To revisit what we talked about earlier, the prevailing thought in *all* the "ex-gay" theories was that men who were attracted to men were products of an environment that, for whatever reason, created a lack of close, non-erotic same-sex friendships as they were growing up. All the ex-gay prominent leaders of the movement agreed that men who were unable to bond with fathers and boys their age would look for those close relationships, once puberty kicked in, through a sexual relationship.

Medinger asserted that the homosexual attractions could be reversed if a man were to formulate the healthy relationships with men that were unattainable during their adolescence. Once the homosexual reconnects with members of his or her own sex in a proper manner, their sexual orientation would begin to shift to a heterosexual one as they bond deeper with the male friend, and over time their need for healthy male intimacy will have been met, which will, in turn, eliminate the sexual desires for members of the same sex.

There is zero scientific evidence that this works.

But I was still hopeful, so I went through the book again, figuring if I just started to tap into the masculinity that I was unconsciously craving for, I'd at the very least, curb the sexual leanings down to a level I could live with. I wanted it to go back to the days when you kids were younger, even if I was now unable to distract myself with all the activities that came with being a dad…and an actor…and a writer…and a producer…and an evangelist. I didn't have a lot of things to fill my time with those days, so I needed a new way to suppress the identity struggles that had been hounding me since I was eight years old.

One afternoon, I was reading Medinger's book on the leg extension machine at the gym, and some dude came up to me and started talking, which, for me, is a typical thing at the gym since I spend a good 25% of my time working out either shooting the breeze with people or playing games on my phone. Or, obviously, reading books.

I wasn't the most dedicated gym rat at the time. That would come later. Which is part of this story.

All I can recall is that he started talking to me. He had been one of those "What's up?" guys you see every day at the gym because when passing them, you'd say, "What's up?" I've made up nicknames for those "What's up?" guys who I tend to run into daily I tend to run into daily, like "Old Man Jim," "Lady in All White," "The Jonas Brothers," "Attitude Guy with Compression Pants," and, my favorite, "Happy Asian Jumping Man." This guy was always jumping on one of those half rubber exercise balls, and he literally has a smile on his face the entire time. It never goes away.

So, the dude who came up to talk to me I had dubbed "Side-bends guy," because he spent a good majority of his workout doing weighted oblique side bends, an exercise I had always labeled as a waste of time, like wrist curls or an elliptical machine.

In the end, I was wrong about those side bends. Do them consistently and you'll have those nice V-shaped obliques every gay or straight guy wants. The closest I ever got to them was a sort of contorted "U."

"Side-bends guy" was Frank. I can't remember exactly why he came up to me and started talking, but eventually the conversation spun to the subject of triathlons. He was preparing for one—of course I had to ask him what a triathlon was—and I knew it had something to do with the number 3 because I'm not a complete idiot—and within seconds, he was asking me if I wanted to join him and some other guys.

Really weird moment. There I was, sitting on a machine reading a "self-help" book dealing with one's masculinity by doing masculine activities with masculine men, and my soon-to-be new Army sergeant, hetero, manly friend Frank, just wanders up and asks me to participate with him and a bunch of other machos in a San Diego/Coronado Island triathlon in about five months.

By the way, don't ever do that at the gym. Don't sit on a machine or a weight bench and go through your phone or sit and read a book, especially if someone is standing there waiting for you to finish your set. It's, like, basic gym etiquette 101.

And I was in. And I took that book home that day and put it back on the shelf because I had everything I needed to know: if ever I could turn heterosexual it would happen by hanging out with this dude. Sure, most of my closest friends growing up were male and very straight, so was my brother, and one could only assume that since I'd spent my boyhood/teenage years surrounded by heterosexuals, their own manly, normal sexuality would have already seeped into my *warped* sexuality, turning me to the good and righteous side…but that had never happened.

Actually, my very first close male friend was Paul, we were in the 9th grade together, and he later became a cop, a pretty manly career choice that surprisingly had no effect on my sexuality. Alex was a surfer and a skater, and yet I did not benefit from some heterosexual osmosis like the ex-gay gurus had assured me would come my way. Chad, my friend from the *Roman and Jorge* and the radio days rode bikes and liked soccer. My friend Cory was a part-time barbecuer. Justin was confident and played the type of golf that didn't require a person to hit a ball through a clown's mouth. And then there was Alex, a surfer.

All these straight guys in my life—who at one time I was as close to as brothers—and yet our bonds did not change my gayness. Not one iota.

But Frank was far manlier than Phil and Alex, right? In addition to all the athletic stuff, he rode dirt bikes and did drywall and could fix his German car when he needed to. Even Alex and Paul couldn't do that. So, ridiculous or not, I still had high hopes that hanging around Frank might act as a conduit to fill that gender gap that the ex-gay movement unequivocally believed was keeping me from embracing full heterosexuality.

So, details regarding our training and the triathlon itself is simply minutiae you don't need, so I won't laden you with specifics, although I will say that even though I performed mediocrely, I ended up being in the best shape of my life because I had never trained that *hard* in my life.

All of this may have risen my natural testosterone levels a bit but did nothing for my sexual identity.

But I figured some bodybuilding supplements might.

Contrary to what you may have heard, the supplement usage for the off-again-on-again year or so I used them was completely my idea; no one offered them to me. No one pushed me to do them. The appeal to get bigger was the driving motivation, and there's really no way to lie about it at this point either: I'm vain and always have been, and I knew if I got cut and shredded or buff and thick, I'd look better. I'd get attention. Vanity was my inspiration, and any serious bodybuilder that tells you something else is probably not being completely honest. I don't know if it's much about the challenge and the ability to lift weights more than the natural body will allow; no, I think it's all about aesthetics and aesthetics is about outward appearance and beauty. I wanted to look good. At the very least, that's why *I* did it.

And I did look good. I was cut and shredded and buff and thick, and while there are no addictive components to most athletic supplements themselves, the addiction comes from the looks and the respect thrown my way, not just at the gym, but by friends, people at work or at the post office. For once I didn't feel like the 6th grade geek that I had never internally let go of, and I enjoyed every bit of the attention I got.

Again, might as well be honest here, I had a confidence that started out as a swagger that grew into a full-blown arrogant stride within the first four months. I had become a full-on attention seeking addict.

Now here is where I'm going to justify my nutritional supplemental usage a tad. Not much, but since I was upfront with the whole vanity issue, try to put yourself in my position and understand that for years I had been told over and over and over that my issue wasn't a *sexual* issue but a *gender* issue. The books and therapists and pastors assured me I wasn't a "homosexual," no, at some point in my life my manhood had just jumped the tracks, so to speak, and I just needed to get the train back on the rails. I needed to understand what made me uniquely male and not *female*, all the experts said, and so while I was busy hitting the weights and preparing for triathlons with super manly dudes, the thought that increasing my testosterone levels seemed like a natural next step to achieving maximum heterosexual masculinity.

Then I found myself thinking, "Why stop at supplements? Why not skip the line even more and get a tattoo? In fact, why not buy a Jeep? And why not take that Jeep and lift it and replace the factory tires on it, swapping them out for the massive monster truck tires so it doesn't look so much like the gym guy with the skinny legs who only focuses on his upper body?"

I got the tattoo. Got the lifted Jeep. Prepared for the triathlon. Ran a couple of 2ks. Went to the shooting range and took you guys out to the desert to shoot mannequins with shotguns. Lifted heavier weight, making huge advancements in my physique day after day.

Of course, after just a couple of weeks I couldn't stick with the basic, "first-step" supplements anymore, of course not, I had to have the most advanced, potent supplements that all the competitive body builders were using. I totally ignored the concept that when looking for a first car purchase you get a Dodge, not a Ferrari. Not me. No, I went to the high end supplements almost right away, never allowing myself to acclimate to the massive changes and burden I was putting on my body. I just decided to go from 25mph to 1000.

And after a good six months, I had become *huge*, muscles popping out in places I didn't know were hiding muscles. I became a weight-lifter that drew the attention of the other gym rats as I caught them watching me out of the corners of their eyes. Besides the bodybuilding, I also became a decent runner and biker—although still a lousy swimmer—and I wasn't bad with a rifle either. I had a cool looking tattoo on sleeveless arms that flashed down on other drivers as I passed them by in a Jeep so tall that short people needed a boost to get into. My fist bump improved. I started carrying my one gallon water jug by the handle instead of the strap.

All of this…and I was still pretty gay.

In fact, with all that testosterone flowing, I was probably even gayer.

None of it had worked.

And when I stared at my huge upper torso in the mirror, little signs of incoming acne dotting my upper shoulders and back, I started to accept the fact that I was never going to experience the change I had been *promised* was coming.

And the raging sense of buyer's remorse was finally beginning to hit me. Hard.

Or maybe all the rage was from the bodybuilding supplements. Who knows at this point?

Love, Dad

Dear Travis,

Remember several letters ago when we discussed—well, I wrote, you read…or I wrote and you burned—the importance of not taking stock into what other people think about how you live your life…to the degree that you can still develop and maintain healthy relationships with the people in your close circle?

Well, I want you to forget most of that advice.

To clarify, reading these letters one after another—which, in one sitting, could be done in three or four hours—might seem as if I wrote them at the same pace in which you could read them in an afternoon. I wish I could say I wrote them in the time span it takes to read them, but the reality is that I started writing to you almost two years ago. I didn't write every day. I sometimes didn't even write once a week.

I am giving you a glimpse into the process only so I can be clear that the dad who may have written to you twenty, thirty letters ago is not necessarily the same dad who is writing to you today, any more than you are the same son you were when I started writing. In the two years that I first wrote to you in the side notes of the Bible that I have now stored away for you, I have been in regular therapy, have rented my own home, put up one of those little libraries in the front yard, got a dog, tried sushi, fractured my ankle (bucket list item), lost friends and gained friends, got down to 9% body fat, injected Botox, dated, fell in love, and got re-married.

With the exception of the Botox, these kinds of life events have a way of shifting old patterns and ways of thinking, and this applies to whether a person is deeply religious or not. Even the staunchest of Christians will witness their non-religious philosophies—and even steadfast theological predilections—morph as time and personal experiences come together. This process is not only a natural part of life, it's a necessary one. Certainly, I don't want to behave and think and act the same way I did when I was twenty…thirty…for my past failures demand I rethink and then act differently based on the knowledge I've acquired through my screw-ups.

All that aside, I need to walk-back some of my earlier advice. At the time, whatever letter it was, I had really wanted to impress upon you that living your life off the opinions of others to the degree where you become one person to one individual and another one to someone else is just a subtle form of narcissism and/or self-centeredness. I still stand by the original advice, but I think it was the wrong *focus*.

It's like spending time trying to find the fastest and best route to get to a Taylor Swift concert when the real problem is that you're on your way to a Taylor Swift concert in the first place. Like a form of triage, deal with the more important matters first and foremost.

Travis, if you find yourself changing who you are to please all the different people who will come in and out of the 80, 90 years that you have left on this earth, put a stop to it. And I don't think you need therapy to realize you're doing it, if indeed you *are* doing it, but consciously or not, when altering the person who is *Travis* in order to be the version of you that exists in the heads of every single person who knows you, you'll be too preoccupied to understand that not a single one of them is actually *you*.

It seems a good a time as any to throw in an inevitable Shakespeare quote, and this one comes from *Hamlet*, the play you and millions of other teenagers across the world left sitting in your backpacks under packs of gum and gym clothes for two months.

Jeesh, in the old days we were at least savvy enough to fake our way through plays and novels by reading the *Cliff's Notes*, but I can't even get students to do *that*.

It's fine, truly. We teachers act all offended when you all don't appreciate Shakespeare, but deep down most of us don't either; we just know we're *supposed* to appreciate Shakespeare, but all we really want to do is lay down and read the latest John Patterson or watch *90 Day Fiancée.*

So even though I'm supposed to be outraged, I really don't care that you skipped *Hamlet*, although I am hopeful you didn't burn the play in the backyard like you did with *Romeo and Juliet.* That was a little…melodramatic.

Really, all you need to know about *Hamlet* is not only is it Shakespeare's greatest play, but it's generally lauded as being the best piece of literature written in the English language, outside of the Bible. That's just some general knowledge you should have.

In Act One, Scene 3, Polonius is giving advice to his son, Laertes, as Polonius is about to leave for "college." Polonius encourages Laertes to "Give every man thy ear, but few thy voice." Now in my estimation, this little homily is far more important than the tired, oft-quoted and more popular "neither a borrower nor lender be" speech which was also given by Polonius to Laertes on that same occasion.

The Act One, "man thy ear" lecture has aged so well and is such a powerful and timely message for the neurotic, self-obsessed Millennials of the Western World, and although I myself am not a Millennial, I have given myself the honorary title.. Essentially, when he lectures his son, Polonius bypasses the advice that I had chosen to give you in a past letter and leaves out the whole "don't change who you are based on what others say of you" in exchange for a far better piece of advice that says, "don't allow people to say anything about you in the *first place.*"

Without the flowery language, here it is, simply put: people can't give your opinions as to how you should think, act, respond, or even *be* if you don't give them that authority in the first place.

I've devoted a lot of time to asking people their opinions on various thoughts I have concerning the business of running my life, and you know what?

If I ask, they tell me.

And if I ask, let's say twenty-five people, for their input on my life, then I get twenty-five different opinions. My next step is then to take those twenty-five opinions and try to find a way to follow every…single…one of them. And when I realize that following more than even *one* opinion is impossible—

shoot, forget *twenty-five*—I find myself manipulating and lying so that the people whose advice I wasn't able to follow won't be insulted that they were ignored! And then if *that* isn't enough, I'll often tell people I *did* listen to them and subsequently turned their thoughts to actions! However, once I do *that*, then the next time I see them I have to live up to that particular version of myself I've given to them so my half-truths and lies aren't uncovered.

Should we be forced to wear masks during COVID? Should there be forced vaccinations? Should there be tighter gun laws? Is climate change a hoax? Health care for all? Raise the minimum wage? Is the Trump presidency a joke? God's love or God's wrath? Calvinism or Arminianism? In-N-Out or Shake Shack? Window seat or aisle? Death by drowning or fire?

My thoughts on those topics and others like them often depends on who I'm talking to at that moment, and while often it's about squeezing a certain amount of approbation from a particular person, more often than not my opinions are formed only after I've figured out how to avoid making someone mad or irritated with me and my ideas.

And the desire to let others do my thinking for me doesn't stop with people I know or people I'm having face-to-face conversations with; I could be reading a book that I'm enjoying, but if I stop by Goodreads or Amazon reviews only to gather that the general consensus is that the book is awful or boring, I'll start to question whether or not it really *is* awful or boring.

I'm 50 years old now. Kind of sick, isn't it?

Kind people might proclaim this behavior is a result of having low self-esteem. Harsher folks might proclaim that it's the result of having a weak character. The Brits might wave an accusatory finger and determine it's the result of being an American.

Listen, I don't know where my desperate behavior to please people comes from nor do I particularly care at this late point in my life; if I'm on the 40th floor of a hotel and it's on fire, I don't care how the fire started—I just need to know how to get out. Maybe later on I can figure out how the fire started, the metaphorical idea being to help others circumvent certain hotels that look as if they might erupt in flames at any time. And that is why I'm being so candid with you as I uncover flaw after flaw that is my life—I don't want you to live in the mental circular hell I've been spinning in from the moment I first realized that disappointing people ignited unpleasant feelings that, being the self-centered kid I was from the very beginning, was to be avoided at all costs.

Finally, the goal here, however, is not to get through life without seeking the counsel from others in certain situations. Of course not. Give some space for some philosophies and ideas other than your own.

Some space. Not all of it.

Trust in the wisdom of your spouse. Your pastor. Your best friend. Listen with an open mind, analyze what is being asked of you…and then make a decision. *Your* decision.

Then live your life.

After all, a man who walks on eggshells to keep people happy with him will eventually become so skilled at it that he makes no sound in life.

Be accountable to God and, like I stated previously, to the person who is paying your bills.

Love, Dad

Dear Travis,

You had a front seat to all the drama the year leading up to my moving out of our home, and even though you may have not understood what was going on behind the scenes, you were probably savvy enough to know there was something very wrong with your dad.

The intensity of my depression and sexual ambiguity, combined with, thanks to the supplements I was taking, a huge jump in my testosterone levels, were soon becoming more than I had been used to dealing with. In the past, I had always been able to keep some amount of depression at bay, and I was very good at compartmentalizing all the various stressors and personalities I had created for myself, but by the time I reached 47, 48, I think, simply, that I was just getting tired. No other reason than that. There wasn't some singular crisis or light bulb moment, I just found myself slowly giving in to the thoughts and questions for which I had never before allowed any space.

Everywhere in life I was coasting. I had settled down at work with no plans to advance into administrative work. I had been teaching the same material for years and could do it without writing one new lesson plan.

I was hearing the same basic sermons at church for almost thirty years, and my mind wandered Sunday after Sunday. I was coasting as a Christian. Show up, do the time, go home.

You boys were pretty much busy with your own lives and didn't require my attention as you had when you were growing up.

So, I began coasting in my role as Dad.

I was restless but didn't know exactly why. I was moody and irritable and didn't know exactly why, and although the supplements got blamed for much of it, I'll keep swearing this until my dying day: they had nothing to do with my acceptance of my sexuality. Nothing.

I worked out harder, sometimes twice a day, and I was *huge*, but the constant exercise did nothing for the stress which was now manifesting itself in panic attacks, which was interesting because while I had researched and *written* about panic attacks for my book, I had personally never had one.

The first one, and worst, came while I was in the bathroom at home. Initially I thought maybe I was starting to cry since the pressure on my chest felt familiar and mimicked the *effects* of crying, but there weren't any tears, and I was having trouble breathing, which I didn't understand because it didn't feel like my airways were blocked. My throat certainly wasn't closing up. It just felt like someone had placed bricks on my chest, like the bricks you used in your construction class—big enough to make breathing laborious but not impossible or life-threatening.

Or maybe it wasn't a *pressure* on my chest but, better, a heaviness was creeping through my upper torso, swirling around, down into my stomach, like a mist in any Dicken's novel: light but still kind of ominous and threatening at the same time. But the really strange symptom was that after forty-some years of breathing 24/7, I had suddenly become *aware* that I was in the *act* of breathing…if that is a better way to describe it.

I sat on the bathroom mat. I remember Mom coming in. She kind of just talked me through it, Mom probably more worried than I was because I was too weirded out by the experience and was distracted enough by the physical feelings so I wouldn't panic about the panic attack. I think by the time we got me into the bedroom it was gone almost as fast as it had come on.

There was one more panic attack but that happened at work one morning before school even started. I was sitting in my Jeep when my chest tightened, and again my attention was drawn to the fact that I was *breathing*. Who does that? We breathe all day without a second thought. With prior experience now under my belt, however, I was able to get through it by knowing it wouldn't last; I needed to simply sit through it. Eventually I was able get into my classroom without even being late for first period.

Now the crying outbreaks were more bothersome because they were far more regular and were very embarrassing. After all, a big man with so much testosterone and a Jeep that stood above most of the cars in our neighborhood shouldn't be crying, much less in public places, and crying in public was starting to become a much too common thing with me.

One night your mom and I went to dinner at Lazy Dog's, and I was eating their fried chicken sandwich and I just lost it. Started crying for no particularly conscious reason. We had to get the check and go home.

I would start to lose it during class sometimes and have to run out, heading straight for the men's faculty bathroom where I could have relative peace inside a stall for a good ten minutes. Good thing there weren't any earthquakes or school shooters running around when I was holed up in the bathroom down the hall from my thirty-five students.

There were a few breakdowns at the gym. Couple of times on the freeway.

Pulled up to work one morning, and I started sobbing in the parking lot, so I just called in sick and drove to Wilderness Park where I sat in my car and spent a couple hours there watching the ducks. Very melodramatic.

By then, Frank and I were pretty good friends and since I worked at Marshall High School with his wife, Lily (who I didn't know was his wife until a couple months after he and I had been working out), we were all seeing each other pretty regularly, either at the gym or at work. Socialized together once in a while, the four of us, as well. Point is, I had come to trust him enough that I could let him know *some* of what was going on. Not everything mind you— we weren't good enough friends at that point to get the *good* stuff, but I knew I had to reach out to someone, and talking to him was an obvious choice since not only was he my friend, but he was a social worker for LAUSD *and* a Christian.

Since I wasn't ready to be completely candid with him about my sexual identity issues, he couldn't do much more than give me tips to deal with the depression, which, in turn, really served little purpose since the issues that were causing the depression and anxiety weren't issues I was ready to confront.

Until I was forced to.

The "beginning of the end," in my estimation, was the day I chose to pop into our emergency room at our local hospital, casually checking in and telling the nurse I had some depression and anxiety and wanted to see a doctor.

One of the first questions they ask a patient who show symptoms similar to mine is whether or not that person is thinking of harming themself. When I was filling out the forms and dealing with the insurance issues, I was asked this question. And the first words out of my mouth were, "Well…"

Now I don't blame the events to follow on Frank because I still don't think I was consciously or unconsciously trying to get myself into a treatment facility without specifically requesting to get myself into a treatment facility. But I had just spent two or three months contacting more than two dozen therapists, trying to find a Christian counselor who would take me on as a patient *and* accept my insurance. It was a never-ending barrage of leaving messages and waiting. To find out, every therapist, Christian or not, had either an extensive waiting list or declined to take patients with insurance. All wanted cash up front.

Having this discussion one day with Frank at the gym was not something I had planned, but I just found myself blurting out in frustration at not being able to find a therapist, especially since I had really good insurance! After I ranted for a bit, he suggested that if I find myself struggling to the degree where I couldn't wait any longer, I could go to the emergency room and tell them the situation. The ER doctor would at least get me referrals and some medication to see me through the time period it was going to take to finally get a regular therapist.

Granted, I know I had told you in a past letter that I had sworn off psychoanalysis years before, and to my credit, I had gone a good fifteen years without stepping foot in a therapist's office, but I knew I was spiraling, and maybe *this* time, maybe now that I was *older* and more mature, therapy might be able to provide a different outcome than it had in the past.

Like a dog returns to its vomit.

When the nurse asked me if I had thoughts of harming myself, I did my whole, "Well…" thing, followed up by, "I'm not suicidal if that's what you're asking. But do I sometimes think about jerking my steering wheel to the right so that I might fly off a steep freeway incline? Sure, but who doesn't?"

In the end, the doctor at the ER never actually *forced* me to go into a "treatment facility;" he just made it clear that if I didn't voluntarily admit myself, he would make that "suggestion" himself.

Semantics.

But I was also promised, and I remember this *clearly*, that since I was "voluntarily" checking myself in, I would have a therapist and medication the same day I was admitted and would probably spend no more than one night away from home.

The offer was an overnight stay at a place Wood Acres College Hospital, a treatment facility that evoked images of comfortable beds, massages, healthy juices, and overstuffed chairs with books lying around plush carpeting? Yeah, if this was going to get me consistent therapy and some anti-depressants, one night was not only worth it but something I was quietly looking forward to.

Fast forward about three hours later. I was in a room that resembled a dorm room—without the mini-refrigerator and pennants. Off-white walls that needed at least a decent cleaning if not new paint. Three twin beds that sit directly on the floor. Functional, commercial carpet, the kind that produces rug burn if one sit-up is attempted, and pretty much nothing else.

There were no slippers and robe waiting for me, not that I was actually expecting that, but I sure didn't think I would have to walk around in that light blue, striped gown they give out in hospitals. You know, the kind that opens in the back and ties unevenly on the side, string and fabric all bunched up so that when you're walking around you look like the back of a computer tower.

Within thirty minutes of realizing I was in an actual mental hospital and not a "treatment facility," I was panicking. Then they told me I wouldn't even be able to see a doctor until the next day. This information was given to me right after they took my shoelaces away, so I wouldn't be tempted to hang myself.

Eventually I was informed that most patients stay for about five days. They had no knowledge of me admitting myself—I had been admitted by the hospital on a "51/50" psychiatric hold and could only leave with a doctor's approval.

I wasn't as panicked as much as…stunned. I walked up and down the fluorescent lighting hallway with a few other patients, feet flopping in loose shoes, the strings in my gown coming undone. I kept grasping at the sides because my boxers kept peeking through the side holes, and I was still in a right enough mind to want some dignity.

I had been crying, too, but that's a given.

Of course, "Things couldn't get worse" is something all people say before things inevitably get worse.

Coming up behind me I heard, "Mr. Elsasser?"

The kid behind me had been in my class several years before, so at least I wasn't coming back to school only to have him sit in my third period class. He was about twenty by this time, and while I didn't remember his name, I knew immediately when I turned around that he had been a student.

To be honest, I can't remember what I said to him. It probably wasn't much since there's not much to say to a student you run into while you're both staying in a psychiatric ward. Since he had already graduated, it would be useless to talk about his current grade. He couldn't ask me for a pass to go to the bathroom. And I'm not sure how appropriate any discussion on Hemingway or Virginia Woolf would be. Upon reflection, I think I was pretty much useless to him, and I jetted back to my room as fast as my flopping shoes would allow me to.

I'll tell you what I *do* remember—when I told the nurse that I couldn't leave my room to go to dinner that night because I was too humiliated to be seen eating half-frozen peas with a plastic spork next to some kid that there was a good chance I had probably given detention to in the 11th grade, they moved him. The next morning a different nurse came to my room to tell me they had moved him to a new wing. A wing, for some reason she felt the need to tell me, that had tighter security measures and dealt with far more mentally ill patients than the wing of which I was currently a visitor.

The move had been generated because I had told the staff that I knew him, and they felt it would be "inappropriate for two people already familiar with one another in the outside world to share this space."

I thought I felt lousy *before*.

I didn't beg, but I came close to it. Not going as far to volunteer to go to the other wing myself, I instead kept insisting it wouldn't be an issue. Just bring him back, I asked. I wouldn't make it a problem.

It was too late, of course, and I never saw that kid again. To this day. I'm not even exactly sure I can remember what he looks like, and, like I said I didn't even know his name, so even if I wanted to, which I do, I wouldn't be able to look him up and apologize.

It wasn't the greatest night's sleep, of course. I had skipped dinner because of that kid and since the nurses had thought I was going to pull some starvation prank, I was periodically checked on. I didn't have my sleeping pills either, and it would take an on-site psychiatrist to prescribe me some. Anything I might have wanted seemed to need approval from either a doctor or a nurse or a receptionist. I couldn't even have a Coke unless the doctor wrote out a prescription.

A prescription for Coke.

So, I spent that first night in a room with two other strangers who *were* sleeping, staring up at a dark ceiling that was too high up for me to see anything but blackness and a red battery light on the fire alarm.

Mid-way through the next afternoon, after having skipped breakfast in silent protest for what they had done to my ex-student, I finally saw a psychiatrist. This was the whole reason I had, seemingly, put myself into this "Wood Acres College" hospital that ironically didn't have one tree or book in sight. Not even a Bible. Later, when I discovered the rec room, all that they had was a few games and a deck of cards.

I went into that psychiatrist's office with so much hope. I'd finally get to meet with the type of therapist who could provide both psychoanalysis *and* medication. All my past therapists didn't have the "MD" behind their names, so all they could do was provide the talk therapy. This guy could give me the drugs too.

I'm going to sum up my conversation with the doctor not because it's too long to go into full detail but because I was in his office for a full eight minutes.

Simply put he asked me why I was there, and I was able to give him a quick run-down. All he responded to was the issue of the bodybuilding supplements. He told me I had to stop taking them. He ignored everything else. Then he wrote in my folder and informed me that he would be starting me on anti-depressants.

When he clicked his pen with a quick flick, indicting this session was already going too long, I knew he wouldn't be giving me any direction or guidance, much less psychoanalysis. I asked him if I could leave and go home.

He responded with, "You need to start dealing with your gender identity issues while you're here. Then we can see about letting you go home."

The guy could have taken my folder and slapped my head with it, and I wouldn't have been more shocked. Yeah, I had briefly told him that I had questioned my sexuality and would rather get to a place where I *didn't*, but who said anything about "gender identity?" I knew I was a man, and that was never an issue. I had never wanted to be a woman; I actually liked being a man.

I looked at the doctor, but I had no idea what to say; all I could think of was whether I now had a gender issue that I didn't know existed before.

He asked me one more question, something about Fair Oaks First Christian, and that was the end of our session. Eight minutes long.

I got my prescription for some anti-depressants, along with an actual prescription for a glass of Coke each day.

My next thought was to get out of that place as quickly as possible. I got the medication I felt I needed, but I wasn't going to get the therapy. I just figured I'd work that out once I got out of there. That was the pressing need.

I made phone calls to your Uncle Jim, your mom, and your grandmother. Besides your mom, no one knew where I was because I had made it clear that I didn't want anyone to know. Of course, now I didn't care *who* knew, I just wanted someone to get me out. It was a gamble checking myself in, and, medication aside, I had lost.

After having a visit from your mom later that afternoon, where she brought me my Bible, a book, and a fresh set of clothes, I was able to sleep better that same night. I also figured the doctor would let me out the next day because I would tell him I would "deal with my gender identity issues immediately." This was my second night here, and I was no longer scared. I was angry and embarrassed. I certainly didn't think I was "crazy," and I didn't believe for a second I was suicidal—which we could debate at another time. I also had stereotypes and preconceptions as to the people who went to mental hospitals, and I *knew* I wasn't one of those people. I was a professional. I had kids and a wife and a home. I needed some...guidance...but I didn't feel my situation warranted being locked up inside of what I was figuring out was basically a prison with nicer guards.

After my morning Coke, I had breakfast. I couldn't appear as if I was staging some sort of hunger strike because that would trigger the doctor that I wasn't mentally stable enough to check out, so I ate and then headed over to the not "mandatory" but "highly encouraged" group therapy sessions where I would smile and nod, so I wouldn't appear belligerent and difficult. All behaviors that would assure me another day's stay.

That afternoon Frank showed up with Mom during the hour allotted for visitors. At first, I was a little irritated with Mom for having told him I was there, but Mom was as legitimately surprised to find Frank there as I was. Still don't know the full story as to how he found out, but once close friends discovered I had "disappeared," I'm sure he used his credentials to find out where they were keeping me.

Frank made a few phone calls after our visit and after a little back-and-forth with my disapproving psychiatrist, I was out by the end of the third day. It was one of the first of many favors Frank did for me. Lily too. Mom picked me up after my doctor signed the release papers and, acting like I had been locked up for thirty years instead of three days, the first thing I asked your mom to do was take me through the In-N-Out drive-through.

The visit had scared me enough to shake me out of my depression. For a time. Like a repeat criminal offender, I left the hospital with a renewed mindset, figuring the experience would change behaviors and feelings and emotions, and I would be a changed man.

A man, not a woman.

But like the repeat offender, I was back to past habits and thought patterns within days. Fear had staved off the struggles, but they would be back.

This would not be my last visit to a mental hospital.

Love, Dad

Dear Travis,

Nothing really to write today; just wanted to say I missed you. I keep wondering how much time will pass before I stop seeing movies or running across words or hear songs that shoot vivid reminders of you or your brothers into my mind. To be honest, sometimes I wish the memories would stop— it's not as if I was simply another parent who gets to look back on the past with bittersweet memories. As time moves on, the sweetness seems to be fading fast, and I'm left with the "bitter" and not the "sweet." I'm sure it's the same for you.

I dream about you at least four or five times a week. That's not an exaggeration. But they're never good dreams. Instead, the dreams, nightmarish in the imagery, are always of you and me shouting at each other, which is weird because even when you and I didn't get along while you were growing up, I don't feel as if we ever resorted to *too* much yelling.

Or maybe we did. I don't know; it seems the further you get away from something, the more acceptable it becomes to bend the truth a little just so you can live with yourself.

Sorry. This letter bummed me out. It was just my intention to say I missed you.

Love, Dad

Dear Travis,

Months went by until I was finally able to procure a therapist in Long Beach. A therapist who would take my insurance *and* was clearly a Christian. Said that right on the *Psychology Today* website. Both Mom and I were relieved—Mom probably more than I; the continual up-and-down mood swings are almost as hard on a spouse as it is on the person experiencing them.

The first forty-five minutes of my initial session was going excellently. I hit it off with this soft-spoken Indian man right away, and when he listened, there was something about his eyes that told me his concern for me was genuine. He wasn't just phoning it in. This time I opened-up and told him *everything*. Gone were the days I told my therapist half-truths or flat out lies to make myself look better. I didn't hold back in that short time; I was more open and honest with him than I had been with any other human being. I told him things I had never said out loud before. And he didn't even have to *say* anything for me to feel some sort of relief. Just speaking the whole truth, without painting a false picture of who I was and what I was going through was therapeutic in and of itself.

When I was finished, he asked me the standard "What do you want to get out of therapy?"

My answer, the same one I had being screaming at God, quietly, inside my head for thirty plus years was, "I want to be a Christian and not be gay."

No big pause. No dramatic movie moment. He just simply said, "I don't think that's going to be possible."

The next week I was given more clarification. When I asked him what he meant, he said, "I don't think you can stop being gay any more than I can stop being Indian."

Travis, this guy was the first therapist who ever had told me "No" when I made it clear that I wanted God and the miracle of therapy to help me get rid of unwanted desires that were literally making me crazy. Unlike previous therapists, he didn't "hem and haw" or do some fancy footwork around the issue. He didn't throw some verses out to me or tell me to read my Bible more or pray or have longer devotional time with God.

He was the first therapist who put the idea into my head that I could be a Christian and a gay man.

But instead of feeling a sense of curiosity, if not relief, I began to shut him out.

I let him talk and didn't argue, but I pretty much had made up my mind right there that this counselor wasn't a "right fit" for me. Which was too bad because he was also the first therapist that not only went the full hour—most are down to forty-five minutes these days—but we had gone over by five minutes the previous week.

Toward the end of that session, which would be the last one, he asked me the strangest question I had ever been asked by a therapist. It was a question I didn't, first of all consider myself, and it was definitely one I didn't think a Christian therapist would propose. At least, he approached the subject carefully. Considering my "struggles," he asked how open Mom would be if I "stepped out" on our relationship once in a while, with her blessing, and took care of my sexual needs by someone else other than her. Specifically, a man.

I want to be as honest with you as possible, but I can also appreciate that you are my son…so I will spare you any more details regarding the rest of our conversation. Long story short, my answer was a firm "No," and there was no more hope that I might be able to make this therapist/patient relationship work.

A next appointment was made. I had no intention of *honoring* that appointment, but I've told you how I try to please everybody all the time, and I didn't want him thinking badly of me, so I told him I would be there.

That week I left a voice message—thankfully no awkward, confrontational one-on-one phone conversation—telling him I didn't think we were a good fit. He never called me back and try to convince me otherwise.

Aaannnddd…back to the therapy hunt.

Not that God doesn't work through *everything* we do, even the mundane tasks that we subconsciously think God doesn't care about, but there is no doubt in my mind that God quickly put me into the path of my next therapist. Who we can all hope will be my last.

Michael was from Biola University and had a practice less than three miles from our house. Like all the past therapists, I had high hopes for this one, and, inwardly, I promised myself he would be the last.

No, *seriously*, I told myself. He *really* will be the last. If he can't help me, then I don't think anyone can. At last count, I had been to 25-30 professionals.

As it turns out—at least as of this writing—Michael was not only my final therapist, but the first person to convince me that I could have a relationship with the same God I had known for most of my life and not have to live in a constant state of fear that He would cast me into hell for being gay. Over a period of seventeen months, Michael was able to help me to, at last, sedate the bats that had been flying around in my head, which had, up until then, been banging into each other and into the sides of my brain.

Through weekly sessions, he would convince me that happiness and joy was not what I had been searching for all these years. It was *peace*. And once I understood the difference, I found myself in a better position to help myself release the anger, the depression, the anxiety, and the control I had put on my sexuality.

He didn't have to convince me that once I released myself from my self-imposed prison that I would be a better man. And a Christian. And a dad.

"Would your kids rather have a gay dad or a dead dad?" he asked after about a month of therapy, therapy that was going nowhere since I had insisted in the first couple of sessions that we deal with the depression and ignore the sexual identity issues. "Because you're headed down one of those roads."

You and I both know which road I would end up choosing, but that road was certainly no "drive up the coast;" it was more like that drive we all made that time coming home from Sacramento with you and Andrew throwing up inside our Tupperware for eight hours in the back of my Prius. That was the same trip where Christopher fell in the parking lot of a liquor store and cut his forehead open.

Man, I thought I had been depressed *before* I chose to go down this route.

I had no idea what was coming.

Love, Dad

Dear Travis,

I've given you my list of pet peeves. It's only fair that I give you a list of things for which I am grateful, and so I would encourage you to create your own list. Humans focus far too much on the things that bother us, so when you are going through something tough or you're feeling depressed, read through your list. It helps.

1. Mountain Dew Zero.
2. One and Quest protein bars.
3. Waitresses who call me "honey."
4. Movies with twist endings.
5. Maine. The entire state.
6. Farce.
7. London.
8. Restaurants that serve soft butter.
9. *In the Hall of the Mountain King.*
10. Anything red velvet flavored.
11. *Old Testament* stories, especially the ones where people don't live up to God's original plan of marriage between one man and one woman and marry a slew of wives or have mistresses but are loved by God anyway. Those are the people pastors ensure us are in heaven to this day.
12. Making up nicknames for people I care about.
13. Dry heat saunas.
14. Falling asleep to a show or movie I like.
15. Laughing at dinner with you guys and me going around the table doing impressions of everyone in our family.
16. Clean sheets.
17. Being a dad.

a.   This isn't a manipulative, schmaltzy way to evoke sympathy or emotions. I generally miss being a dad because, like I've stated earlier, I was good at it! If I was a more than decent hockey player or was an excellent moirologist and I stopped doing it, I would miss it. Same thing applies here.

Love, Dad

Dear Travis,

Don't ever leave change (quarters, dimes, etc.) in your car where people can see it from the outside. It isn't worth having someone break into your car over .68.

Also, speaking of cars, if you want to save gas money, keep your air conditioning unit off and windows open if you are going under 40mph. Air conditioning on at speeds greater than 40.

Throw in a couple of ice cubes or a wet washcloth into your dryer; it will remove wrinkles off t-shirts.

Although it isn't currently in style, don't hang a bunch of stuff from your car's rearview mirror (except maybe a parking pass); you'll get a ticket.

Finally, if you ever need kindling and you don't have any wood, use Doritos. Works just as well.

Love, Dad

Dear Travis,

In the past, I would always cry out Yeah, ok!" whenever I would hear stories on Dr. Phil or Dateline from people who experienced trauma only to claim later the experience was forgotten after the person consciously "blocked it out." I didn't get it nor believed it because, after all, my trauma was always playing front and center in my mind like that black-and-white Mickey Mouse cartoon that runs all day on Main Street at Disneyland. Jeesh, I was *never* fortunate enough to experience the blessed relief that must come from blocking certain memories out of existence.

The day I moved out of our house was bad. A couple days later when I had to go home and tell you and Andrew *why* I had moved out was the worst day of my life.

Understanding that it probably was one of yours as well.

But while sitting here now, trying to recall the conversation we had that night, I'm finding myself not searching for the right wording or looking for ways to justify myself, instead, I'm truly having a hard time remembering how that hour or so conversation went down. Am I trying to avoid pain by blocking it out like those Dr. Phil guests? Am I pretending to forget the specific details of the running monologue I delivered that February night in 2019 so I don't have to relive the worst moment of my 50 years all over again?

Right now, I don't know, and I no longer have a therapist who I can run these thoughts by, but logically, I probably took the content of all these previous letters and summed them up that night in a conversation in which I did most of the talking, so there's no need to rehash that day any further.

I left right after our "conversation" and went back to the room I was renting from a former student, Daniela, who is now an assistant principal for our rival high school. Her house was a convenient seven-minute drive from yours, and I went home, laid down on my bed, and broke down.

For weeks, I had prepared for that speech, even though at the time I had no idea how long I was going to stay in my marriage. I was coming to a crossroads, so to speak, faster than what I was prepared for, and I was psychologically weary from the previous six months where I had been obsessively thinking about the subject of death… *death,* not necessarily suicide, since it wasn't as much about the act of dying as it was thinking about what life would be like for you guys if I wasn't around. For weeks, and most days, a death "motif" hovered over my life when I woke up and it stuck around until I went to bed…at 5:30pm, of course. Trying to picture a future for you and your mom and brothers without me around became my top priority, and I needed to make sure you all would be taken care of.

One crazy Sunday, after Googling "the most dangerous cities in Los Angeles," I took off in my brand-new Jeep, that monster green Sahara beast I've talked about which still didn't have license plates yet, and I drove to the seediest part of that "dangerous" city. It was right in the middle of the day when I pulled over to the side of the road, left my keys in the ignition, rolled down my windows…and waited. I sat there for a good three hours, hoping and praying someone would come and carjack me.

I had it all planned out. A gun-toting criminal would ask for the keys, I would refuse, and it would be over.

Crazy, huh? Yeah, well, I was pretty much out of my mind in those days.

After a nice elderly man who was sweeping the sidewalk outside his church waved at me, I figured nothing was going to happen, so I drove home.

However, in therapy, Michael and I had been spending a good amount of our sessions working through different scenarios of what life might look for you guys if I *did* stick around. And what life might look for me. And your mom. By December, I had already decided that you guys would rather have a gay dad than a dead one, and so slowly, the constant barrage of death scenarios were replaced with ways I might be able to have a relationship with my kids even though we wouldn't be living together as we once had.

Thinking I might even be able to have a relationship with your mom, although we wouldn't be together, was a romantic ideal but ultimately a delusional one.

In the early court papers Mom filed, she had written that once I moved out, I was running around "acting like a teenager." That was one statement I couldn't argue with. She was right—those first months I practically *blew up*, and when I wasn't either working or crying while watching *Lost* on repeat while laying on my new, strange bed in a new, strange house, I went out and did whatever I could to make-up for all those years where I had chosen to portray a counterfeit version of myself that those in my world, who meant the most to me, would find acceptable. I was like a jack-in-the-box that had been winding up for thirty years instead of thirty seconds, and when the top popped open, I jumped out of that confinement with a lot of exuberance, a lot of newly discovered idealism, and a lot of expectations.

Remember that time at the park when we opened-up a two-liter bottle of soda and slipped in a packet of Mentos? The fountain that shot out of that bottle was the closest thing we ever came to conducting a science project while you were growing up.

Now imagine taking that same bottle and placing it in one of those electric paint can shakers for 3 hours *before* you put the Mentos in—to be painfully dramatic, that's what it felt like once I had finally unscrewed the cap of my mind. When I finally freed myself, I just exploded.

Like many gay men and women finding themselves free after decades of suppressed identity, I went out those first six months and made mistake after mistake after mistake, but even though I was aware that I was acting contrary to the biblical beliefs I had upheld and for which I had my whole life argued zealously with those who didn't share these same beliefs, I didn't care. Understand that I had been told for so many years that Christianity and homosexuality was by no means compatible, so I had to just accept the dogma that I was no longer a Christian and just adopt the position that since my Moral Compass was now gone—unless I never had a true relationship with God from the beginning as my Calvinist friends would argue—then what difference would it make if I now adhered to my own standards of morality?

Like my non-secular friends, I would now determine what was right and wrong based on my own personal set of ethics.

So, was I acting like the teenager Mom claimed? Was I having a good time relishing in my newfound "freedom" masked as youthful rebellion? Did I get a rush out of dating, setting up an online profile, or going to bars where'd I meet men and women who had stories and histories not unlike my own? Honestly? Sure.

Now I am fully aware that you heard rumors and half-truths and full-truths of how I was living my life during those messy months, and I know some of my behavior and actions just deepened the wounds I had created when I moved out of the house. For this, I will forever regret, and I don't even think an apology can make up for the price you had to pay in order for me to be "free." Some of it was inexcusable, and I won't justify any of it, nor will I try to soften the truth as it concerns that period of my life.

What I *will* do is spare you the specific details of my many "adventures" because just like I don't want to know every aspect of your adult private life, I, likewise, should be able to retain a measure of privacy. You're almost an adult at this juncture of your life, but when it comes down to it, I'm still your dad, and I need you to primarily think of me in that role. Just think of my behavior during that time as if it were one of our multiple trips we took to Paris: each time we went, we saw the same sites over and over and over again. The Eiffel Tower. The Louvre. Notre Dame. We always made sure we saw the most important, impressively beautiful sites that represent the city, but we never have time to go into the catacombs to see the decay.

I will also ask you to give me a chance to rectify the damage done during that time. Today I may not be able to heal the *wound*, but, if you give me a chance, I may be able to stop the bleeding.

So, while ignoring specifics, I can admit that I embraced a lot of foolishness; however, at the time it was an easy justification on my part because now that I had God taken out of my life by those who claimed I was now "lost," I was going to do whatever I deemed necessary to finally bring me a sliver of peace. No matter what, no matter how drastic, I was going to be comfortable with the truest version of myself that—at least by 8 years of age—I had decided was horribly incongruent with the original "Greg" that God has designed.

Eventually, the rumors of my behavior got back to me, and one of the comments I kept hearing repeatedly was that I was "acting out of character." This floored me and although I answered very few of my detractors, choosing, for the most part, to keep myself from jumping into defense mode, I still fought the urge to let people understand that claiming I was out of character was a little ironic since I had been in character my whole life.

What I didn't understand at the time, but is very clear for me now, is that by throwing God out of my life, I just became a different, fake version of myself, replacing the previous, fake person. I wasn't anymore "authentic" than the last Greg I was pretending to be. I *was* a Christian—God had assured me of that time and time again, through His word and through the "fruit" through the "fruit" of my walk with Christ. Me pretending *not* to be a Christian, which is who God *made* me to be as opposed to me *making* myself a Christian, is as fraudulent as a person pretending he is heterosexual when he clearly knows he is not.

But while I was hurtling through this new life with such blundering, brash—and callous, certainly—exuberance, for lack of a better word, I was also experiencing raw grief for the first time in my life. Sure, I had gone through intense depression and a couple mediocre attempts to take my life, but I hadn't known true grief up until then. All my grandparents were dead, so I was familiar with sadness and loss, but I had not known the grief that comes with losing a child. And while I'm aware that I didn't experience the grief that comes with the finality of a child's *death,* the pain was still acute. It certainly was as painful as anything I have ever experienced up until then.

Over time, you wouldn't be the only son I lost. Within a year or two, I would lose all three of you, for a block of time, and when that happened not only was I losing my mind, I panicked. I would worry about potential issues from everything like "How will they keep up their grades without me there to push them?" "How will I keep them from being disrespectful to their mom?"

"What if there's an earthquake?" "What if a burglar breaks in?" "Who's going to watch *30 Rock* with you guys and explain the satire?"

Remember: all of this was going on pre-COVID. Once COVID hit and thousands of people were dying, my often irrational fears were immediately legitimized. In the end—although we are still currently at some risk—I never found out if you had COVID…if you were exposed to COVID…if you were vaccinated.

I don't even know what you looked like in a mask, and for some reason, that's something that bothers me as much as not knowing if you were ever *sick*. I don't know—I'm weird.

But let's backtrack.

You and I lost contact in July of 2019; I had moved out the previous February. At first, things seemed to be ok with you and me. You would still stop by my classroom once in a while to hang out. We went to lunch occasionally. While things certainly weren't normal, you seemed to be working through any confusion and resentment.

By March, the worry, the stress, the guilt—oh, so much guilt—and the idea that I was about to go through the next several years without living with my sons broke me. I was at rehearsal one afternoon and arguing with your mom over the phone, and by the end of that conversation, I knew I would be moving back home.

That night…or maybe the next day…I came back home, the Jeep's trunk only a quarter filled with stuff I had taken back in February. I don't know—maybe I knew deep down that this was a temporary return. I really can't tell you what I was thinking. Based on what happened that night, I wasn't thinking at *all*.

By the time Mom got back from work and you guys were home from school, the awaited sense of relief I'm sure we all expected was non-existent.

The arguing started almost immediately. Andrew, unfairly having been forced into taking the position of "Man of the House" since I had been gone, started the argument. Recriminations, anger, and a general build-up of sadness and pain all erupted from Andrew, Mom and me. Christopher ran into the other room.

I hated that day. Writing about it now is difficult. There's something extra difficult about writing down painful memories in lieu of talking about them.

Everyone was shouting. In the last couple days, I've come to the conclusion that it doesn't matter *what* we were shouting about—it's the *why* that seems more prevalent. And we all know why we were shouting.

The one thing I clearly remember was the role you took that night. You didn't yell. You remained calm, and at that moment, *you* became the "Man of the House" as you kept your voice even, refusing to give in to your emotions. You were standing in the kitchen, right up against the refrigerator, and you attempted to reign the rest of us in when you stopped and said, "Everybody stop yelling. You're only going to drive him away again."

It was around dinner time by then, and I was already falling back into past habits—I was ready for bed. I was crying by then, and I apologized once more for everything I had put the family through, and then I asked everyone to leave me alone for the rest of the night. I just wanted to go to sleep.

The decision to end my life was made as I walked into my old bedroom and got into bed. This wouldn't be a cry for help this time either. The gun I had bought about eight months or so before had been given to Frank, but I'm not sure I would have used it anyway—I may have been suicidal, but I was thinking with enough reason to understand I couldn't do it that way.

In the home with you guys one room over.

I'm also way too much of a coward to use a gun. There's no way.

There was an almost brand-new prescription of sleeping pills in my overnight bag, almost thirty pills, and I had at least twenty-five to thirty anti-anxiety drugs on me too. I took the bottle of whiskey from off the bookshelf and put the pills in a dish in my drawer. I can't remember what I did with the empty bottles of medication, but I know I hid them well; the thought was to make it more difficult for any emergency crews to determine why I was unconscious in case they got to me before I had died.

I made a couple of cryptic, melodramatic phone calls, which only undermines the theory that I was 100% serious about taking my life. I was probably making one last attempt to reach out to someone to fix me. Actually, I'm sure of it now.

Finally, I did one last thing before I downed my cocktail. I wrote you a quick note. To this day I don't know if it was given to you or not. It was short, and I stuffed it in the middle of the journal I had been writing in for some time. It just said something like, "Travis: thank you for sticking up for me."

The stories of the next thirty-six hours have come in fragments, and, over time, different people have filled in different parts of the events, and even though I was the one asking for the details, I'm at the place now where I wish I could have remained ignorant.

Travis, I've spent a lot of time in my letters seeking your forgiveness for many of my self-centered behaviors you had to witness, but like the saying goes, in some situations apologies truly aren't enough.

For acknowledgment purposes, I do apologize directly to you for attempting to take my life in *your* home with *you* in it. All attempts at trying to make excuses for it would be foolish because no matter how bad I thought I had it at the time, nothing can take away from the brazen, self-centeredness of my act. I can never apologize enough, and the only thing I have to offer you is time.

Time can and will, I believe, lessen the pain I unleashed on the family, and I'm also a logical enough person to know that the scars I left will never completely heal. You yourself will remember that night and the following days until you're an old man.

Here's to praying that someday you'll give me a chance to help you work through the leftover trauma that is a part of your history, trauma that is taking a primary position in your life.

One of the things I pray for, when I'm praying for you, is that you will soon get to experience the accompanying power that comes when you forgive someone, whether it's me, or an enemy, or your spouse, or even your children, because the most powerful human experience that runs secondary to love is forgiveness.

I do ask for it not just for my benefit but also for yours. You're going to have to trust me on this one.

The several hours I spent in the ER is a memory I do not have, and I am grateful that it is buried away in the dark recesses of my mind that I hope no psychiatrist ever tries to summon up. Last thing I remember is going to bed, and my next conscious memory after going to sleep that night was being wheeled into my second psychiatric hospital about 24-30 hours later. I was strapped down, and once they got me off the gurney, I was taken to another room that looked very familiar. Blank room. Three beds close to the floor. Nothing decorating the walls but the red light of the fire alarm. I soon found out it was a different hospital, but it might as well have been the same.

However, I have no memory of the day prior. Or was it the morning of *that* day? Not sure. To this day, I'm not sure how many hours I was in the ER before they transferred me to the mental hospital, and according to the various accounts of the people who were there, I was in a state of "consciousness" while they flushed the drugs out of my system, but I was also, as Uncle Jim describes it, "out of my mind."

It was Uncle Jim and several others who have since filled me in on those lost hours, so the story is strongly credible. I'll put them down here as if I was a *witness* to these events as long as you understand that I really was not.

Like I mentioned, I had sent a few cryptic messages before I overdosed. One was to my friend Charlotte and one was to Frank. Kyle, a friend to both Charlotte and I, was elected by Charlotte to go by the house and check on me— something was "off" about our conversation, she noted. Sending Kyle instead of going over herself made sense since Kyle lived around the corner.

You remember Kyle—he was the drama teacher that took over my position at Marshall when I wanted to work exclusively within the English department. He and his friend spent the day with us that time you and I went to New York.

Anyway Kyle showed up at our house around 7 or 8 and knocked. Mom answered the door.

It was a quick conversation; Kyle stayed just below the steps and asked if everything was ok. He asked if he could see me. Mom told him I had gone to sleep early and would be out for the night, which, Kyle told me earlier, set him at ease. It was common knowledge amongst my friends and family that I went to bed early most nights. He figured if I was asleep, I was ok.

Frank was nervous and told Lily who insisted Frank drive by the house to find out what was going on, which he did. Sort of. He drove by the house and parked in front, rolling down his window to see if he could hear anything unusual.

The lights were on in the kitchen, and the house sounded peaceful. He chalked my behavior up to my usual melodrama and went home.

My cousin Sandi may have received a text from me, and there is a possibility she called your mom that night to check on me as well. Sacramento is a long way from Los Angeles so even if there was something wrong, the only help she could give would be through Mom.

Early the next morning, I was stumbling around the bedroom, into the bathroom, falling down. I'm sure there is a medical name for the state I was in, but since I have never asked a doctor what I was experiencing that morning, I can just equate my behavior to that of movie zombies—there was enough brain activity to keep my body moving, but all sense of consciousness and coherent thought had been overpowered by the effects from the pills and alcohol.

Your mom was able to lift me to some degree, dragging my body from the hard bathroom floor to the carpeted bedroom—no small feat for a 5'2" woman and a 6'4" man who was thrashing around like the walking dead.

Once Mom had me safely on the floor, she continued to get ready for work. That's when the phone calls began, I believe. the first to call was my friend Mike from Living Waters. Not sure how Mike had found out that something was going on in our household—maybe I had sent him a text the night before too—but he was calling early to check in with me and couldn't get a response since I had shut off my phone right after I took the pills.

According to Mike's account, your mom told him I had taken some pills the night before, although she didn't know what or how many since I had hidden the empty bottle pretty well, and she wasn't able to get me to a full conscious state to ask me. As he was talking to her, Mike got into his car and headed to our house.

He told Mom to call 911.

Next, my cousin Sandi called Mom. Mom gave her a run down as well, but the conversation was a short one since Mom was getting ready to go to work. Sandi also urged her to call 911.

In order of where Uncle Jim's call to your mom fell amongst the other ones, I'm not sure, but the conservations were similar to the others.

It was Mike who called 911, sending the paramedics our way. He and Uncle Jim must have been talking because when Uncle Jim found out the paramedics were on their way, he called you.

It was this part of the events of that day that I wished I had never been told. It pains me to my core that Uncle Jim had to tell you to wake Christopher up and take him to the park down the street, so he wouldn't have to see his dad being wheeled away in an ambulance.

When you took that call, Mom had already left for work. As a result of our family fight the night before, Andrew had left that night to go spend the night at your grandmothers, so, with an ambulance on its way, you were left alone in the house with your little brother and a father dying in the next room.

Looking at this in print now, I'm shocked that you didn't stop talking to me sooner. It was the most atrocious thing I've ever done to you."

Not sure if you made it to the park, but Uncle Jim got to the house around the same time Mike and the ambulance arrived. Somehow he found you, and now that it was safe to be in the house, he left you and Christopher at home while he and Mike drove to the hospital.

I had no idea that after twenty-three years in our home, I would spend my last few minutes inside of it being strapped to a gurney.

In the ER and completely out of my mind, but now having the ability to talk and move like a half-bred human/zombie, I started yelling at everyone. I guess I yelled at the doctors or nurses and even Mike, who I told to his face that I didn't want him in the room with me. Since I was hollering that I also didn't want to see my parents or your mom, only Uncle Jim was allowed to stay as they poured that same charcoal substance they had administered to me twenty-five years ago down my stomach, neutralizing the effects of the pills, thus keeping me alive.

In a couple of days, the psychiatrist would tell me I was lucky to be alive. The combination and amount of the prescription pills I put into my system should have killed me, he claimed.

I don't know why I specifically demanded certain people stay out of my room that morning. I know in the past I've put a lot of blame on my parents for the root causes of my sexuality, and I know I was very angry at your mom for what we had been going through since the separation. Her friend Cathy picked Mom up at work and drove her to the ER later that morning, but word got to her that I had a whole list of people I didn't want to see, so they left quickly.

I don't know why I was so harsh on Mike, for he had done nothing but show me kindness since the beginning of our friendship, so I think I chose to take the pent-up frustrations that I had with the church and other Christians over the issues of homosexuality and decided to elect Mike as their representative.

I've since apologized to Mike, but I know the sting of my words will stay with him for a while. Whoever made up that whole "sticks and stones" aphorism had obviously never been the recipient of cruel words, and I was especially cruel that day.

Barking demands and spouting some pretty hateful words, all while black and white chalky spit ran out of the sides of my mouth, was what Uncle Jim had to sit through until the hospital declared me neutralized from the pills. Since he had been the one to have to deal with me and the doctors, he was most likely relieved when they finally sent me to the psychiatric institution.

Whereas my first visit to a mental hospital was semi-"voluntary," this trip was considered a 51/50, a slang term for the California code law that allows the state to commit a person to a psychiatric facility if they are deemed a danger to themselves because of mental illness. There was no way I was getting out in two or three days this time, and I knew that from the start.

I also knew how to play the game a little better this time around. There would be no pouting in my room and not eating. I would have to go to every group session, even if the topics didn't apply to me. I'd have to socialize. I'd have to try and not give my psychiatrist attitude.

By the next morning, I was up and eating breakfast. So far, this "visit" wasn't as traumatic as it was the previous time; it was almost like I was getting used to it. I wasn't even humiliated that I had actually tried to kill myself again, although underneath the veneer of disappointment, there was a sense of relief. The minutes leading up to the attempt, I was convinced that it wasn't a "cry for help" this time. Waking up alive proved otherwise.

As I began to settle into my surroundings, you guys were left at home to work through the second mess I had dragged you through. Outside of the death of your grandfather, this was the biggest challenge you had faced in your fifteen years. I often wonder what you and Christopher talked about when you guys were alone the day they took me away in the ambulance, strapped to a gurney. Did you have to lie to him? Did you try and distract him until Mom got home from work? Did you realize right then and there that you were the one who would have to step up and protect your youngest brother from the dysfunction of the world around him only having to explain to him that it was his father that had created the dysfunction?

As bad as things were, the next day they would get worse. I don't know if Mom had you or Andrew figure out how to break into my iPad, but then again, in this case, the devil really isn't in the details.

Speaking of the devil, we often blame him, or Satan, whenever life crumbles around us. How Old Scratch must roll his red eyes when the finger is pointed at him by the human hands that truly cause most of the problems in our world. In fact, I always warned you guys not to give Satan so much credit for the sin you bring to the table, for our own personal human corruptness is capable of far more damage.

You, your brothers, and your mom found out about my relationship with David once you guys figured out how to get into my iPad. While the pictures you discovered were 100% innocuous, there was some evidence that might raise eyebrows. However, I hadn't told you about David before this because I was not ready to speak to you and your brothers about him, nor did I feel you were ready either.

The day Mom came to see me at the psychiatric facility was the defining moment in our marriage. Before the visit, I think both of us had small notions in our heads that we might be able to somehow salvage our relationship, although on my end the prerequisite for a reconciliation still depended on God's Divine intervention, fixing my sexuality once and for all; a notion I completely knew was not a rational one but one a tiny part of my psyche clung to.

Even after all that had happened and all that I had experienced, wouldn't I still want to be straight if God granted it? I'd still have a marriage for which complete fulfillment could be met, and I'd be back in the home where I could see my kids every day. Not to mention the appealing idea that half the circle in my world would stop hating me—as long as I renounced my sexuality and declared it sinful. On the flip side, my liberal, non-religious friends and family would still love me like they had chosen to do so after the separation, but if my marriage was restored, I'd have my Christian friends back as well.

Life could go back to normal. If only God could fix me.

Before we could go over our marital options that day at the psychiatric hospital, Mom first needed to tell me she knew about David. She told me about the iPad picture she found of me and David sitting outside a restaurant; later she would send that picture to yours and Andrew's phone, which was then forwarded to mine…all during the five days I was locked up.

Your mom showed an amazing amount of grace that day. Although the picture you all found could be explained away without much effort, I could have simply said David was a new friend I had met during the two-month period I had been out of the house, but I didn't see the need to lie about the relationship. David and I were not serious, but we were exclusive by that time. And while there was some embarrassment on my part upon learning you all knew about him, I was more ashamed that I had met and started dating him within a week of moving out. What lack of self-control I had exhibited by moving out and dating within days while you guys were left home, grieving over the breakup of our family! It was a self-centered move on my part and beyond insensitive. Now, I could make excuses for myself and make a defense for the pent-up identity-crisis that had finally exploded, rendering me incapable of rational behavior, but you and I both know that I am fully able to exhibit self-control.

After all, for the most part, I had relied on self-control my entire life.

Essentially, your mom told me that even though she knew about me and David, she would forgive me and take me back. It could all be forgiven, which, regardless of whether or not leaving my marriage was a question of immorality, the affair I was having *was* just that. I *did* need forgiveness for that affair, and I will always love your mom for making that offer. It was a selfless proposal and ran contrary to my selfishness of the past two months.

It got to me when she talked about you and your brothers, and I found myself less assured of what I was doing with my life when she told me how much all three of you had missed me. She talked of Christopher crying when he went to bed every night which was effective, almost sealing the deal right then and there, and an old debate was given new life—Christopher was 11 at the time.

Again, *maybe* I could make it until he was at least 18…

She specifically mentioned you as well, telling me of the newly formed family devotional time she began with the four of you every night after dinner, and how you stuck up for me yet again saying, "If there's one thing about Dad, he owns his screw-ups."

The most serious conversation your mom and I would ever have in the almost thirty years we had known each other had to be condensed into fifteen minutes due to the visiting time limit imposed by the hospital. When our time was almost up and without actualizing it, I knew I was still on the fence. Leaving the family and the consequent emotional price I was paying was wrecking the little sanity I had left.

The resurging temptation to return and get my family back was at its peak. I figured it wouldn't be difficult to slip back into the façade, picking up where I had left off, but I also knew that if I *did*, the façade would have cracks visible enough to see through the invisible Scotch tape I'd have to use to patch it all up. Everybody would know what had happened and what I was hiding.

Up until that moment, I could have gone either way, and then your mom, right before our time was up, said something to me that sent me flying over the side of the fence on which I had been straddling. And although she probably wouldn't like to hear this, I am grateful she said it because starting with the end of that visit, I never thought of returning to a life of dishonesty with any level of real sincerity.

She said, "Greg—you haven't received healing from God because you just won't let Him. You haven't tried hard enough."

Listen, in a long-term marriage like the one I had with Mom, both people, Christian or not, say a lot of nasty things to each other. But what she said to me across that table, in what would be the last full conversation your mom and I would ever have, wasn't meant to be hurtful or rude. It wasn't a last minute "dig" to get me riled up or to give her the satisfaction of having the last word. Your mom truly thought she was giving me sound, godly advice that if I just took seriously and applied to my struggles, would usher in the healing I had been looking for but had somehow overlooked.

Since you're not a real fan of movies in general, I'm pretty sure you've never willingly gone to a sad movie. Like a *really* sad movie where a person dies or a dog gets hit by a bus. But some day, if you find yourself sitting in a theatre where something like this were to happen to a character or his pet, you might notice that instead of *crying* someone might *laugh*, especially if the scene is very quiet or at its most dramatic moment.

Laughing, when crying is more appropriate, is very normal behavior. Human beings are emotionally complicated creatures and when we find ourselves uncomfortable, we often exhibit a reaction that doesn't match up with the emotion we are experiencing at that particular moment.

People will laugh at funerals. Or cry when happy. It's not uncommon for people to become angry and lash out at the nearest person when they're scared.

When I walked back to my room that day, after that last conversation with your mom, I started crying. This in and of itself was not unusual—after all, I had been crying for a good two years, but for once I wasn't crying out of that familiar gnawing depression or sense of helplessness. I was pissed off.

Then I started laughing. I seriously did. Then I was crying again. Then I was back to being pissed off.

I hadn't tried hard enough? I screamed in my head. *I hadn't let God* help *me?*

If there was any *one* person that had witnessed me struggle and fight over the years, attempting to switch my sexual desires to more societal acceptable desires, it was your mom. She had stood by me when I had repeatedly talked about it with her. She was a captive audience, given front row seats to the decades of depression and angst and anti-depressants and therapy and books and suicidal ideation and dog excrement and moodiness, and so I became so angry that morning, not because she had *told* me those things but because she *felt* those things. She really did believe I hadn't done enough to "heal" myself.

Not done enough? I had tried to kill myself to put an end to my sexual "dysfunction."

What was left to do?

I got to my room and ignored my two roommates, a young ex-Marine and a college-aged kid who always said "touché" in conversations where "touché" made no sense, and I laid down on my bed, throwing my arm around my eyes to stop the tears from slipping out.

Now obsessed over the idea that people might see my actions over the previous months as just another typical mid-life crisis, I replayed the scene with your mom and me over and over. She was the one person who understood my struggle more than any other, and I was mortified that she had looked and spoken to me like my behavior was just a result of a human nature that only wanted to enjoy the sinful pleasures of a secular life. And nothing more.

During that short walk to my room, I had come to the conclusion that no matter how hard I might try, I wouldn't be able to make anyone understand my reality. I couldn't switch brains with people for five minutes so they could experience what had been in my head since I was a kid, consequently giving them an opportunity to display a little compassion, perhaps giving them an opportunity to understand that this wasn't merely an issue *who I wanted to sleep with!* And if Mom wasn't even convinced of the intensity of the battle I had been waging after all that she had been dragged through, others definitely wouldn't.

No, I would simply be labeled a prodigal who wanted to indulge in the flesh, a rebellious man who had pushed Jesus off the stoop at the door of my heart while He stood there knocking away, just waiting for me to let Him in.

Ridiculous.

Not even suicide and two mental hospitals could make people stop and say, "Wait a minute. I think this isn't just an issue of sex. This is so much deeper."

That was the last time I debated the prospect of a future for my marriage.

Love, Dad

Dear Travis,

Before you sign up for service with any company—phone service, internet, satellite, insurance—call them up first and then follow my advice below:

1. When the automated system picks up, dial "0" immediately. If you get a "Sorry, you have selected an invalid option," hang up and pick a different company.
2. Put your phone on speaker; if the computerized operator interprets your background neighborhood traffic noise as you try to speak your selection, and the voice keeps saying, "Sorry, I don't understand," hang up and pick a different company.
3. If the system offers to hold your place in line and call you back, don't fall for it. They'll never call you back.
4. When you get to a live operator and they pick up by saying something like, "Thank you for calling _____, my name is Judy, operator 783928407568082389-AA-L45. How can I make this the best call of your day and make your experience with us more meaningful and enriching by making you smile and answering every concern you might have?"…hang up. You don't have time for all of that.

Love, Dad

Dear Travis,

The rest of the week in the hospital went by quickly even though it was only four days, two more days than my first trip to a psychiatric facility.

This time around, the hospital set me up with a therapist who actually talked me through some issues, and I still had a separate psychiatrist who prescribed medication and met with me for about five minutes a day.

They pulled the therapist in from another unit in the hospital. Since this therapist was a gay man, the psychiatrist put us together for the benefit of having me speak to someone who would understand my specific issues. For several days, we spoke about being gay, about being a Christian—which he was—and about the process of transitioning to a new life not only as a gay man, but as a man whose entire family and social structure had changed almost overnight. It did help some.

During those four days, I interacted more with the people around me…much more than I had done at the last place.

I spent some restless nights sitting on a chair outside the nurse's station talking to the nurses about education and philosophy, and our conversations made me feel like a human being instead of a mentally ill man who was under mandatory medical treatment like some character out of *One Flew Over the Cuckoo's Nest*.

A couple nights I talked to my roommates, although outside of suffering from depression, I didn't have a lot in common with them. A couple times I had to play "adult in the room," but most of it was in good fun.

During the day, I went to group sessions and played cards during the prescribed free time. Although we were missing two or three cards, I'll never, *ever* forget teaching a meth addict and two bi-polar girls how to play Hearts. The meth addict kept starting our games with the 2 of spades instead of the 2 of clubs, and I was losing my mind by his 3rd or 4th attempt, but I held back my irritation, thinking it would be a good idea to refrain from getting snippy with a guy who hadn't had any methamphetamines for a couple days. The girls were quiet, archetypically dark and brooding, and several times I avoided throwing the queen of hearts on them lest it triggered something and thus keeping them at the hospital longer than they needed to stay.

I'm not trying to be funny; I really did do that.

On my 3rd day, the doctor told me I could go home the next day, as long as I promised both the therapist and psychiatrist one thing: I was not allowed to go back home. To your home. I had to assure them I'd stay away from the house and go back to Daniela's. I was still too "mentally fragile," they said, and going home could put me right back where I was.

The next day I checked out, and Lily picked me up. Like I said I would, I went straight to Daniela's. Since the day the paramedics wheeled me away, I've only seen the outside of what used to be our home.

It's surreal and depressing. Because of the way I left, because of the brokenness I left behind me, all the memories I have are laced with guilt, and I find myself unable to reminiscence, focusing on the good times we had in that house. There's a part of me that feels I lost that privilege. Maybe the pain that accompanies my memories are a kind of penance but temporary, like purgatory, and these memories will eventually become bittersweet instead of just bitter.

But I think about the good times regardless of the pain that accompanies the memories. The hours, and I mean *hours* we spent playing the Wii. The wrestling matches when you guys were little. You as a toddler crawling after Andrew trying to bite him. Demolishing the kitchen in preparation for a remodel. The living room and bathroom addition. Me hiding the fart machine under your bed and then operating it with the remote control I had in my bedroom.

The sex talk I gave you and Andrew that you were probably *way* too young for. When I finished, you guys just looked at me, cracking up at the whole idea of it.

Putting those plastic capsules into warm water and watching them turn into dinosaurs and police cars.

Taking that wooden back scratcher and giving you guys a "scratchy-scratch" while we watched TV.

Knocking on our adjoining wall to say "goodnight." You guys knocking back. Man, that kills me.

And I am truly saddened that I'll never see that faded, greasy "T" that stared at me every night from the brick on the bedroom fireplace, a "T" that a past owner had created before you had even been born. A "T" that will always stand for "Travis" in my mind.

Go in and look at that fireplace; the "T" is smeared into one of the bricks on the right-hand side.

Love, Dad

Dear Travis,

Within a couple months, after the events of the hospital, you were no longer speaking to me. Your visits to my classroom were becoming less regular. We only went out to eat once. On my birthday, you, me and your brothers all went to lunch, and it would be the last time we'd all be together. So glad I took a picture.

By July 2nd, I stopped hearing from you. My texts and phone calls were blocked, and when I'd see you during summer school, you wouldn't look my way.

I'd like to claim ignorance and say I didn't know what happened between us, but when I try to look at all of this through your perspective, putting together the pending divorce, the affair, and the attempted suicide, I can claim with all truthfulness that I "get it." I understand your position and can even side with you a little. After all, in the past, I've been known to cut my father off for a lot less.

The week of July 2nd also saw the end of my relationship with David. Now looking back with some measure of neutrality, I can appreciate that it wasn't a healthy relationship from the beginning, and while David understood he was dating a man who was grieving over the loss of his boys *as* he was coming to terms with his sexuality *and* drinking too much *and* having a sincere crisis of faith, it still wasn't fair to ask him to wallow through the wreckage that was my life; emotionally a disaster or not, I was still a grown man and knew better than to start a new relationship under these circumstances. In fact, we had only been dating less than two months when I was put into the mental hospital, and yet when I got out, he was still there for me.

When we finally broke it off in July, I'm sure his friends and family congratulated him on dodging that particular bullet. I would have.

In the meantime, I was still seeing Christopher on a regular basis, each weekend and on Tuesday nights. Ironically enough, I was spending more time with him while living outside the home than I had when I had lived there. Although in the past we had never gone to Disneyland together, I had become a "Disneyland dad," or better yet, "Knott's Berry Farm dad," and we were out-and-about constantly.

That whole first year, he and I spent our time together talking through a thousand things, and most of it wasn't about the divorce or his feelings, although that had to be addressed from time to time. It was about time I got to know my son, and my only regret was that it was happening while his mom and dad were getting divorced.

Besides bi-monthly trip to Knotts, I introduced him to the classic films of the 80s. We hit Hollywood and Los Angeles several times. We bowled and went miniature golfing. I took him to that abandoned, "haunted" asylum, those same boarded up buildings we used to bike to when you and Andrew were little. We visited his grandparents and cousins quite a bit.

I also bought him tons of presents that spoke volumes to my love for him and for the shame I felt at having hurt him; in fact, after it got back to me that the third or fourth large purchase were declared "guilt presents," I told him, "Of course they're guilt presents. I feel guilty."

I suppose I can't attest to what was going on in Christopher's head to any degree of certainty, but I thought he was dealing with the divorce as best as any kid could considering the unique circumstances of our particular family dynamics. There was no doubt in my mind he'd have to have some talk therapy at some point in his future, but I didn't sense he was unduly suffering. I know he had friends whose parents were divorced, but I'm sure he was the only kid whose parents had divorced because his dad was gay, and I get that these "special circumstances" brought on an extra burden that no 12-year-old should have to carry. However, he was always talkative and had even started to adopt that funny, quirky sarcasm that I had worked so hard to model.

We had just finished an evening at this "upside down" museum in Hollywood one Friday night when Christopher accidentally let it slip that you had been robbed at knife point some months earlier. Since he had been sworn to secrecy, I got very little information out of him other than some guy pulled a knife on you outside a pizza place and took your backpack and phone. An old buddy whose mom was working with your mom had more details for me, and he told me the guy was caught, and your mom or grandma was going to take you to court to testify against him.

A dropping-away sensation in my insides made its way up from the bottom of my stomach, twisting my gut right there on Hollywood Blvd where we stood somewhere between Janis Joplin and Charles Chaplin's star on the Hollywood Walk of Fame. But the panic was only partly due to having a knife pulled on my kid; even more sharp was this biological instinct to help my son even though much time had passed since the incident, and he was no longer in immediate danger. No, for me this was all happening as Christopher was telling it, and all I could think to do was grab you and stand between you and this guy, creating some distance between you and a weapon.

There aren't enough adjectives to describe the helplessness. Have a kid, picture the scene, and no words will be necessary.

I'm looking forward to the day we can sit at Chic-Fil-A or Chipotle, and you can share the events of that day and its aftermath with me.

Yes, I know I'm not supposed to eat at Chic-Fil-A, but I continue to do so. I'm a bad gay.

Love, Dad

Dear Travis,

Unless you're the Unabomber, an all-in-one shampoo, conditioner, and body wash shouldn't be in your shopping cart. Spend the extra money and buy them separate. And while I'm sure you know this already, Axe Body Spray and all Axe products should have been retired when you graduated 8th grade.

Also: choosing a bar of soap shouldn't be a matter of looking for the cheapest brand—I don't care how much it costs, you have to use an anti-bacteria bar of soap for your armpits. Dove moisturizing cream was made for your mother.

Love, Dad

Dear Travis,

Running around making new friends, dating, and beginning the life-long process of getting comfortable with who and what God had made me wasn't how I was spending the entirety of my time. The social portion of my life may have gotten the most "publicity" in the various circles your mom and I had been a part of, but the majority of my time, besides fighting to extremes to still be an important part of my children's lives, was spent throwing myself back into work.

I had not been the greatest teacher during the previous two years. I had collected a myriad of absences and when I *did* show up to work, I was phoning everything in. Many days I was nothing more than a paid somnambulist, sleep walking through lectures, meetings, student interactions. In that first terrible year, I was having occasional breakdowns, but I always first made it into the private men's bathroom adjacent to my room.

A couple months after your mom and I had split, I found myself, once again, crying in the bathroom, but I found I couldn't pull myself together like I usually would. I had to call Lily's classroom, and she left her students to come talk me down—in the middle of the men's restroom. We sat on the bathroom floor for about half an hour while I just blubbered.

Side note: contrary to what you may have heard, neither Lily nor Frank nor *any* of my friends and family were responsible for the choices I made, either before the separation or after. The only collective goal they all shared was to lend support, and whether or not they agreed with the decisions I was making is a moot point. No one told me to go out and "be gay" any more than they would have told me to go home and be with my family. Those who stood by me strictly wanted to see me at peace. They wanted me alive.

One night, I went into a CVS. While I was standing there waiting, the guy in front of me at the register was buying some snacks and a bottle of gin. There was an exchange between him and the checker—a male employee that had to use a cane to get around, and I began to pick up bits of the conversation between the two that implied the guy didn't have enough money to buy all his items. So instead of putting some things back on the shelves, the guy simply took the food and alcohol and walked out.

The CVS employee started yelling something to the man about stealing, and right away I started following the guy out. I don't why I did it; it was just an impulse.

I caught up to the guy outside and used my charms and ability to reason, trying to encourage him to go back in and pay for the items he *could* afford. Charm and reason wouldn't work in this case, however—the guy was high as a kite. He took the $5 I offered him, smiled back at me, and then just floated away into the parking lot.

Back inside, I paid the man's tab, ignoring the protests from the CVS employee. Then I walked back to a different register to pay for *my* stuff.

The female CVS employee was almost finished ringing me up when she said, "Can I have your CVS membership number, and that was a very nice thing you did. You're a good person."

I pulled out my credit card and slipped it into the card reader. I didn't even realize I had started crying until I saw her face that I caught staring at *my* face.

We both froze up while my credit card payment was processing. She didn't know what to say, and I certainly didn't know what to say; here I was, a 6'4" aging man crying at a drugstore counter while purchasing rice cakes and a box of Frosted Mini Wheats. Before I broke down completely, I just took my 12-foot receipt from her hands and said, "Trust me. I'm not a good person." Then I left.

I had been crying off and for so long that it was becoming habit, like biting one's nails or alphabetizing groceries in a pantry. A lot of things set me off in those days, but nothing upset me more than someone telling me I was a good person when they had no idea what I had done to my family.

Good person indeed.

Ugg, enough talk about crying…jeesh! Back to teaching.

I was determined to step up my game in the classroom once again. Or at least aim to be a teacher who threw out some free extra points once in a while and smiled and joked around with his students. Two years prior, the Masons had awarded me with their Teacher of the Year plaque, but now I was spending my teaching days showing instructional YouTube videos while laying my head on my desk.

The worst was when I had to teach *The Great Gatsby* in my English 11 class with your brother sitting five feet in front of me. There I stood, talking about the classless, scummy, wife abusing, cheater that was Tom Buchanan while my son quietly took notes in his notebook, lecture delivered by his junior English teacher/father who was going out to dinner on the weekends with men…while still married to his mother.

To his great credit, he never *once* confronted me with personal, family issues; instead, he stayed in student mode from February to May, leaving our battles to be conducted outside of school hours.

By the end of that spring semester, a good many students knew I was getting divorced and many of them had figured out why. Tight-lipped from the beginning, I still wasn't surprised when the rumors began to spread, and the gossip flowed not only through the student body but the faculty as well. Both kids and teachers were asking me questions, and the previously vague answers I had been giving for months were no longer cutting it.

In the past, your mom and I were sometimes "victims" of various rumors, some true, some half-true, but I was known to take a different approach to the gossip, bypassing the usual outraged indignation and shrugging it off, while, of course, not relying on the pat response, "it is what it is." I would handle it this way not because I had some kind of thick skin—which you know I don't—but because I have the ability to recognize that Mom and I have spent a good period of our lives gossiping about other people (in the evangelical world this is often called "prayer requests"); that makes it so we are ineligible to complain when people do the same thing to us.

So, unless you're a human anomaly and you've never once in your life said a negative thing about another person to *another* person, don't get all hot and bothered when people gossip about you and it returns to you…especially if what they're saying is true. Like I said before, "Own it." Sometimes when people come up to me and inform me that they've "heard some whispers," I generally step up right away and say, "Well, whatever it is, it's probably true."

Get in front of stuff.

And cut out all self-righteous moral superiority when people gossip about you; you've been a victimizer as often as you've been a victim.

So, for me, when I could no longer avoid the staff rumors at work, I addressed them.

However, during that spring semester, I never said *anything* to the students. I don't know how they found out, but I would *never* have said a word about our family situation to my students. Your peers. Your friends. The rumor and verification mill were just running overtime.

So how else did I spend my time when I wasn't working, going out on weekends when I wasn't with Christopher, or re-watching *Cheers* and *Arrested Development* on a loop, the familiar one-liners and laugh tracks numbing my mind, in partnership with Skyy vodka?

Well, I plotted. A lot. In between TV shows, grading papers, and rehearsals for my latest play, my mind would free up the blockage I had put in place to guard my rapidly deteriorating psyche from any further pain, and I would summon up the most outrageous plans and schemes to get you back.

In my top ten favorite books of all time, ranking at #6, sits Stephen King's *Pet Sematary*. Besides making my top ten list where it has stayed for over thirty years, *Sematary* remains to this day as the most distressing, traumatic book I've ever read.

Not sure if it was a King movie I let you guys sit through, but *Pet Sematary* tells the story of Louis Creed and his family who move to the fictional town of Ludlow, Maine when Louis takes a job as a university physician. Behind their house lies this cute little pet cemetery. Behind that lies another cemetery, one that isn't so cute.

The essentials: the Creed cat dies. Louis buries it. Cat comes back as a cat/demon. Their three-year-old son dies. Louis buries him in a normal cemetery.

But overwhelmed with grief with grief, Louis digs him up and reburies him in the *bad* cemetery.

Whether or not you've seen the movie or not, you can figure out where this goes. Kid comes alive—10x times the demon the cat was—kills the neighbor, and then kills his mother. Louis, grief-stricken, realizes the mistake he has made, and kills the son that-isn't-really-his-son.

Of course, he's completely out of his mind now, so he buries his dead wife in the cemetery with the bad track record.

She comes to "life" and kills him. End of book.

Super disturbing. I've read it three times.

I didn't understand Louis Creed when I finished the book for the first time in 9th grade. I didn't get closer to understanding him the 2nd or 3rd time either. The 1990s film version didn't help either.

But when I saw the newest film version, which was awful by the way, don't bother, it resonated with me unlike the story had in the past. Cradling his recently buried dead son in his arms as he plots to bring his kid back to life, even though he knew the kid would probably be this satanic shell of himself, Louis makes sense.

How had he not before?

Well, he never made sense before because I never had a *kid* before, and I, now, understand the lengths I would go to have my son back.

No need for me to rehash my past letters where I've listed all the crazy stunts I undertook to reunite us. But those were the things I *tried*. Those are the things I *told* you about. You have no idea what "thinking out of the box" looks like in my head.

To me, Louis Creed is an amateurish chump, and all I can say at this moment, hopefully on the tail end of our estrangement, is that tackling grief by bringing a kid back from the dead is, literally, child's play.

I can do so much more.

Travis, you can metaphorically kill me and bury me, but for me, dead and buried isn't the end. It's an obstacle, and you and I have been fighting different obstacles our whole lives.

And you and I are good at overcoming them.

Love, Dad

Dear Travis,

One thing I can't really spend too much time on are the specific details regarding my divorce from your mom, which would also be a waste of time since I know you've already been a first-hand witness to several unfortunate events and behaviors that began from the day I moved out.

Here's what I can do. I can give you some solid advice: avoid divorce at all costs. It's single-handedly the second hardest thing I've done in my life, and I can guarantee you I will never put myself and my loved ones through it again.

If you can, fight through the urge to end a marriage. You don't want to end up like me, a 7pm drunk, balancing off a Lazy Dog barstool after a brutal preliminary hearing. Unashamedly and publicly sobbing, I sat there while another ex-student perched close by, buying me drinks and telling me how I was the teacher who had given him the most detentions in an otherwise stellar educational career.

Leaving that Lazy Dog and laying down on the grass in front of the space center, propping myself up against what I think was a model of the moon, or Mars, I called your uncle, ranting and cursing, inwardly begging him to take away the persistent hurt, hurt that I had partially brought on myself.

After one rigorous week of drinking, I woke up one morning and couldn't stop hiccupping. I hiccupped on and off for twenty-four hours before I finally went into the emergency room. I thought I was having some sort of breathing ailment related to stress. The doctor came in and one of the first questions he asked me was about alcohol intake, a connection I still hadn't made. I really thought the divorce was making me hiccup. When I told him that I'd pretty much had four to five drinks a night for, you know, four or five nights in a row, he left. While a nurse hooked me up to an IV bag to hydrate and flush out the toxins in my system, the doctor returned.

He gave me a pamphlet for AA and left the room without saying anything.

Divorce stinks, Travis. I can't emphasize that enough. So, if you're going to get married, do everything in your power to keep it together. You, Son, are extremely stubborn. When it comes to your marriage, use that to your advantage.

I'm sitting here concluding this letter, sitting on my too tiny chair in my classroom, the school day having been over for several hours. A while ago, I leaned back too far in this chair on the third day of school, and I fell backward to the ground. Right in front of my third period class.

Anyway, my second story room overlooks the parking lot and the construction ed tech class where you spent almost all of your high school elective credits laying brick and building framework that would be torn down at the end of each school year. Five minutes ago, I watched two brazen racoons skitter across the roof that holds up the chain-link fence cordoning off the backyard wing of the building; I think they hang out in that area to eat the Koi out of the pond from the teacher's lounge patio.

Even though this is Southern California and not Montana, have at it, racoons. I've heard Koi is the filet mignon of the fish world.

Love, Dad

Dear Travis,

Years and Years was an HBO show that I came across at a time when *Modern Family* and even repeated viewings of *Roseanne* was getting old. It was May of 2019, and I saw an ad for a British limited series and noticed my favorite actor, Russell Tovey, was in it.

Tovey's an excellent, underrated actor, but that aside, I tend to be a fan of actors and actresses who aren't "big" yet. For some reason, once they hit 1 million Instagram followers, I lose interest in their career, and I move on to someone else. It's almost as if I feel they need my support when their career is getting off the ground, but once they've "made it," my services are no longer necessary.

Man, that was one bizarre series. It's the first show I've seen that switches gears at the end of the first episode, almost, mid-story, completely changing genres. It would be like having Ferris Bueller start hacking off his friends' body parts the moment they arrive in Chicago.

You can IMDB the details if you're interested, but, I guess I have to warn you, there are spoilers ahead. Tovey played a guy named Daniel Lyons, a happily married gay man who falls in love with a Ukrainian refugee before this refugee is deported by an "evil Trump-like," right-wing prime minister.

Lyons is actually kind of a scum. On the brink of World War III, he literally runs out on his husband to carry out his affair with the Ukrainian, but since he drowns in a later episode, it's fine—punishment is doled out, the lesson is proclaimed, clearly, and all morality is set aright.

Putting aside the affair for a moment, the viewer becomes a witness to the price Lyons pays for falling in love with a refugee whose whole reason for his deportation in the first place lies in the fact that he is gay. For three episodes, Lyons gives up every bit of his life, cashes out, sells everything, all in an attempt to smuggle his partner back into Britain…only to drown sometime later in episode 4.

Tovey's storyline ended there but there were two episodes left. Odd episodes too. However, after they killed him off, and the focus shifted to the newly single Viktor, the Ukrainian, my interest faded a little.

I began watching that show with very little judgment aimed at Tovey's character because after all, I can no longer judge anyone for anything anyone ever does ever again. You lose that moral sense of superiority when you spend your years preaching for a return to biblical values and scruples and then leave your wife and kids to marry a man.

But once a man's highly-regarded moral standards are ripped off his body, a body clothed in pretense, he can sit with a little more humility as he, for example, watches Walter White destroy the lives of people that "Heisenberg" determines are far eviler than he'll ever be. And if it's "just a TV show" that same naked man can watch a character leave his husband for another man, fully aware he needs to shut his mouth and say very little.

And I'll say this for having lower standards of morality—it makes going to the movies a lot less battle of the mind: now I can silently root for the shark in *Jaws* over the human victims with a little less guilt.

Lyon's affair with Viktor was the most emotional story I had come across since Adam Sandler and Drew Barrymore's relationship in *50 First Dates*. I don't know, maybe I was just at a weak moment in my life, emotions easily manipulated as I stood at a crossroads of my life, still *slightly* weighing whether I should slip back into that outfit of judgment and high-standing morality that had never seemed to fit quite right and return to your mom and the God who would start speaking to me once again.

Fictionalized story or not, I still wanted to experience the kind of love that existed between Lyon and Viktor. Between Westley and Buttercup. Homer and Marge. Between that old couple who drowned together on the *Titanic*. The kind where a life is sacrificed without hesitation just as long as there was love, and even if it was for a short period of time.

And I didn't just want this for *me*, Travis, I wanted this for your mom too. I swear, this is not a weak attempt to appear magnanimous, for I had truly *loved* your mom, and throughout our marriage I was aware that she had been ignored for far too long. It was her turn to have someone love her with a ferocity that I was unable to provide from the beginning. I wanted that for *her*. I want that for you someday. For your brothers. And I wanted that for myself.

So in a way, yeah, a TV show might have been the final factor in my decision to accept that my marriage was over, and this time for good. I'm also very aware that leaning on the entertainment industry to make such an important decision might seem trite, but historically, art has always been a powerful force, and all it did in my case was act as a good therapist should, beaming some light on a spot in my soul that I had forced into the dark a long time ago.

A few days after I watched episode 4, I knew I wouldn't be going back to your mom. I would no longer experiment on her heart and mine, not when there was a possibility that both she and I had the potential for experiencing real love.

However, my passion for fatherhood hadn't waned; if anything, your silence made me appreciate what I had left behind, and I would no longer take for granted the role I have been given as your dad. Separation or not, I would fight hard for you, harder than I had been, like Louis Creed, and while you may have been winning the battles thus far, I know I will eventually win the war.

But first I had another fight I needed to turn my attention to. Real quick.

Love, Dad

Dear Travis,

Over the years and mostly through experimentation and trial-and-error, I've picked up a few things about working out and overall health. I may not have gathered enough information to write a book on the subject—there are too many of them as it is—but it was always a goal of mine to pass on to my sons what I know about eating right and general fitness.

Here are just a few basic strategies and concepts to get you started; I've heard rumors that you've been thinking about buying a gym membership. Someday, when all of this is behind us, I look forward to working out with you, training you, and walking you through a more complete, thorough diet and exercise plan.

1. My favorite rule: don't bother with abdominal work until you've gotten your diet under control. Core work is great, but exercises that targets the abs can wait until your body fat percentage comes down. Once your bf% comes down, you can exercise your abs, unlike other major body parts, every single day; there is very little chance of over-training them.

2. When you begin training with weights, concentrate more on perfecting the correct form for all exercises. Once you've done that, you can focus on adding more weight to your regime.

3. Do a leg exercise every single time you have an upper body day. And you should *still* have a leg day of its own.

4. Pre-workout is a waste of $50; you can receive the same effect if you buy caffeine pills on Amazon. They are about $10. Most supplements are unnecessary unless you plan on competing.

5. You should be eating one gram of protein per pound of body weight.

6. Don't avoid carbs. Ever. If you want to slim down, avoid *sugary* carbs. That includes fruit. An unpopular opinion, but a diet doesn't need fruit as long as you are eating plenty of green vegetables every single day.

7. If eating properly, you will never need another liquid in your life other than water. I talked to you earlier about the scam that is fruit juice.

8. Avoid creatine. By using water, creatine pumps you up temporarily, but as soon as you stop taking it, the water in your body disappears and you usually look the same as you did before you started taking it. It's also hard on the kidneys.

9. A high protein, low carb, low fat, low calorie diet, combined with weights and cardio, will get you cut up faster than if you just rely on the old "calories in, calories out" mantra.

10. If you're at the gym and someone is waiting to use the bench/machine that you're currently using, ask them if they want to work in with you. I don't care if it slows you down, it is courteous and kind. Do it every time. Who knows, you might meet your future wife in the gym.

I have many more tips. Call me.

Love, Dad

Dear Travis,

By September of 2019, I started seeing a change in Christopher. At first, I chalked it up to him just being a pre-teen; he was bound to be quiet and dark. A little moody. I had bought him a phone for his birthday, a "guilt gift" that would pay off for me since I'd be able to talk to him during the days he wasn't with me. Naturally, any kid with a new phone is going to spend a lot of time playing around on it and not talking to Dad, but as August past he was texting and playing games more often than he had been, suddenly disinterested in riding bikes or playing the classic Mario games with me on the Wii.

We were also running out of the good 80s movies and while we had moved on to the 90s, I could tell by his body language that his heart and energies were someplace else; my house—where he had his own room for the first time—may have had his dad, a dad who was *always* present, but his home was where his mom and brothers lived. He was becoming more and more distant with each visit.

There were some serious discussions with Christopher about whether he wanted to spend more time or less time with me, and when he'd express a desire to cut down our weekly time together—which equated to about 20% of his week—my hurt feelings often took control over my mouth, prompting me to lecture him several times. He was shooting for less time and here I was trying to push for 50%!

He would often start crying as soon as I would pick him up. Then I'd feel guilty and turn right back around and take him to his mom's.

There was that one time he was supposed to come with me, which I know you remember, but he didn't come out of the house. So, I called the police, filing a complaint that I was being kept from my son. I let them know that I had legal, partial custody at the time, but when the police came out of the house to let me know that—custody or not—if a kid didn't want to go with the other parent during his or her custodial time, they wouldn't drag him out, kicking and screaming. With about zero sympathy, they then proceeded to warn me that even with a legal custodial agreement, if I went into the house, creating a scene trying to get my kid, they would arrest me.

By mid-October, Christopher told me he didn't want to see me anymore, period, and then he stopped taking my calls and texts. I'd still show up every Friday to pick him up from school, but he stayed in Mom's classroom until I would give up and leave. I did that for two months before I stopped showing up altogether.

Months later I did file a second complaint with the police, and I know they went to go and talk to Christopher at school, but they never called me back nor followed up in any way. I was getting the impression that there was nothing I could do.

Divorce is ugly. Like Danny DeVito says in my seventh favorite movie of all time *The War of the Roses*, "In divorce, there is no winning. There are only degrees of losing."

Looking back, do I regret making those drastic, overly-dramatic decisions to get my kid back? I don't know, depends on what I'm feeling on any given day. Sometimes I'm proud of myself for showing Christopher how hard I was fighting to see him. To visually show him that his dad would never give up on him.

On other days, I'm ashamed that I put him through all of that. A kid who was already struggling with the breakup of his family did not need his dad bringing him more trauma-inducing chaos.

But if I didn't fight for *his* rights to see his father, wouldn't that make me one of those loser, deadbeat dads?

Only time and therapy will tell.

Love, Dad

Dear Travis,

I will always wrestle with my relationship with God in some fashion, periods of peace followed by periods of questioning and doubting, and this is something that I've not only accepted, but with the advantage of time and reflection, I can see the value of the struggle. Maybe it's the way I avoid complacency in my walk with Christ; it forces me to work at it much harder than I normally would, and, for me, when things get too easy, I tend to drift. I get bored.

It's almost as if I *need* the drama that comes with my faith, and since God Himself made me a certain way, He utilizes the passionate back-and-forth of my faithfulness in order to further His advantage and highlight His glory.

Between the thousands of hours I have clocked, engaged in internal debate over the decisions I've made since February of 2019, I have doubled those hours engaging in silent arguments with God. I have more questions at this point in my life than I have in any other previous incarnations of "Greg." I have always been told that the Bible has all the answers I would ever need, and I, too, had parroted that popular slice of "Christianese" for years, but I'm sorry, that's a pat response by people who are unwilling to admit that the Bible *doesn't* cover all the life questions we are going to have from birth to death.

Travis, all I wanted to do was follow God, be a father, and find love. Why is this such a drastically disgusting, immoral, diseased, depraved, and wicked desire in the eyes of evangelicals around the world? The evangelical response to me wanting to follow God but accept my homosexuality, demonstrating it in a monogamous, committed marriage, is that it's *impossible* for me to have both. Essentially, it's the Christian version of "you can't have your cake and eat it too."

Well, what the frick is a cake good for if you can't even eat it?

Might be a lame example, but to me, enjoying God and delighting in the way He made me but at the same time rejecting *who* He made me to be is like swallowing a raspberry whole just so I won't get the seeds in my teeth. The evangelical Christian says, "Do that. Those are bad seeds. Swallow that raspberry. Or better yet just eat a blueberry."

But what if God created me with an aversion to blueberries?

A week before we left for our yearly trip to Europe, two parents of one of my student travelers, an evangelical Christian couple who I had known and had socialized with on one or two occasions, pulled their son out of the trip claiming he had to "study for the upcoming AP exam."

A week before that they had found out through the "prayer request" circles that I was gay.

Of course, I didn't fight it, but I did find it interesting that as a perceived "straight man," no parent of any *female student* had previously shown any concern that I would be taking their teenage daughter on a field trip across the world.

Now that I was gay? Hide your boys, evangelicals! They're out to get you!

Think I'm exaggerating? I remember years ago there was an east coast lesbian couple who had split up after one of them had become a Christian and had decided the relationship was an offense to God. During their relationship, the couple had a child together and once they split, the newly "ex-lesbian" Christian gal decided it was better for her to excise the other parent out of her daughter's life because the mother was a lesbian.

As a church, we prayed that the ex-lesbian would win. We prayed that the child would lose the right to see her mother because her mother was gay.

These religious questions and thoughts were just some of the theological conundrums I had running through my mind on a nightly basis, interrupting my *Galavant* flow, sucking the joy out of the vodka/anything buzz I would start chasing about 4pm each day while sitting on my oversized bed in my tiny room at Daniela's house.

When I wasn't thinking about you guys, I was thinking about God. About religion itself. About trying to be straight. About accepting who I was.

I thought about Mom. About my parents. About the friends I had lost.

Many of those people and situations I could do absolutely nothing about. Their responses to my situation were out of my hands, and for once, I wasn't able to manipulate the problems in my immediate vicinity. I just had to let them go.

But I could still pray, and I could still talk to God, and I could still read my Bible. *Those things* were under my control. And that's what I did—I just picked up with Him where I had left off. In some ways, I spent more authentic time with God than I had in the past, and I believe it's because there was no expectation of a "quid-pro-quo" anymore. No more "I will pray and be obedient if You just make me straight." My prayers were simply, "I want to follow You, and even if my homosexuality keeps me from knowing You, I'm going to do it anyway because that's what I want. I want to be Your child."

The fact that I decided to behave as if God still loved me was a source of chagrin for some folks in my old evangelical circle. I know this not because of anything that was said to me directly but because I know the thinking. I know the theology. I know their silence was communicating their disapproval.

Not all of my past evangelical and church friends disappeared; a few stuck around, trying to keep up some form of a relationship, but there was always a hidden caveat in their outreaches. From what I could tell, lunch requests and phone call made to "check in" were always tainted with objectives to "bring the prodigal home." At least, that's what I assumed. I suppose I could be wrong, since, to be fair, I hardly ever responded, but I don't think any of my friends were simply interested in meeting up just because they missed me. No, they had a mission to restore me to God, and once I had gotten to the point where I was secure in my salvation as it stood, there was no need for me to reestablish relationships with people who only had an interest in seeing me "return" to the faith.

The friends I lost would argue with all of this claiming *I* was the one who cut them out of their lives, not the other way around. I would say, yeah, I *did* cut them out but only because I only desired to have people in my life who loved the entirety of me. I wasn't interested in having relationships with people who considered our friendship a "mission field."

I also lost a pretty big endorsement when I came out. My book, *The Field Trip*, was published by the same publishing house that Ray Comfort used for his books and scripts so having Ray's endorsement on the front cover of my book was a *huge* plus. "One of the most original and entertaining Christian novel in years!" he had authorized in bold, yellow font right above the title, on both the print and the e-book copy. However, once it came out that I was a gay man, the print copy had to be "pulled" from the Christian market, although the e-book, for reasons I didn't pursue, was allowed to remain on Amazon.

As of this writing, you can find the book on Amazon if you type "Greg Elsasser the Field Trip" into the search box, and while the title, my name, and that horrible book cover still appear as they did the day the book was published, Ray's endorsement has disappeared. It was taken off for obvious reasons, but the book is an evangelical, solidly Christian novel that has nothing to do with homosexuality. In the end, I suppose Ray and his ministry couldn't be associated with a known homosexual, so his name and his endorsement were removed.

When your mom and I first separated, I did not return to the church I had called my home for almost thirty years, Fair Oaks First Christian, nor did I expect or demand they allow me to come back if I was still a "practicing homosexual." I knew and respected their stance on the issue, and I say this next part without any bitterness—I truly didn't want to go to a church where I wasn't wanted. I knew I would eventually land at a church where I would be welcomed and felt comfortable.

But this *next* part is where the bitterness comes in. A full-on sour, angry, resenting bitterness that I *know* I will hang onto for years to come.

When one of the pastor's daughters showed up to the various divorce hearings as a show of solidarity with Mom, I totally understood. Actually, at first, I was thankful for this woman's appearances because I knew your mom was in her own version of hell and needed the love of her friends; she also needed the support of her church. This woman filled both needs.

But a little over a year later, I decided to reach out to the church myself.

The concern I had at the time was that the church wasn't making an effort to reach out and offer help to you and your brothers. Without going into too much detail on paper, I had heard from various people how you especially were struggling with all of the changes within our family, and it is the church's duty to step up and offer, at the very least, some counseling. I knew Mom was getting help, but you went to Fair Oaks too, and you deserved their assistance.

Over a period of a few days, I emailed and/or called three pastors from the church. One called me back, and when he did, he let me know he was no longer with Fair Oaks First Christian, but he did assure me he would reach out to the pastors personally and then they'd be in touch.

Nothing. No responses. I never heard anything back from any of them. I was "anathema." I had been *that* cut-off.

Super angry at this major slight, my initial thought was, of course, for myself. The pastors had no idea why I was calling, I had just requested a return call. What if I accepted my "prodigal" status and was seeking forgiveness, wanting restoration?

I can only suppose these things didn't matter to them, but I guess it isn't fair for me to judge their silence because I don't know their rationale for ignoring my calls.

But for me, that was strike one.

Strike two came sometime later, and while I don't always have my dates correct, it was about a month, maybe two, after the last message I left at the church when one of the pastor's wives called me up. Now this is rather interesting when you think about it, for not *one* pastor did what his pastoral position required him to do; not one of them took five minutes to come "running after his lost sheep."

But a pastor's wife did. A pastor's wife stood up and took it upon herself to fulfill her husband's responsibility, even though she is biblically denied any official pastoral role. Instead of deferring to a male pastor in the duty of "shepherding a wayward believer," she should have been "attending to the children and other women." That is, if I am reading the Bible correctly.

But I digress. Claire called me up one early evening to discuss my situation and new "life choice" I had made for myself and to also speak on another issue that had been brought to her attention.

Let me fast track the "other situation" for you.

There was a female friend of mine, Miranda, who had grown up at Fair Oaks but had left years ago; we had been on a few church missions together when I was in my twenties, she in her late teens.

Over thirty years ago, a relative of Miranda and a church volunteer/leader with Fair Oaks had molested Miranda while she was a pre-teen. The abuse continued over a period of years. When the molestation was exposed, the church elders confronted this man, Chuck, about the abuse, but all he would admit to was that he'd had an "inappropriate relationship" with Miranda. The girl, a teenager by then, was then brought in front of Chuck and the elders where, standing there exposed and scared out of her mind, she balked and recanted the severity of the accusations.

In the end, no legal charges were brought, Chuck was forgiven by the church and restored to ministry, and the girl went on with her life.

As is so common with other victims of abuse, time and adulthood prompted Miranda to re-open the issue and all the old wounds that accompanied them. She would still see Chuck from time-to-time, and she now had the maturity and life experience to realize that an abuser often does not stop at one victim.

She started by contacting the police who contacted the DA. In the end, the DA declined to press charges—too much time had passed. Memories were getting "foggy." But *my* part of the story doesn't end here.

Right after the DA closed the case, Miranda reached out to me after she had read a Facebook rant I had posted on my wall—a regrettable rant about my divorce that did *not* showcase the better parts of my character. I have always heavily criticized people who post personal family issues on social media, and that day I became the very person for whom I had reserved so much self-righteous judgment. I really do feel a little warm flush of my cheeks when I think about that post.

Oh, and one other post. That was a bad one during a bad moment as well.

After catching up with Miranda, she told me the whole history between her and Chuck. She was completely broken that the DA has declined to pursue the case, but now she was turning her anger on Fair Oaks First Christian. She had spoken previously to Claire but felt like her concerns of the past were pushed aside.

Accepting the legal defeat, Miranda wanted to know how Chuck, her abuser, had gotten away with legal prosecution but could still actively be a part of a church where he held a couple different leadership positions.

We talked for a bit, and a few days later Claire got a hold of me. I was, and am, 100% grateful that she reached out and then spoke to me without an ounce of condemnation or disappointment. By then, your mom and I were smack in the middle of an ugly, *ugly* public divorce and custody battle of which the details the church was very familiar with, but not once did I feel like she was taking sides nor preparing to "throw any stones." She was gracious and cordial even when we had to go through the whole tired, "we love you (the sinner) but hate your homosexuality (the sin)" platform, but when we got through that, the conversation switched to Miranda.

Claire was clear that she and the church wanted to do everything they could to rally behind Miranda, but she had little to offer in terms of actual *action*. I remember she mentioned counseling, but I honestly don't think they had any other suggestions to give this girl, now a full-grown woman, any *concrete* plans of action to rectify what had been done to her.

Counseling?

That's when I and Claire got into it. In script form, this is *basically* how the discussion went and will act as a summary in lieu of an actual word-for-word conversation.

GREG. Claire, why is this guy still in a leadership position at Fair Oaks? Thirty years ago you had, at the very least, legitimate accusations in front of you followed by a confession that he had done something inappropriate with a young girl. Why wasn't he removed?

CLAIRE. Because, Greg, as you know, just as well as I do, there is *no* sin a Christian can commit that he can't be forgiven for. Once there is a confession, full restoration to ministry and the church is not only appropriate but is what's specifically commanded in the Bible. We're all sinners, but it doesn't make a person ineligible to serve God within the body of Christ once there has been a confession of sin.

GREG. Wait a minute…wait a minute. You and I just spoke about homosexuality and the church's "black-and-white" stance on the issue. Are you telling me that if my husband and I came to Fair Oaks First Christian to worship God, as a couple, maybe even as my husband, maybe holding hands, someone in leadership would ask us to leave, *but* a known child molester could serve in that same church for *thirty years* without question?

CLAIRE. Because he confessed his sin. It was forgiven. *You* are embracing a lifestyle of sin without repentance, and the biblical response is to not condone openly sinful lives. If the person isn't repentant, they cannot be a part of the body of Christ. Why are you acting like you don't know or understand this? You yourself once believed this same thing!

Ok, so this was a very good point, and both then and now I've had a hard time confronting my own hypocrisy. Did I now have a right to blanketly call certain behaviors "righteous" when just a day before I had called them a sin? Did I now have to recuse myself on issues of right and wrong, on subjects concerning ethics and morality, if I changed my mind on how God views homosexuality?

Let's detour once again and talk further about this issue of hypocrisy. It's always been somewhat of an irritant for me when people fall back on the "I don't go to church because it's full of hypocrites" argument, as if they can't see that if they *did* go to church they'd be sitting there shoulder-to-shoulder with just another fellow hypocrite.

The truth is, we *all*, in one way or another, tell people to live their lives in direct contrast to the way we live them. Smokers tell other smokers they shouldn't smoke. The sexually immoral person will always, albeit silently, condemn others they see as sexual deviants. Democrats will always accuse Republicans of violating the same ethical standards they espouse. Republicans will secretly engage in acts that the party on the other side of the aisle publicly preaches against. Parents will *always* preach to their children the importance of kindness and respect, patience and tolerance, two minutes before they start screaming and fighting with each other, in full view of those same kids.

My point is, every human being that has ever lived were and *are* horrendous hypocrites, but my feeling is that the whole "do what I say and not as I do" carries some validity. I mean, after all, if we all stopped teaching, correcting, or judging people altogether, the only viable option left for humans is to surrender to anarchy. Even our whole judicial system would be on shaky grounds, since every single judge and juror have all participated in a *stockade* of illegal activity. Jeesh, on my way to work this morning, a seven-minute drive, I probably broke five laws.

We judge others with the full knowledge that we, too, commit the same, if not similar, acts that we find so deplorable. But the *true* hypocrisy is how we feign outrage when those same acts are performed by others.

This kind of human behavior explains why we sit and watch a movie, eating our popcorn and Milk Duds, and barely flinch when the antagonist blows away hundreds of people. But when that same antagonist kills a dog, everybody in the movie theatre freaks out. Why the discrepancy? Because there's something going on in our subconscious that recognizes that while animals are completely innocent creatures, human beings are rotten at their deepest levels. When random humans get knocked off in films, we kind of just think—without *consciously* thinking it—"yeah, we deserve that."

So for me to begin screaming "hypocrisy" when churches label homosexuality as sin and remove those church members when their homosexuality is finally revealed—typically after long, trauma-induced inward battles—wouldn't necessarily be hypocritical of me. Yes, I once declared it a sinful human choice, and, yes, I voted for California's Prop 8, and, yes, I *did* join our church in prayer against that lesbian mother but I've since learned I was in serious error.

Simply that. We grow up and we go through a bunch of hardships and we change our minds. We're allowed to do that; we're allowed for as many shifts in perspective that come our way. In fact, there's almost a comfort in knowing that I may not think the same way tomorrow as I do today. It's humbling knowing I don't have all the answers, and I'm ok with accepting that those answers might be different next week. Next month. Ten years from now.

Don't forget: the church itself has had moments of reflection and have been allowed to change their minds. I think about the Reformation. About women's roles in church. About slavery.

The church is wrong for ostracizing homosexuals, denying them a place in their church. When it all comes down to it, and this is strictly my opinion, the church is a private entity and can keep the LGBTQ community out. That's their business, and I'll take my business elsewhere, thank you very much.

On the contrary, that doesn't mean the modern, non-accepting evangelical church isn't in error on this issue, and I can say, most assuredly, that the church has been misled in thinking that the LGBTQ person cannot walk with Christ. The Bible says trust and faith in Christ alone are the only requirements for salvation, and so I have chosen to shut everyone else's voice out and believe that.

But until the church comes around, they can act as they see fit; it's not as if there aren't other churches out there that haven't opened their doors to the LGBTQ community.

However.

HOWEVER: the church is *not* entitled to keep the gays at bay while letting a self-confessed child molester freely sit in her pews and serve communion to her people.

That is where the hypocrisy argument has major merit.

And that's why I stood with Miranda outside Fair Oaks First Christian one Sunday morning in protest. I wasn't there requesting LGBTQ reform, but I was *demanding* that Fair Oaks see the sheer ridiculousness of denying church entrance to homosexuals while ushering in the child molesters.

The night before, we were gracious enough to reach out to Claire, giving the church an opportunity to release Chuck from ministry positions before we showed up with our flyers and signs. We weren't even asking for him to be kicked out of the church, we just made it clear that Chuck should not be in ministry.

Claire, again speaking for the church, declined to remove him.

Unfrickenbelievable.

Within four hours of our protest the next morning, in January of 2020, Chuck was removed. Miranda was the quintessentially brave victim having spent those hours telling her story to church members who would walk out to the sidewalk and hear what she had to say.

She also had to stand there and listen to people scream at her, labeling her a liar, and many of those folks hurled "LIAR" at her before she was even able to share one part of her story with them. They just saw her carrying a sign, deeming her an anti-Christ and therefore untruthful.

Unfrickenbelievable.

While it goes without saying, my relationship with Fair Oaks had taken a huge hit after this second strike, but there was still a place in my heart that held on to hope that a major miracle might happen in the future. Even as a gay man, maybe the doors would open back up someday. Maybe I'd be the guy who would bring the LGBTQ and evangelical community together.

Then there was strike three.

As I stated previously, I was grateful to the pastor's daughter when she sat next to your mom through our divorce proceedings. I even watched her try to play both sides, often coming over to hug me to tell me she loved me and was praying for me. Trust me, it was appreciated.

It was too good to last, however. Once the financial disputes were laid aside in order to deal with the custody issue, the ugliness went to a whole new level. By then, you had made your choice not to have any contact with me and since you were of age, I didn't try and seek a custody ruling, forcing you to come see me on a weekly basis. No judge would have ordered that anyway.

That being said, I was fighting pretty hard for Christopher's rights to spend a good portion of his week with me; however, when it came to my understanding that—considering that I was a homosexual man—the preferred amount of custodial time was at 0 percent, I panicked. I whole-heartedly freaked out. The fight was to keep Christopher permanently away from me.

Similar to the situation in which I prayed against the East coast lesbian mother (maybe it's true what they say about karma), I began hearing whispers and rumblings about Fair Oaks First Christian prayer circles being formed with pleadings being offered to God that would keep my son from being exposed to such wickedness.

Soon after that, Christopher started pulling away.

And even with the full knowledge that it was the primary goal to completely separate me and your brother, your mom's friend, the pastor's daughter, kept coming to court. She saw herself as a confidant and support to your mom. I saw her as a representative of Fair Oaks First Christian.

In the end, I was granted about 20% custody of Christopher, which, ultimately, didn't really matter because by that time, he had cut off our relationship. Just like you had. And like you had done as well, he severed the relationship with my parents and his uncle and his cousins. The 20% judgment may have been final and legal, but at 12-years-old, the true decision lay with Christopher, and I guess those Fair Oaks First Christian prayers worked—my evilness was just too much for him.

With this latest stunt, combined with the handling of the Chuck/Miranda tragedy, I began to sympathize with those who point their finger at the church and the evangelical community at large, citing blatant hypocritical behaviors. No longer was I feeling that those excuses were always that—excuses! There are legitimate concerns non-Christian folks have with Christians, and I think it is time we stop waving these "excuses" away and *listen* to what is being claimed.

With that in mind, I started compiling a mental list, a list not unlike the one Santa composes each December. I examined the people in my Christian circle, past and present, who were blatantly living lives contrary to what the Bible commands. Many of these same people who adamantly state that my lifestyle will send me to hell would argue that their particular sins are just the natural by-products of being a "struggling Christian."

Here is a portion of that list:

1. In direct contradiction of 1 Corinthians 3:16-17, I know *countless* Christian men and women who are overweight due to overeating, their weight placing undue stress on their heart, thus slowly destroying their "temple."
2. I can't think of many Christians who don't drink coffee—and among those, I can't think of any who drink *decaf.* Caffeine is labeled an addictive drug (trust me, I know), and when it hits the blood stream, it manipulates mood, putting people at odds with Ephesians 5:18 which commands Christians to be under the influence of the Holy Spirit and not alcohol…which, logically, would include drugs.

On that note, many of the folks in my Christian circle drinks alcohol to excess, putting them under the influence of something other than God. Same thing with medication, and, man, do I know a ton of Christians that live by the belief that as long as that drug is in an orange container with a pharmacy's label on it, then they are good with God! Can I get an "Amen?"

1. There's a few anxiety-ridden believers among the Christians I know. Philippians 4:6.
2. Every single Christian I know gossips. James 1:26. Proverbs 11:13. Proverbs 16:28. To name a few.
3. "Now the works of the flesh are evident:…enmity, strife, jealousy, fits of anger, rivalries, dissensions, divisions, envy…and things like these. I warn you, as I warned you before, that those who do such things will not inherit the kingdom of God." Galatians 5:19-21. Know any angry Christians, Travis?

Oh that's right. These are things Christians *struggle* against…they aren't sins that they openly *embrace*.

Really? I know Christians who embrace these things every day, and the church hasn't kicked *them* out yet.

1. Ephesians 5:3-7 (and several like-minded verses) is a good read, basically listing every single sin a human being can commit, then ordering the Christian not to take a part in these very sins or involve themselves with the people who *do* commit them. So then, for consistency's sake, every single Christian who watches any Hollywood movie or TV show directly violates this command. Shoot, forget *Game of Thrones* or even *American Horror Story*, to truly be obedient, a Christian must even avoid *G rated* movies. There's a lot of "foolish talking" in a Pixar film. Lots of sex in PG movies. Plenty of evil doing in the black-and-white classics.
2. A "struggling Christian" friend of mine goes to strip clubs and shady massage parlors once in a while. It's ok because he asks for forgiveness after.
3. One of the friends I lost has a father who murdered someone on the side of a road and was never caught. Now, due to *my* being gay, I don't have that friend anymore, but to this day my old friend still visits his dad. A murderer made the cut, but the gay guy didn't.

Travis, why do my friends and family members I mention above get a place in heaven with God while I get damned to hell? Why are those who practice certain sinful behaviors on a regular basis "good" in God's eyes, but me who "practices homosexuality" is an unrepented sinner who will not "inherit the kingdom of God?"

Again, in the believer's eyes, it's all a matter of what a person fights against verses what a person accepts. To them, I gave in to my "sin," while they just give in to their desire to gossip, get angry, get jealous, cause strife and division every single day but claim it's just a part of the "battle."

Must not be a very bloody battle.

After Christopher's decision to cut me out of his life, and after discovering many people within our church had a profound influence on this decision, I took that small vestige of hope I had for reconciliation with Fair Oaks and squeezed it until it popped. And while it *is* true that although Claire and her pastor husband, for which I am thankful, urged your mom to give in to the judgment of 20%, many, many church members lent their support to the opinion that Christopher should not have a homosexual father in his life, and they actively prayed for this very thing.

Because of this, and not unlike the way Christians excuse their individual sins as "acceptable sins," I embraced my new-found disgust for Fair Oaks First Christian, and I did it with loads of bitterness, enjoying every last ounce of resentment and hatred I had for that place. I loved it then and I wallow in it now.

Just like I am seeking forgiveness from others, I will eventually need to forgive them.

Just not yet.

Love, Dad

Dear Travis,

Today was mine and my husband's wedding reception. While we were married back in July, we chose to hold off on the reception so we might celebrate with friends and family.

The reception was technically yesterday since it's now after midnight, but it was important that I might be able to talk to you on the day I celebrate my marriage because although you may not be here physically, your presence was felt by *everyone*.

At first, I wanted to set out three extra chairs for you and your brothers, knowing they wouldn't be filled. However, I was relying on the symbolism of three empty spots, and it gave me a little boost knowing the chairs were there.

Regardless, you are my son, and present or not, you guys were the most important guests from the beginning, and while I was a little depressed that neither my children or my parents came to celebrate with us, it didn't take away from the fact that I have three sons that I get to love... even if it's from a distance.

A distance of only three miles or so, but it's still a distance.

In my second favorite play of all time, *Marvin's Room*, Bessie has a conversation with her sister in Act 2, Scene 5. For twenty years, Bessie has taken care of her ailing father and aunt, choosing to stay home as nurse and caretaker while everyone around her grew up, moved out of their childhood homes, married, and had children. However, now Bessie has been diagnosed with leukemia and is relying on her sister, Lee, to step up and continue the job she will no longer be able to finish.

As she openly faces the reality that the leukemia is going to take her life, Bessie talks to Lee about the love she's experienced in her adult life, despite the fact she never had a husband or children of her own.

BESSIE. "I'm lucky to have Dad and Ruth."

LEE. "Mm-hmmm."

BESSIE. "I've had such love in my life. I look back and I've had such love."

LEE. "They love you very much."

BESSIE. "I don't mean—I mean I love them. I am so lucky to have been able to love someone so much. I am so lucky to have loved so much. I am so lucky."

When I first read that years ago, it struck me. When we talk about the love we have in our lives, we usually refer to the love people have for *us*; our self-worth is often measured by the amount and intensity of the love people in our lives have shown *us*. But this woman considered herself lucky because she was able to love other people; her joy and life's purpose came from the act of loving someone, not for someone loving her.

As your father, it, too, has been my privilege to love you, and that is regardless of your love, hate, apathy, or ambivalence for *me*. If indeed our paths never cross again, I can still die a complete and satisfied man because I have been graced with the opportunity to whole-heartedly love three other human beings, for many years in the past and for an unforeseeable amount of years in the future.

I am lucky.

Love, Dad

Dear Travis,

About six months after I had come out, a friend at work said to me, in an email, something along the lines of "welcome to your new life." I read the email twice, and while it was a nice sentiment, I wasn't sure the phrase really applied to me. Sure, I had heard similar expressions many times, have probably used something close to them on someone else, but when it came to me, I didn't think it was appropriate for my situation.

The implication in her email was that my "coming out" process had created a new person; I was slipping into the skin of a someone new even though I was simply becoming the person I was supposed to have been in the first place.

Since my colleague's message, I've come to the conclusion that all of the radical changes in my life did not constitute a new life but acted as the "act three" in a very long play. In the third act of any play, the same characters appear, but by then, the protagonist has faced enough conflict to have instituted an inward change, a transformation that precipitates growth and sees character maturity.

As opposed to a whole new play, my life currently rests in act 3 because while I'm not the same person I was three years ago…two years ago…last *week*, I have very much carried over the person that I was in acts 1 and 2, and I can't be in an entirely new story because the people I love are still in the *old* one. If I leap into a new play instead of carrying on the plot of the old one, I lose all those characters that helped define me in the first half of the play. I won't do that. I'll go through 235 acts of this play before I start writing a new one.

Besides, even if I had wanted to, there's no way I could ever become a "whole new person" now that I've had the experience of having children. As of this writing, my relationship with your oldest brother, Andrew, is the best it has been since this all began, but I still have two other children out there who are the other joys of my life, past and present, so I am happy to live with the old parts of me that define me as a father.

I'll never let go of that guy.

And, like I said in a previous letter, while I can still move forward, I will always be unable to move on. Think of it like this: when a person loses an arm or a leg or perhaps goes blind later on in life—like Mary on *Little House on the Prairie* (remember that episode?)—life can still be as enjoyable as it was before, however, adjustments will need to be made. Dealing with the loss of sight or a limb will naturally require some adaptations, but it can't be argued that the person will ever *physically* become whole again.

Travis: *you* are the sight that I've lost. For two years, I've been blindly running around, adapting to a world that is completely dark, 24/7, and while I can find some "color" in this new world I've leapt into, without you my newfound freedom isn't as joyous as I had hoped.

And while some people might offer their left arm to get their sight back, I find myself unable to do that—that arm went missing when I lost you and Christopher.

Without my boys, I will never be whole. Doesn't mean I can't have a life; I'll just have to make some adjustments in order to live with some emptiness. And I am not special either; hundreds of thousands of men in my same position are doing it as we speak, living, and not by choice, without their children, day after painful day.

There was an elderly man, a retiree, by the name of William who would get up every morning and walk two miles before he started his day. A man of obstinate routine, a firm believer in the German ideal that a satisfied life should always run with precision and efficiency, William was out the door by exactly 7:00am each day. He never took a different route, and he never stopped for any reason whatsoever. If a neighbor stopped to comment on the weather or such nonsense, he either flapped a hand a hand at him or pretended he was hard of hearing and moved on.

Once a bird with a broken wing fell in his path and he stepped over it.

He did this every day, even on the weekends, and was usually back on his front porch by 7:30am sharp.

There was only one small barrier to keeping his routine exactly as he approved it: rigid and assured. As part of his route, William had to cross a semi-busy street, but three years before, a set of traffic signals had replaced the four-way stop signs, and since he could never count on the green light always working in his favor, his 7:30am deadline often stretched to 7:31am.

That bugged him.

But what bugged him the most was that on the weekdays, at least two to three times a week, a red Mustang would barrel past him, generally enjoying a drive at about ten-twenty miles over the speed limit, the owner's head staring into his lap at what, William figured, was a cellphone. In addition to the speeding and distracted driving, and on more than one occasion, William witnessed the Mustang blow through the intersection, even when the light was *clearly* red, and several times William had to pull his foot out of the crosswalk lest he became old man roadkill.

After months of witnessing this reckless behavior and incensed that the Mustang skated through its drive each morning without any punishment, either by the law or, at the very least by an irritated honking of collective horns, William decided he himself would do something about this outrage.

Bad acts should always be penalized. That was as important to him as it was to live on a tightly regimented schedule.

Here's the clever plan William came up with: on his next morning walk, he would carefully time his steps so that when the car ran the red light, William would already be in the crosswalk. He would map out those steps beforehand to perfection so that the car's bumper would barely clip his left side, and if it all went like he expected it would—like everything else in his life did— William would receive little, if no, permanent injury.

You're a smart boy; you can figure out what happened next.

The Mustang driver, an 18-year-old high school kid, was found guilty of reckless driving and for driving without a license. He was sentenced to six months in jail—which was suspended—and was ordered to pay the victim's hospital bills, on top of a $150,000 pain and suffering fine awarded straight to William, fines of which 80% were paid for by the kid's parents. Jack, the driver, paid the other 20%.

William, now paralyzed from the neck down, spent six months in a kind of jail as well—a rehab hospital where he spent his days strapped into various leather and metallic torture contraptions, treatments that doctors assured him would bring him some form of mobility in the future.

The pain was at its worst during the night, and after the opioids were administered and his television was turned off either by a nurse or a late visitor, William would lay there until the meds began to work their magic, and only then would he allow himself to ponder over the failed plan that put him in a hospital bed, unable to move 90% of his body, unable to feed himself. Unable to take his daily, regimented walk.

And when he finally had the chance to think over the events of that day, undistracted, without some tube or strap poking him in the face, William would smile. Now a smile does take some muscular effort, and it certainly was a challenging feat coming from a man whose body only worked from the neck up but make no mistake: the look on William's face couldn't be interpreted as anything else. He was smiling. That broken, 72-year-old man spent an hour or so each evening, post *Seinfeld* episode—which he insisted on playing each night without fail—grinning, and it wasn't because he found *Seinfeld* that amusing either. In fact, he had told two nurses he found the show "annoying" and was super disappointed that *Mash* repeats weren't a thing anymore.

Even before the full effects of the opioids could be enjoyed, William would smile because even though he knew he would never walk again, William had peace in his heart because William had "won."

The boy was punished. Through William's selfless actions, the law had caught up with that thoughtless, inconsiderate deviant! Sure, the kid didn't actually have to spend a minute in jail, and the monetary punishment didn't affect him much, but that was inconsequential: justice had been met! The boy had been found guilty! The world that had momentarily slipped off its axis could be righted again.

Cool story, huh?

I made it up.

However, a good made-up story can often make a finer point better than any well-spoken speech or lecture, and, since I'm an English teacher it really works for *me*, I'm hoping you'll read the story again carefully and come back with the realization that you, Travis, are the William in my little allegory.

You are William and your dad is the reckless driver.

At some point, in the aftermath of my moving out of the house, you, understandably, felt your dad needed to be punished. Your world had crashed, it was burning, you were stunned and then angry, someone needed to stand up for your mom, and the only way life could be made right once again was for justice to be handed down, complete with a wagging shake of your index finger.

I was punished, I was punished good, and if the end goal was to see me miserable, goal accomplished. You won. And if you took this story to extremes, you could make me not only the driver of that Mustang but the neighbors that William slighted each day. Even the freakin' bird he stepped over that time.

But Travis, you're the guy who proved a point—you saw a wrong and made sure justice was meted out, but now you lay in a bed, paralyzed from the neck down, a fellow victim of your own punishment.

You've done what you sent out to do, and as a result, I have lived with the sentence you've handed down.

Now how much longer are you going to punish yourself?

How long will you go before you let go of this anger and resentment that can only cause partial injury to me but will completely destroy *all* of your life. It will suck out the joy and happiness and peace that you've had coming to you since the day you hurled your way into the world.

Travis, I acknowledge that when it came to the divorce, I had, from the beginning, made irrational, stupid decisions that only compounded the injuries you had already endured from my absence, and instead of being a true man who could step up and stop the bleeding, I just took my knife and dug into the wound, over and over again. But you are robbing yourself of so many wonderful things, Travis—a strong, important relationship with your dad being only one of them. Please listen to me, learn from me, and don't hurt yourself any further. Forgive and then let go. Yeah, there will be some days you'll need to forgive and let go over and over again but start trying it now.

And listen: I know there are some crimes I've committed against you that I've failed to mention in these letters, some unspoken hurts for which you feel entitled to an apology, but I've purposefully left some things out for a couple of reasons.

First, there are some things that all of us in our family have done to each other over the years that *none of us* wants in print. No need to comment on that further.

Second, I want to look you in the face and let you tell me what you're feeling. And then I want to apologize to you in person, man-to-man. I think you deserve that. Your silence has backfired in the sense that it doesn't really help me understand to what extent your pain has manifested itself in your life. It's time you began using your words.

Most importantly, I just want to sit in a room with you, just me and you, over food or a drink, and just talk with my son, no matter the words, no matter the emotions. No matter the outcome.

I just want to look at the kid that I helped turn into a man, and then I want a quiet moment to myself in order to brag about him in my head.

And before he goes, I want to get a chance to explain to him that life is not "like a box of chocolates." No, life is instead like a three-foot smart phone charging cord because every single time you go to charge your phone, the cord will, no matter how you hold it, be upside down.

So, you'll turn it over, and that too won't work.

Then you'll you flip it back like you were holding it in the first place, and it will finally slide in nicely.

Makes zero sense, but for some reason, we all accept it anyway.

Love, Dad

Dear Travis,

A dentist's office does not belong in a strip mall. Go somewhere else.

Love, Dad

CPSIA information can be obtained
at www.ICGtesting.com
Printed in the USA
JSHW010731290623
43918JS00001B/2